The Roma Café

Human Rights and the Plight of the Romani People

István Pogány

Pluto Press

LONDON • STERLING, VIRGINIA

First published 2004 by Pluto Press
345 Archway Road, London N6 5AA
and 22883 Quicksilver Drive, Sterling, VA 20166–2012, USA

www.plutobooks.com

British Library Cataloguing in Publication Data
A catalogue record for this book is available from the British Library

ISBN   0 7453 2052 X hardback
ISBN   0 7453 2051 1 paperback

Library of Congress Cataloging-in-Publication Data
Pogany, Istvan S.
   The Roma Café / Istvan Pogany.
      p. cm.
Includes bibliographical references and index.
   ISBN 0–7453–2052–X (cloth) — ISBN 0–7453–2051–1 (pbk.)
   1. Romanies—Europe, Eastern. 2. Europe, Eastern—Ethnic relations.
I. Title.

DX210.P64 2004
305.891'49704—dc22
                                                    2003023261

10   9   8   7   6   5   4   3   2   1

Designed and produced for Pluto Press by
Chase Publishing Services, Fortescue, Sidmouth, EX10 9QG, England
Typeset from disk by Stanford DTP Services, Northampton, England
Printed and bound in the European Union by
Antony Rowe Ltd, Chippenham and Eastbourne, England

Contents

Acknowledgements

Research grants from several bodies enabled me to familiarise myself with the conditions in which many Roma live in parts of Central and Eastern Europe, to conduct lengthy, semi-structured interviews and to work in specialist libraries. I should like to thank, in particular, the Airey Neave Trust, which awarded me a fellowship to work on the minorities problems that have arisen in Central and Eastern Europe since the end of Communism, the British Academy, the Nuffield Foundation, the University of Warwick's Research and Teaching Development Fund, and its Legal Research Institute.

This book could not have been written without the help and encouragement of numerous friends and colleagues. Dr Péter Szuhay of Budapest's Museum of Ethnography patiently instructed me in ethnographic techniques. He also shared with me his vast knowledge of the Roma of Hungary and Romania. Péter and Bea's hospitality, at their house in Tök, has been extraordinary. Suppers (and breakfasts) at their village home have been some of the most memorable, if girth expanding, experiences I can recall. The distinguished film-maker Edit Kőszegi, who has directed several highly regarded films and documentaries on Roma themes, helped me in innumerable ways. Chapter 4 draws on a documentary that she is making with Péter Szuhay about Roma naive artists in Hungary. Dr Zoe Waxman, Lecturer in Modern European History at Mansfield College, University of Oxford, deepened my understanding of oral history and kindly read a draft of my chapter on the Roma Holocaust. She helped me to appreciate both the potentialities and pitfalls of oral history as a medium of historical inquiry. Dr Paul Gready of the Institute of Commonwealth Studies, University of London, kindly discussed with me the use of personal testimonies in socio-scientific research. Professor Judith Okely of the University of Hull gave me invaluable advice on a range of topics. Professor Harry Arthurs of Osgoode Hall Law School, York University, Ontario, Canada, challenged my sometimes excessive enthusiasm for rights and for the judicial process as a means of helping disadvantaged groups.

In Romania, I benefited from the help, kindness and hospitality of a wide range of people, not all of whom can be named. I should like to thank, in particular, Dr Eugen Baican, Dr Levente Salat and Dr Virgiliu Târău, of the University of Babeş-Bolyai, Áron and Kati Balló, Maria

Cheregi, Dan Doghi and his family, István Haller of Liga Pro Europa, Florin Moisa, Alex Negrea, Géza Ötvös, Andrei Szantó and the staff of Wassdas, Marius Titi and his family, Julia Todea, Levente Tolas, as well as my indefatigable research assistants, Mihaela Chiorean and Alina Ghergha.

In addition to Edit Kőszegi and Dr Péter Szuhay, I relied on assistance and support from the following in Hungary: Jean Garland, Jim Goldston, Ioana Banu and other past and present staff at the European Roma Rights Center, Aladár Horváth and colleagues at the Romani Civil Rights Foundation, Dr Gábor Halmai of the Human Rights Information Center, Dr Gábor Kardos of the Eötvos Loránd University, Budapest, and Dr Szilveszter Pócsik of the National Institute of Criminology. Attila Hunyádi, Adél Pomázi, Gabriella Szabó and Judit Szabó variously collected Hungarian-language research materials, transcribed tapes of interviews and provided other forms of research assistance. Miklós Mádl took the photographs included in Chapters 2, 7 and 8 of this book. I am grateful to him for allowing me to reproduce them. Dr Éva Horváth not only contributed to this project in countless ways but also eased my (re)entry into Hungarian life, helping me navigate various bureaucratic obstacles when I decided to purchase a small apartment in Budapest. This book is dedicated to her in appreciation of her warm and unstinting friendship.

At the University of Warwick, I benefited from research assistance by Oby Agu and Thérèse Lepicard, and good-humoured secretarial support from June Green and, latterly, Aileen Stockham. Irene Blood and her colleagues in the University's Finance Department have had to deal with a bewildering array of invoices, including one for the hire of a horse and cart – literally the only way to reach an isolated Romani farmstead several kilometres from the nearest surfaced road at a season of the year when the ground was treacherous with thigh-deep mud.

Several friends and colleagues have been kind enough to read one or more chapters in draft and to offer their comments. I should like to thank, in particular, Professor Upendra Baxi and Dr Andrew Williams of the Department of Law, University of Warwick, Professor Robert Fine of the Department of Sociology, University of Warwick, Dr Erika Harris of the Department of Politics, University of Leeds, Dr Eric Heinze of the School of Law, Queen Mary and Westfield College, University of London, Dr Boldizsár Nagy of the Faculty of Law, Eötvos Loránd University, Budapest, and Dr Marcia Rooker, formerly of the Faculty of Law, University of Nijmegen. My wife, Ruth Pogány, a practising lawyer who also holds an MA in English Language and Literature, read various chapters in draft and offered valuable legal and editorial advice. I should also like to thank the anonymous academic referees who reviewed my manuscript for Pluto and who made several very helpful suggestions. However, my greatest debt is to the hundreds of Roma whom I met, especially in Romania and Hungary, while researching this book. In particular, I should like to express my appreciation to the Romani families who accepted me into their homes, whenever I called, and who conveyed to me some sense of their lives and concerns at this critical juncture in the history of the Roma. If any readers would like to support Wassdas, an NGO that has been working with the destitute Roma of the Pata Rât settlement in Romania, funds can be sent to the following accounts:

(in EUROS) SV 9499501300
(in US $) SV 6734671300
SWIFT: BRDROBU
Banca Romania de Dezvoltare, Sucursala Cluj,
B-dul 21 decembrie 1989, Nr. 81–83, Romania.

Wassdas, Str. Tipografiei Nr. 28, 3400 Chij-Napoca, Romania

An extract from Chapter 6 was published on 11 June 2001 in *Szabadság*, a Hungarian-language daily newspaper in Transylvanian Romania. An earlier and shorter version of Chapter 3 was published as 'Memory and forgetting: The Roma Holocaust' in Paul Gready (ed.), *Political Transition* (London: Pluto, 2003), Chapter 5. An article, 'Refashioning rights in Central and Eastern Europe: Some implications for the region's Roma', was published in March 2004 in *European Public Law* (Vol. 10, No. 1), incorporating extracts from Chapters 1, 5, 6 and 8.

István Pogány
Warwickshire and Budapest, September 2003

For Éva

1
Introduction

THE TRANSITION FROM COMMUNISM

Since the collapse of Communist regimes in Central and Eastern Europe (CEE) the region's 6 million Roma, or Gypsies, have rarely been out of the news.[1] There has been a disturbing pattern of unprovoked assaults on Roma, of severe beatings inflicted on Romani suspects in police stations – several of which have resulted in fatalities – and of 'pogroms' in which Romani-owned houses have been set on fire and their inhabitants variously beaten, lynched or chased from villages in which they were settled, sometimes for generations.[2]

The squalor and destitution in which a large proportion of the Roma have lived in the CEE countries, particularly since the end of state socialism, has also attracted attention.[3] All too often Gypsies are to be found in overcrowded tenements in the poorer parts of towns and cities across Central and Eastern Europe. In rural areas, Gypsies frequently occupy substandard houses many of which are located, pariah-like, at the edge of villages.

Hundreds of thousands of Roma, particularly in Slovakia, Romania, Bulgaria and in parts of the former Yugoslavia, live in settlements with limited access to clean water, sanitation or basic medical care.[4] Many of these settlements, like the one at Pata Rât on the outskirts of the city of Cluj-Napoca, in Romania, pose additional health hazards for the Gypsies living there. Known as 'Dallas' by its residents, who have evidently not lost their sense of humour, Pata Rât is located next to Cluj-Napoca's sprawling rubbish dump.

Lacking running water or flushing toilets, the shacks of Pata Rât are built of thin planks of wood, scraps of tarpaulin, anything that comes to hand. Women fetch water in buckets from a couple of water taps installed a few years ago with aid from a foreign charity. Mouldering piles of rags, plastic bottles and rusting cans delineate part of the settlement's boundary; half-wild piglets scamper amongst the refuse. Pata Rât resembles a Third World shanty town transplanted to the heart of Europe.

'There are 386 people living at Pata Rât right now', Géza Ötvös told me when I interviewed him in Cluj-Napoca in the cramped basement

1   Romani children at the Pata Rât settlement, Cluj-Napoca, Romania

offices of Wassdas, the Roma rights NGO that he has run since it was founded in 1997. 'Clean running water is available from two taps and there are eight communal toilets.' The water pipes and toilets were paid for by Médecins sans Frontières.

The Gypsies of Pata Rât earn a precarious living by picking through the refuse at the nearby dump. They collect glass bottles, metal, cardboard, anything that can be sold for recycling. Until a few years ago children worked alongside their parents, combing through the mounds of stinking rubbish for items of value. Now most of the children attend an elementary school built by Wassdas in Someşeni, a nearby suburb of Cluj. 'There are currently 56 pupils from Pata Rât attending the school, aged between eight and 15', Géza Ötvös said, reeling off the figures from memory. In all, there are 76 children studying at the school; several of the teachers are Roma.

The severe problems experienced by millions of Roma in Central and Eastern Europe, since the ousting of Communist regimes in 1989, cannot be viewed simply as a function of the abandonment of centrally planned economies and of the switch to often exploitative forms of capitalism. Down the centuries, poverty, low levels of literacy and social marginalisation have characterised the lives of most Roma in the region. A poem entitled 'Childhood', published in 1937 by the Hungarian poet Antal Forgács, vividly conveys the semi-destitute conditions in which many Gypsies lived as late as the eve of World War II, and the irrational dread that they evoked amongst Gadje or non-Gypsies:[5]

> Until now I haven't mentioned the Gypsies,
> Oh, how I feared them as they came round, dressed in their rags!
> …
> They begged and they sold all kinds of goods
> Mushrooms, iron nails and huge wooden bowls;
>
> They eat children, or so it was rumoured!
> And if they turn their gaze on you, you'll break a limb;
> Their skin has turned brown from drinking blood, it was said!
> Whenever I could I ran away from them.
> …

Elderly Romani men and women whom I met in Hungary while researching this book recalled that, as children in the 1930s and 1940s, they had lived in crude dwellings consisting of a single room carved out of the bare earth with a simple roof placed on top. Entire families were squeezed into such gloomy, subterranean hovels. Rózsi, a Vlach Romani woman, recounted the following details of the dwelling in which she was born after her parents settled in the Hungarian village of Patakrét where she has lived most of her life:[6]

> [My parents] moved from Elek to Patakrét. They didn't live in a house, it was just a hovel. It was a hovel that they'd built underground. And there they had 18 children...of the 18 only four survived...There was a row of such hovels where the Gypsies lived when they settled here.

In terms of literacy, the gulf between the Roma and much of the rest of the population of Central and Eastern Europe was already apparent in the 1890s. In 1893, a detailed census of the Gypsies living in Hungary – an area that then encompassed Transylvania, Slovakia and Serbian Vojvodina, in addition to present-day Hungary – was carried out. This found that whereas over 60 per cent of all men in the territories controlled by Hungary could read and write, the equivalent figure for Romani men was 6.54 per cent.[7] The proportion of Romani women who were literate was fractionally under 5 per cent, as against 46.5 per cent of all women in Hungary. In territories further to the east, levels of literacy amongst the Roma would have been appreciably lower.

The harsh reality of Gypsies' lives in much of Central and Eastern Europe – as well as ideological unease at the entrepreneurial habits and/ or nomadic lifestyle of some Gypsy 'tribes' or subgroups – prompted newly installed Communist regimes to institute programmes of forcible integration for the region's Roma, beginning in the late 1940s. As a result, the bulk of the Roma were provided with jobs, improved housing and access to public services, including health care and education.[8] Even so, by the 1970s, levels of Romani illiteracy remained high.[9] A long-held scepticism amongst the Roma about Gadje notions of education, as well as Gadje teachers' low expectations of their Romani pupils, go some way towards explaining this phenomenon.[10]

Since 1990, in the transition from command to market economies, Roma poverty and social exclusion have worsened dramatically, swiftly reversing the painstaking socio-economic gains experienced by many Gypsies during the socialist era.[11] Levels of unemployment amongst Gypsies in the CEE states have soared since 1990. In Hungary, for example, it has been estimated that 70 per cent of Romani men of working age are currently unemployed as against less than 10 per cent of the non-Romani male population.[12] The extent of Romani unemployment in other CEE states with significant Roma minorities,[13] such as the Czech Republic, Slovakia, Bulgaria and Romania, is comparable.

Spiralling unemployment amongst the Roma – particularly at a time of economic transition when former Communist states have been shedding many of the subsidies and welfarist structures that were introduced during the socialist period – has impacted massively on Roma living conditions throughout the region.[14] Unable to keep up the rent on apartments or to meet the rising cost of utilities many Roma have vacated their homes, moving to flimsy shacks in overcrowded settlements or squatting in unoccupied buildings that often lack proper sanitation, water or electricity.[15]

During the latter years of the socialist era most of the Gypsies now living at the Pata Rât settlement worked as labourers for agricultural co-operatives in the locality.[16] As well as paying the Gypsies modest wages, co-operatives, which were established by the Communists throughout the CEE states, using land and livestock 'voluntarily' contributed by peasants, provided simple housing for the Gypsy labourers and their families. During the 1990s many of Romania's agricultural co-operatives were disbanded as a result of legislation permitting the restitution of land to the peasants.[17] In the process tens of thousands of Gypsies, including most of those who eventually drifted to the settlement at Pata Rât, lost their jobs, their homes and the only way of life that they knew.[18]

Communist policies towards the Roma varied significantly from country to country, particularly after the mid 1950s. Nevertheless, there was a general, though far from uniform, effort by Communist authorities to try to integrate the Roma, as far as possible, providing them with jobs, housing and access to public services.[19] Under Communism, the bulk of the Roma in Hungary, Romania and in the former Czechoslovakia grew accustomed to working in factories, as construction workers or as labourers on the agricultural co-operatives. Over time, many Gypsies became increasingly reliant on the state as a source of ready employment and of automatic (if meagre) social provision. As a middle-aged Gábor Gypsy, whom I interviewed in Târgu-Mureş in the Transylvanian region of Romania, put it, most of the country's Gypsies 'didn't have special skills. What the state put in their hands, that was their "trade".'[20]

Numerous studies have drawn attention to the fact that, in addition to enduring social exclusion, racist assaults, dwindling employment opportunities and a general deterioration in their standard of living, Roma in post-Communist states are frequently denied full or equal access to public services.[21] For example Romani children in the Czech Republic have been systematically allocated to 'special' schools intended for the educationally subnormal without regard to their individual abilities.[22] As a detailed report of the Budapest-based European Roma Rights Center notes:[23]

According to reasonable estimates, Roma are at least fifteen times more likely to be placed in remedial special schools than non-Roma. A student who has completed remedial special school has greatly restricted choices in secondary education compared to a student who has completed mainstream primary school. Romani children are thereby effectively condemned from an early age to a lifetime of diminished opportunity and self-respect. In addition, the segregation of Roma in inferior schools is used as constant legitimation for discriminatory attitudes and actions by members of the majority society.

These practices in the Czech Republic are currently the subject of a complaint to the European Court of Human Rights. In Hungary, a recent study of elementary schools found that pressure from non-

Romani parents had resulted in the allocation of large numbers of Gypsy pupils to 'special classes'.[24] Researchers, who examined 192 Hungarian elementary schools, concluded that almost 85 per cent of the children in 'special classes' were of Roma extraction.[25] The teachers assigned to 'special classes' are often poorly qualified and the standard of instruction provided to the mostly Romani pupils in these classes is frequently unsatisfactory.

The worsening poverty amongst the Roma in the closing decade of the twentieth century, quite apart from institutionalised discrimination, also contributed to increased levels of educational segregation. As large numbers of Roma were forced to find cheaper housing, whether in rural areas or in poorer districts of towns and cities, the proportion of Romani children studying in elementary schools in the localities affected rose dramatically. This process was accelerated by the 'flight' of much of the non-Roma population from the areas subject to increased Romani settlement. For example, in twelve elementary schools located in run-down parts of Budapest the proportion of Romani children rose from 22.7 per cent in 1989 to 49.1 per cent in 1999.[26]

Poverty and social marginalisation have also affected the degree to which many Roma are able to take advantage of state-funded medical services in the CEE region. For example, Gypsies living on settlements, such as Pata Rât, often face severe difficulties in trying to register with a family doctor, despite chronic health problems compounded by poor nutrition, unsatisfactory housing and adverse environmental factors.[27] A report published recently by the Open Society Institute confirms that such problems are commonplace in Romania.[28]

In the final decade of the twentieth century, following the end of Communist rule, there was a steep increase in crime throughout the CEE states. All too often, the Roma have been blamed for much of this upsurge of criminal activity. In the popular imagination, across much of Central and Eastern Europe, the Roma are seen as work-shy and as having a 'natural' propensity for petty crime. Such starkly negative stereotypes, which reflect ancient prejudices, are often reinforced by the local media. Both electronic and print media in several states in the region regularly draw attention to the ethnicity of Romani defendants who have been charged with various offences, thereby encouraging widely held assumptions about the 'innate' criminality of the Roma.[29]

In Western Europe and North America, the Roma of Central and Eastern Europe have come to public attention chiefly as migrants and asylum seekers. Tens of thousands of Roma from the former Yugoslavia, Slovakia, the Czech Republic, Romania, Hungary and elsewhere have sought asylum in the west since 1990.[30] Frequently, the western media has chosen to portray the Romani applicants as economic migrants eager to take advantage of generous social welfare schemes, rather than as genuine asylum seekers fleeing persecution in their countries of origin.

Of course, it would be quite wrong to view the effects on the Roma of the transition to market economies and to liberal(ish) democracies, in the CEE states, in purely negatives terms. A number of Romani traders and businesspeople, often belonging to less integrated, more entrepreneurially-minded Romani subgroups such as the Oláh, in Hungary, or the Gábor and Kalderash, in Romania, have flourished in the new economic climate.[31] These individuals have established thriving businesses, accumulating considerable personal wealth in a way that would have been inconceivable under Communism with its severe restrictions on private commercial activity. Roma possessing flair, commercial acumen, ambition and a measure of capital are now free to pursue their economic goals. Prosperous Roma have financed the construction of luxurious homes for themselves and their families, ostentatious symbols of their wealth.[32]

The removal of Communism, with its panoply of ideologically-fuelled restrictions on individual freedom and self-expression and its general reluctance to accommodate ethnic difference, has also given Roma in the CEE states the opportunity to establish a wide variety of cultural and political associations. In accordance with the new or revised constitutions adopted by every country in the region the Roma are now free to assert their legal rights, both as individuals and as members of an ethnic minority, to advance political claims and to explore and foster their sense of cultural identity.[33] These are far from negligible gains. Under Communism, freedom – including the freedom of the Roma to assert their minority status and culture – could only be exercised, if at all, within narrow, shifting and prescribed limits.[34] In addition, a small but potentially influential Romani intelligentsia is emerging in the region as increasing numbers of Romani students, encouraged by scholarships and by other forms of institutional support, enter universities and colleges. Though tiny in comparison with the huge, poorly educated and mostly casually employed underclass of Roma in the CEE states, a Romani middle class, composed of teachers, social workers, journalists, businesspeople and assorted professionals, is slowly taking shape.

Nonetheless, any 'balance sheet' would reveal that, overall, the Roma have been spectacular and catastrophic casualties of the transition process. The number of successful Romani businesspeople in the CEE states remains extremely small, while the bulk of the Roma are experiencing acute problems in finding regular employment within new market-driven economies and in maintaining modest living standards. As noted by a recent World Bank report:[35]

> Roma are the most prominent poverty risk group in many of the countries of Central and Eastern Europe. They are poorer than other groups, more likely to fall into poverty, and more likely to remain poor. In some cases poverty rates for Roma are more than 10 times that of non-Roma. A recent survey found that nearly 80 per cent of Roma in Romania and Bulgaria were living on less than $4.30 per day...Even in Hungary, one of the most prosperous accession countries, 40 per cent of Roma live below the poverty line.

There is broad agreement that the already precarious economic position of the Roma has been undermined in the transition from Communism and that Roma 'gains' in other sectors remain limited, at best. Notional rights of political participation and of legal redress for the Roma – in the newly democratised states of Central and Eastern Europe – have to be judged in the light of widespread institutional resistance, as well as pervasive antipathy towards the Roma amongst the general public. More fundamentally, political or cultural engagement represents an unaffordable 'luxury' for many ordinary Roma who are preoccupied with more urgent material necessities such as feeding and clothing themselves and their families, paying the rent on apartments and meeting the soaring cost of utilities.

Beginning in the late 1990s, governments in Central and Eastern Europe began to introduce wide-ranging programmes aimed at alleviating the most acute socio-economic, cultural, legal and political problems experienced by Romani minorities.[36] In part, these initiatives were a response to mounting pressure exerted by international organisations, including the European Union, the Council of Europe, the World Bank and the Organisation for Security and Cooperation in Europe (OSCE), as well as by human rights NGOs such as the European Roma Rights Center and Human Rights Watch.[37] In addition, CEE governments have been forced to come to terms with their legal obligations under a variety of human rights treaties including the International Covenant on Civil and Political Rights, the International Convention for the Elimination of all Forms of Racial Discrimination, the European Convention on Human Rights and Fundamental Freedoms and the Framework Convention for the Protection of National Minorities.[38] Since 1990, the organs responsible for monitoring compliance with these treaties have repeatedly emphasised the acute problems experienced by the Roma of Central and Eastern Europe. For example, in August 2000, the Committee on the Elimination of Racial Discrimination adopted General Recommendation XXVII on 'Discrimination against Roma'.[39] Paragraph 12 of the General Recommendation calls on states:[40]

> To ensure protection of the security and integrity of Roma, without any discrimination, by adopting measures for preventing racially motivated acts of violence against them; to ensure prompt action by the police, the prosecutors and the judiciary for investigating and punishing such acts; and to ensure that perpetrators, be they public officials or other persons, do not enjoy any degree of impunity.

In a series of high-profile and (for the defendant states) acutely embarrassing judgments, the European Court of Human Rights has drawn attention to the casual disregard of even the most fundamental rights of Roma living in some of the CEE states.[41] A number of cases now pending before the Court are likely to result in findings that the Roma have been victims of institutionalised discrimination by public services in the region, and that criminal justice systems have failed to safeguard Romani communities from pogroms instigated by non-Roma or Gadje.

AIMS AND RESEARCH METHODS

My principal aims, in writing this book, have been to provide an overview of the formidable difficulties confronting the Roma of Central and Eastern Europe in recent years and to convey some sense of how they understand their lives and problems. Too often, the perspective of 'ordinary', poorly educated Roma has been overlooked – even by the policy makers and scholars who are committed to improving their conditions – as if the opinions of the Roma are of no conceivable interest.[42]

In writing this book, I was anxious not to portray the Roma as faceless statistics or as impersonal and perennial victims of harassment, social exclusion and economic dislocation. I wanted to reveal them as individuals who defy glib generalisations. All too often, Gypsies, like Jews, have been reduced to disparaging stereotypes. I wanted to liberate the Roma from these two-dimensional clichés and to present them as I knew them – people possessing the full range of individual traits and qualities, good and bad, found amongst any other national or ethnic group.

In addition, one of the central aims of this book has been to emphasise the cultural and social diversity to be found amongst the region's Roma, or Gypsies. This is a 'minority' made up of a kaleidoscope of minorities with very different values, levels of income, occupational specialisms and degrees of social acceptance. Neither religion nor language constitute defining characteristics of the Roma of Central and Eastern Europe. In general, Gypsies have tended to adopt (often with certain permutations) the religion of the people amongst whom they have settled, although a number of evangelical Protestant sects are currently attracting numerous Romani converts. In terms of language, a significant proportion of Roma in the region no longer speak any of the dialects of Romani, the Indic language of their forebears.[43] In Hungary, for example, almost 90 per cent of the Roma had adopted Hungarian as their mother tongue by 1993, as compared with 71 per cent in 1973.[44]

In truth, the Roma comprise a *multiplicity* of minorities with little sense, as yet, of a common identity.[45] Very largely, they are a 'people' only in the eyes of Gadje, to whom they often appear almost indistinguishable. However, amongst themselves, identity is often sharply and narrowly defined, frequently in opposition to other so-called Gypsy groups. As Sir Angus Fraser has commented, '[t]here is…no single Romani word corresponding to "Gypsy"…Each Gypsy grouping tends to look upon itself as being the authentic Gypsies.'[46]

Finally, I have sought to explore the impact of successive phases of Central and Eastern Europe's modern history on the region's Roma. What policies have governments in the CEE states adopted with respect to their Romani minorities during three distinct periods: (1) the inter-war period and the War years; (2) the Communist era, and (3) the post-Communist transition? And how have successive regimes been perceived by the region's Gypsies? It seemed probable that the Roma, as a despised and mostly impoverished minority would have experienced these distinct historical phases quite differently than the bulk of the Poles, Czechs, Slovaks, Romanians, Bulgarians, Hungarians, and others amongst whom they lived. Major historical events – the rise of Nazi Germany and of political movements based on theories of racial exclusivity, the brutal imposition of Soviet-style Communism after the War and, finally, the introduction of 'liberal' democracies and market economies since 1990 – were likely to have impacted very differently on the Roma compared with the region's predominant national groups.

The answers to the questions posed above cannot be found within a single academic discipline. History, cultural studies, political science, sociology, ethnography, anthropology and law have all contributed to our knowledge about the Roma of Central and Eastern Europe and the dilemmas they face. Perhaps it's presumptuous of an academic lawyer (even a wayward one) to imagine that he can avail himself of the literature and research tools of the social sciences and the humanities. However, I could conceive no alternative. Whatever my limitations as an ethnographer or an historian I believed it essential to attempt a broadly based, interdisciplinary inquiry in order to present a meaningful picture of the region's Roma at this critical point in their history.

In addition to reading much of the available literature on the Roma of the CEE states,[47] I made numerous field trips to the region. In Hungary and in the Transylvanian region of Romania I recorded lengthy, semi-structured interviews with a wide variety of Romani families in both urban and rural locations. I revisited many of the families as often as two or three times a year. Sharing their meals, occasionally visiting local bars with some of the men, I was gradually able to achieve a degree of intimacy, enabling me to construct a picture of their lives and concerns at a time of painful economic and social transition.

Inevitably, factors such as gender, age, ethnicity and occupational status created a distance (albeit variable) between myself and many of my Romani subjects. This was something that I attempted to bridge with various stratagems intended to establish a rapport between us. These included adopting a relaxed and friendly demeanour – spending time with the families rather than bombarding them with a list of predetermined questions.[48] I hoped that, over time, I would come to be seen not as a typical Gadjo, but as occupying some intermediate status. Achieving a good rapport with the Romani families was greatly facilitated by the fact that I liked and readily empathised with most of them.

In accordance with normal academic practice, I have changed the names of most of the Roma who are mentioned or quoted in this book. The names of villages have also been altered, although not their approximate geographical location. However, in the case of Roma who are already public figures in their own countries, such as Aladár Horváth, Director of the Romani Civil Rights Foundation in Budapest, Géza Ötvös, Director of the Romanian Roma rights NGO Wassdas, in Cluj, the Hungarian naive artist András Balogh Balázs, or the Romanian musician Kálmán Urszui – none of whom spoke to me on a confidential basis – there was no need to alter their names or details.

Observing people in their homes and neighbourhoods, over a lengthy period, frequently proved as informative as their answers to my questions – something that will come as no surprise to any ethnographer.[49] However, the many hours of recorded interviews also constitute a rich source of material. I have incorporated as much of it as possible in this and in the following chapters, allowing the Roma to express their thoughts about their lives, communities and the changing world around them.

Qualitative research of this kind – that focuses on individual lives and testimonies – has a number of critical advantages, particularly when used in conjunction with other approaches.[50] A recent study of Romani poverty, commissioned by the World Bank, emphasises the unique contribution that qualitative research can make to an understanding of the problems affecting the Roma in Central and Eastern Europe:[51]

> While quantitative research shows that Roma poverty is distinctive, it does not provide an adequate basis for understanding the particular dynamics that underlie Roma poverty. Here, qualitative research has the greatest impact. Qualitative research can identify social processes, mechanisms, and relations between social variables that are difficult to discern by looking at numbers alone...Therefore qualitative research provides a sharper picture of Roma living conditions in different communities, to emphasize the diversity of Roma populations and better understand interconnections between causes of poverty.

Through semi-structured interviews – and by spending time – with Romungro, Oláh, Beás, Sátoros and Gábor Roma, as well as urban Roma in Transylvania who often described themselves simply as 'Romanian Gypsies' to distinguish themselves from Hungarian or Romungro Gypsies, I was able to gain some insight into the cultural dynamics of these strikingly different Romani subgroups, particularly concerning their respective attitudes to education, appropriate types of work for members of their community and the roles of women and children. Without this kind of detailed information it is impossible to understand some of the root causes of Roma poverty and social marginalisation in the CEE states. Of course, the attitudes of Gadjo society – particularly teachers, employers, police, judges, social workers, media and health care professionals – towards the Roma have also been crucial in shaping the constricted social and economic space within which the Roma function in Central and Eastern Europe.

Legal scholarship has become a vital tool for understanding many of the problems experienced by the Roma of Central and Eastern Europe, particularly since 1990. Post-Communist states assure their citizens – including the Roma – a range of constitutional rights, including the right not to be discriminated against on grounds of national or ethnic origins. These rights are reinforced by numerous treaties and by international commitments of a more political character. However, in practice, access to public services in the CEE states – or treatment by overloaded criminal justice systems – often hinges, at least in part, on an individual's ethnicity. It is widely recognised that Gypsies, or Roma, have been routinely denied basic rights and that they have been treated less favourably than non-Roma by bureaucracies, courts and police in much of Central and Eastern Europe.[52]

There is also an extraordinary lack of congruence between many of the rights with which the Roma have been invested, since 1990, and their actual needs. Under Communism, the Roma along with other citizens enjoyed a series of basic, socio-economic entitlements. A large majority of the region's Roma would happily trade their new-found rights to democratic participation and freedom of expression for the material securities (guaranteed employment, subsidised housing, utilities, basic foodstuffs and so forth) of the socialist era.[53]

Modern scholarship in law and the social sciences often prizes unintelligibility, or so it seems. The near impossibility of establishing the meaning of a text is frequently seen as proof of its intellectual merit. Judged by this criterion my book will disappoint. I have deliberately chosen to write in a simple, accessible style uncluttered, as far as possible, by technical jargon. I wanted to produce a text that, while still eminently useful for policy makers, university teachers and students, would not immediately alienate the intelligent general reader with an interest in current affairs, human rights and the plight of Europe's largest ethnic minority, the Roma.

Many of the chapters in the book have a narrative quality, tracing the lives and concerns of 'ordinary' Romani men and women. Wherever possible, I have incorporated the actual words spoken by my Romani interviewees. Some of these techniques – as well as the focus on a marginalised social group – are well established in academic disciplines such as oral history and ethnography.[54] It has been argued, for example, that:[55]

the most distinctive contribution of oral history has been to include within the historical record the experiences and perspectives of groups of people who might otherwise have been 'hidden from history', perhaps written about by social observers or in official documents, but only rarely preserved in personal papers or scraps of autobiographical writing.

If ever a people has remained 'hidden from history', particularly European history, it is the Roma. Very few books on the history of Central and Eastern Europe contain so much as an index entry for 'Roma' or 'Gypsies', despite the centuries-long presence of large Roma communities in the region. The silence of most historians about the Roma has been compounded by the virtual 'silence' of the Roma themselves. Until comparatively recently very little writing of any kind was generated by the Roma because of chronically low levels of literacy and an overwhelmingly oral culture.

For the most part, the individual life stories presented in the following chapters have been selected because they are illustrative of problems or outlooks that characterise significant numbers of Roma in Central and Eastern Europe. Unemployment, lack of formal education, difficulties over housing and access to welfare benefits, harsh and unsympathetic treatment by police and criminal justice systems represent all too familiar features of the current predicament of the bulk of the Roma of the region.

However, even apparently 'ordinary' lives cannot always be reduced to a few simple truths. For example, the retired Romani labourer living in the town of Salgótarján in northern Hungary, whose life I describe in Chapter 4, became an accomplished artist. His paintings hang in the Museum of Ethnography in Budapest. Yet, despite his comparative celebrity, he lives on a modest pension from the County Waterworks and sometimes cannot afford to buy oil paints or canvas.

In opting for a jargon-free style – and in focusing on individual lives as one of the means of conveying the experiences of an entire people – I was influenced, above all, by a literary genre that has been well established in parts of Central and Eastern Europe, including Hungary, since the inter-war period. Known as *szociográfia* in Hungarian, it can perhaps be rendered as 'sociography' in English. It represents an amalgam of socio-scientific method and data, occasional personal observations and an accessible, sometimes literary mode of expression.[56] Sociography is broadly concerned with the lifestyle of social groups, communities or localities.[57]

Some works of fiction, such as the 1934 novel *Kiskunhalom* by the Hungarian writer Lajos Nagy, are generally classified as literary sociography. Using withering social satire, *Kiskunhalom* traces 24 hours in the life of an imaginary (but all too realistic) Hungarian village of the early 1930s.[58] However, many sociographic texts are entirely factual. For example, Gyula Illyés' *Puszták népe*, or 'People of the Puszta', first published in 1936, describes the harsh lives of farm labourers employed on Hungary's great estates in the inter-war period.[59] Kept in isolation from virtually every facet of modernity by their masters, the labourers and their families frequently lived in unimaginable ignorance and squalor. In the 1970s, Zsolt Csalog, a sociologist and writer, published a sociographic work whose appeal extended far beyond the academy in Hungary. In *Kilenc cigány*, or 'Nine Gypsies', Hungarian Gypsies of various levels of education and social integration describe their lives in often richly idiomatic language.[60]

I have sought to emulate some of these outstanding works of sociography in the sections of this book that describe the lives of Romani musicians, painters, labourers, traders, publicans, smallholders and pensioners, living in cities and villages across Transylvanian Romania and Hungary. However, overall, this book does not purport to be a 'pure' work of sociography insofar as the case studies, which form a central part of several chapters, are discussed in the light of the revelant anthropological, sociological, historical, legal and political science literature. Thus, the degree to which the Roma families highlighted in this book are representative of the experience of the Roma of Central and Eastern Europe, in the transition from Communism, is examined at some length. Such 'erudite' discussions are absent from conventional works of sociography.

In discussing the problems of the Roma one is led, almost inevitably, to invoke the language of human rights. Standards of conduct regarding the treatment of individuals and minorities, as incorporated in treaties, national legislation or 'soft-law' instruments – and as applied by courts, ombudsmen or other bodies – are increasingly couched in terms of rights. Human rights have become the ultimate (sometimes the exclusive) standard by which a state's treatment of its citizens is judged – especially by lawyers. We live in a rights-centric era, in which the language of human rights has become central to both political and legal discourse. Although I would not dissent from the intellectual tradition that sees human rights ideology as emancipatory and as a vital potential check on 'the barbarism of power',[61] it may be important to recognise that the growing focus on rights may have partially obscured other modes of analysis and understanding.

Undoubtedly, the experience of the Roma during the post-Communist transition in Central and Eastern Europe bears witness to the widespread denial of those rights with which the peoples of the region were supposedly invested as new democratic constitutions were drawn up and as the two halves of Europe were reunited.[62] The predicament of the Roma, since 1990, also illustrates the sometimes catastrophic consequences of the hasty reconceptualisation of rights that took place in the region, leading to the brusque withdrawal of those socio-economic entitlements on which many Roma had become reliant. Much of this book is inevitably taken up with a detailed catalogue of the failure of post-Communist states to uphold the legal rights of their Romani citizens. Yet, aside from human rights, there are other ways of conceptualising the problems of the Roma of CEE countries. To put it another way, the chronic difficulties experienced by many Roma, including under-education, unemployment and social marginalisation, are not simply a function of the denial of rights. Though the enforcement of basic rights, including rights to life and non-discrimination, constitutes a necessary and important goal, it will not, of itself, tackle many of the underlying problems that the Roma are experiencing.

THE STRUCTURE OF THE BOOK

The current predicament of the Roma of the CEE states can only be understood by examining the history of this sizeable and growing ethnic minority, particularly over the past hundred years. The impact, successively, of ideologically-driven persecution during World War II, of enforced sedentarisation and proletarianisation during the Communist era, and of the sudden collapse of employment opportunities and of welfarist structures following the ousting of Communist regimes in 1989 provides indispensable background information.

Chapters 2, 3 and 4 are intended to provide the reader with an historical overview of the experience of the Roma in Central and Eastern Europe from their first appearance in the region, in the Middle Ages, until the final collapse of the Communist administrations. In addition, Chapter 2 introduces the reader to several key aspects of traditional Roma culture(s), including notions of property, attitudes to work and towards Gadje, as well as perceptions that Roma have of themselves and their history. The chapter begins with a story recounted to me by Rózsi, an elderly Vlach Romani woman living in the village of Patakrét in Hungary. The story, which was no doubt improvised for my benefit, borrows freely from various sources including the Bible. Rózsi's tale was intended to explain the origins of the enmity that exists between Gypsies and Gadje, and the circumstances that had led most Gypsies, particularly in the area under consideration, to abandon their nomadic way of life. Although a product of her imagination Rózsi's story is illuminating, reflecting many of her (and her community's) tacit assumptions and values.

An entire chapter (Chapter 3) has been devoted to the subject of the Porajmos, or Roma Holocaust.[63] In recent years, the persecution of the Roma during World War II has attracted increasing scholarly and even literary attention. Nevertheless, the number of Romani victims and the genocidal intent of the Nazis and their allies remain mired in controversy. In addition to examining the burgeoning academic literature on the Roma Holocaust, the chapter draws on the recollections of elderly Roma whom I interviewed in Hungary and in the Transylvanian region of Romania about this terrible period of Roma history which, until recently, was almost entirely neglected.

Chapter 4 concludes the historical introduction by considering the impact of Communist administrations on the Roma after World War II. The chapter focuses on the life of a retired Romani labourer, András Balogh Balázs, who lives with his wife in a modest apartment in the mining town of Salgótarján in northern Hungary. His starkly unsentimental description of life during the Communist era tells us much about the treatment of many ordinary, poorly qualified Roma under state socialism. The chapter goes on to trace the differences that gradually emerged, from the late 1950s onwards, in the handling of Romani minorities by the region's various Communist regimes. In middle age, András Balogh Balázs became known as a gifted naïve artist. The chapter discusses his late-blossoming career as a painter and the difficulties experienced by Roma visual artists in the region.

As indicated in the first part of this chapter, the current predicament of the Roma in Central and Eastern Europe raises a wide range of issues – social, political, economic and legal. The most important of these are tackled in Chapters 5, 6, 7 and 8. As before, the case study method is used so that the experiences of a Romani individual, couple or family are considered as a preliminary to a general examination of specific issues affecting large numbers of Roma in the region. Such issues include poverty, attitudes to work or education, exclusion from the labour market and experiences with the criminal justice system.

Sometimes, as in Chapter 5, themes are introduced in combination.[64] Chapter 5 begins with a brief portrait of an eminent classical musician, living in Transylvanian Romania, who is of Roma extraction. The chapter describes the rich and varied contribution that the Roma have made to both classical and folk music traditions in Central and Eastern Europe. A number of Romani musicians whom I interviewed, while researching this chapter, were reluctant to reveal their ethnicity to outsiders or sometimes even to their own children. The chapter considers the significance of this extraordinary (if understandable) diffidence, particularly in terms of the relevance of schemes of minority rights for the region's Roma. The creation of minority rights regimes has been a conspicuous feature of the transition process in Central and Eastern Europe. However, while such regimes may be potentially important for economically stable, educated and cohesive minorities, such as ethnic Hungarians in Romania or Slovakia or ethnic Germans in Hungary or Poland, they are arguably of much more limited utility to a people such as the Roma who are overwhelmingly poor and who are often too ashamed even to admit their ethnicity.

Chapter 6 begins with a description of the lives of Eszti and Lajós, a middle-aged Romani couple in the Romanian city of Cluj-Napoca. I first met Eszti several years ago when she and her husband were living in a tiny, unheated shed on a Romani settlement in a suburb of the city. Eszti's landlord, a Gypsy, found the couple living rough on the streets and offered them his shed as a temporary home. During the Communist era, Lajós worked for over 25 years as a semi-skilled construction worker, earning a decent wage. The couple and their two daughters lived in a one-room apartment that they rented from the municipality. Now Lajós and Eszti subsist by collecting cardboard for recycling. Their elder daughter died some years ago in an accident. The younger daughter was placed in an orphanage when the couple were evicted from their apartment for non-payment of rent.

The disintegration of Eszti's family has many causes. But, in their descent from a near ordinary working-class family into destitution and a precarious life on the streets, Eszti and Lajós can be listed amongst the numerous casualties of the political and economic transformation of Central and Eastern Europe. Along with millions of other Roma in the region (and of course non-Roma), the couple have seen the withdrawal of social and economic rights formerly guaranteed by the state and the creation of market economies in which they are ill-equipped to compete. The chapter goes on to examine the approach adopted by both governments and constitutional courts in CEE states to social and economic rights in the transition from Communism.

In Chapter 7 I look at the situation of Romani women. Often expected to assume a significant role in generating income for their families Romani women invariably have many domestic responsibilities as well, including caring for the children, looking after the home and cooking. Traditionally, in Romani culture, women were regarded as of much lower status than men, although a limited exception was made in the case of older women who were no longer capable of bearing children. Such attitudes remain commonplace amongst poorly educated Roma and may account, at least in part, for the relatively high incidence of domestic violence.

However, as ever, generalisations should be treated with care. In the course of researching this book I was entertained several times at the luxurious home of a Romani matron in Transylvanian Romania. She was subsequently revealed to be a high-level 'fixer' in the criminal underworld. The press in Cluj described her as 'the notorious head of a mafia gang'. Her mild-mannered husband all too visibly lived in her powerful shadow. The chapter begins with a case study of a middle-aged Romani woman in a Hungarian village, Patakrét. Defying all the stereotypes, Anikó is neither meek nor subservient in her relations with her husband and with the other men in her family. Her life story – her mother was an ethnic Hungarian – also tells us something about the construction of Roma identity.

Chapter 8 examines the failure of criminal justice systems in the region to respond to an upsurge of assaults on the Roma since 1990. The chapter begins with a case study of an attack on the the Lambada, a scruffy, Romani-owned bar in a village situated some 30 kilometers north of Cluj in Transylvanian Romania. The owner of the bar, Olga, is a Romani widow in her mid fifties. Most of her customers were Gypsies from the Roma quarter of the village.

Since the attack on the bar and its customers by three Romanian brothers from the village, in February 1999, the Lambada has remained closed and Olga has lost her only source of income. She is highly critical of the police investigation into the incident. Olga also says that an offer of compensation from the defendants, which led her to ask for the case to be discontinued, has not been honoured in full. Olga says that the three Romanian brothers who attacked her and her customers often taunt her as they pass by her house. The chapter examines the limited access of poor and ill-educated Gypsies, such as Olga, to courts and to criminal justice systems in Central and Eastern Europe. In practice, many of the region's Roma live outside the full protection of the law.

The chapter goes on to consider the growing impact of International Law on the CEE states, with particular reference to their treatment of Romani minorities. Obligations assumed under multilateral human rights treaties as well as pressure exerted by international organisations such as the European Union, the Council of Europe and the OSCE are playing a part in inducing the CEE states to improve their domestic policies and practices concerning the Roma, whether in terms of criminal justice systems, education or health care provision.

The concluding chapter summarises the principal challenges confronting the Roma in the transition from Communism and offers several policy recommendations, taking account of recent studies including a report on Roma poverty commissioned by the World Bank.[65] Finally, the chapter asks whether Europe, after the Holocaust/Porajmos and the ethnic cleansing that disfigured the former Yugoslavia, can finally learn to accept and even celebrate cultural and ethnic difference.

A NOTE ON THE TERMS USED IN THIS BOOK

As yet, there is little consistency in the terms used to describe the people or peoples who form the subject of this book, or their ancestral language. In some recent texts words such as 'Gypsy' (or its Hungarian equivalent 'Cigány') have been retained, in defiance of the commonly held view that such terms are inherently pejorative. In the anthropological literature, 'Rom' is occasionally used to designate a man and 'Romni' a woman belonging to the 'Roma' (or 'Romani') people. Quite commonly, 'Roma' is used as a noun (singular and plural) while 'Romani' becomes an adjective. Another approach, favoured by Ian Hancock, a noted Romani scholar and activist, is to use 'Romani' as both an adjective and a noun; 'Romanies' is Hancock's preferred plural of Romani.[66] However, the World Bank report mentioned above on the causes and cures of Roma poverty, uses 'Roma' indiscriminately as both noun (singular and plural), adjective, and even as the name of the ancestral language of the Roma people.[67]

Although certain communities, such as the Sinti, do not consider themselves to be 'Roma', the latter term is now widely regarded as applying to all so-called Gypsy groups. I have therefore used 'Roma' as the plural noun and 'Romani' as the singular noun in this book, while generally favouring 'Romani' as the adjectival form. In some cases, however, 'Roma' has been used as an adjective where this corresponds to general usage. For example, it is customary to refer to the Roma (not Romani) Holocaust.

I have felt free throughout this book to employ 'Gypsy' as a synonym for 'Roma' and 'Romani'. There is a limit to the number of times one can repeat the term 'Roma' or 'Romani' in a single sentence or paragraph, particularly if the passage also contains one or more references to 'Romania', 'Romanian' or 'Romanians'. For the ancestral language of the Romani people I have used the term 'Romani'. Interestingly, when conversing in Hungarian, Roma in Hungary and Transylvanian Romania often refer to speaking *cigányul*, that is, 'in Gypsy'.

2
The Hairy Thing that Bites, or why Gypsies Shun Gadje

It was late December and we were sitting in Rózsi's overheated *nappali*, or sitting room, its walls decorated with a jumble of religious prints and family photographs. A Vlach Gypsy in her late sixties, Rózsi lives in Patakrét, a village in south-eastern Hungary just a few kilometres from the Romanian border. At this confluence of cultures many of the locals speak both Romanian and Hungarian. Vlach Gypsies, like Rózsi, also speak Romani, which they use amongst themselves. Romani, which has affinities with Sanskrit and with several contemporary Indic languages, hints at the Indian origins of Gypsies.[1]

We had known one another for some years and I judged that Rózsi wouldn't fob me off with misleading answers. So I came right out with it and asked her why Gypsies are said to shun Gadje or non-Gypsies. At the time, I was sceptical of the explanations offered by anthropologists who suggest that Gypsies avoid unnecessary dealings with Gadje because they regard them as a potential source of impurity or shame.[2] Somehow these intellectualised accounts didn't tally with my own experiences amongst Gypsies, many of whom seemed totally ignorant of the beliefs that scholars impute to them.[*] It was only later, when I became acquainted with several Gábor Romani families in Romania, whose lives are still regulated by the tenets of an intensely traditional culture, that I began to find evidence of a preoccupation with ideas of 'shame'.[3] Though notions of 'pollution' or 'shame' may once have represented universal and defining features of Romani culture(s) there is hardly a trace of them in the lifestyles or memory of increasing numbers of Roma in Central and Eastern Europe. As a recent book

---

[*] In Transylvania, a young Romani social worker whom I befriended, visiting him and his family frequently at their home, was genuinely perplexed when I asked about Romani notions of 'pollution' or 'shame'. Hoping to learn more about these allegedly crucial Romani beliefs, I found myself giving an impromptu lecture to my host. On another occasion, a Romani woman in Transylvania happily posed for a photograph, with her teenage daughter, under a washing line on which several pairs of freshly washed female knickers had been hung out to dry. Yet, according to various anthropological accounts, the Roma consider it shameful for female undergarments to be seen by a man.

2 Elderly Vlach Romani women in a Hungarian village

about the region's Roma notes, 'most East European Gypsies no longer live by the old customs; they are not, as it were, "orthodox Roma"'.[4]

Instead of answering me directly, Rózsi launched into a story. At the time, I didn't pay it much heed although, out of politeness, I recorded it anyway. I had hoped for a 'proper' explanation of Romani attitudes towards Gadje. It was only later, when I played back Rózsi's tale on my cassette recorder, that I realised its significance. Rózsi had answered my question although she had done so in her own way, by means of a fable. This is what she said.

It happened in the old times, before the Communists, when the world was run by dukes and counts. Gypsies led a wandering life back then with their horses and wagons. One day, a band of Gypsies came upon a wood. They stopped, put up their tents, lit fires and cooked themselves a meal. The Gypsies stayed in this spot for a long time. In winter, if a child was born, they washed it in snow. If they needed water for cooking or for drinking they'd melt some more snow. If they were hungry they foraged in the woods, while the women went out to beg at the local farms.

One day the Gypsies found a little Gadjo boy who had run away from home. The child was the grandson of the Count who owned all the land thereabouts. The Gypsies felt sorry for the lad and took him in. He was looked after by an elderly couple who treated him as if he were their own son. That's always been the Gypsy way. If someone comes to them in need, even if Gypsies have nothing themselves, somehow they'll always find a way to help.

Several months went by and the Gypsies were still camped beside the wood. One morning, the old woman was baking some potatoes for her family in the ashes of a fire. The little Gadjo boy, who was very hungry, grew impatient. He took it into his head to help himself to one of the potatoes, squatting down next to the old woman, who was standing by the fire. All of a sudden, the boy looked up and saw underneath the old woman's skirts.

'What's that hairy thing?' cried the little boy. 'That hairy thing bites!'

'Get away from there!' the old woman shrieked, striking the child.

Soon afterwards some *gendarmes* called at the Gypsy camp. The little Gadjo boy went up to them. 'Take care', the boy warned the *gendarmes*. 'That old woman has a big hairy thing and it'll bite you all! You'd better get away from here!'

I wasn't the only one who was puzzled by the story. Rózsi's daughter Ilona had been in the room with us the whole time, nursing her baby in her arms.

'So what was this big hairy thing?' Ilona asked her mother.

'It was her *pina*!' snorted Rózsi, using a Hungarian word I didn't know.

'*Pina*?'

Ilona giggled. 'You know, it's what a woman has.'

'It's a woman's body', suggested her mother.

'Her whole body?'

'No, it's what a woman has down there!' Ilona enlightened me. She laughed at my ignorance and asked me what *pina* was in English. But let's return to Rózsi's story; she was eager to get on with it.

Eventually, the *gendarmes* went away. Not long afterwards, the old woman's husband came back. He had been collecting firewood some distance from the camp.

'Why are you looking so miserable?' he asked his wife.

'Of course, I'm miserable', she told him. 'You were the one who decided the Gadjo kid could live here with us. Just now he peeked up my skirt and saw what I have there. He even had the cheek to tell me it bites!'

The old woman wouldn't be comforted. 'I'm going away', she told her husband. 'I'm leaving you.' Realising that he'd lost his wife because of the little boy's uncouth behaviour, the old man became angry and chased the kid away.

The Gadjo boy was forced to leave the camp but he soon found another band of Gypsies who had set up their tents not far away, further along the edge of the wood. Although these Gypsies got to hear of what had happened with the old woman, they accepted the Gadjo boy into their midst and raised him up. The kid was smart and the Gypsies taught him everything they knew. At night, the boy went out with the men to steal from the farms so there would be food for the children. Imagine, they even stole from the Count! When he was a little older, the Gadjo boy led these expeditions himself. And what happened to him when he grew up? He became a *gendarme*!

Dressed in his new uniform, the Gadjo went back to the old Gypsy couple who'd looked after him when he ran away from home. He beat the old man without mercy and he kicked the old woman again and again. He hurt them so badly that they no longer recognised themselves. He smashed their wagon and ripped their tent to shreds. Then he took a piece of fatty bacon and cut it into two thick chunks. 'Suck on that!' he said, shoving the pieces of bacon into the old couples' mouths. Amongst Gypsies, that's an ugly thing to say. Since that day, Gypsies have kept away from Gadje!

Well, the old man recognised the *gendarme* straight away. He knew he was the little boy that he and his wife had looked after all those years before. The old man laid a curse on the lad, 'As you leave this wood, may you be struck by a bullet without ever knowing where it came from!' And that's exactly what happened. In those days if a Gypsy cursed you, then something bad happened. Gypsies were very powerful back then because they were without sin. The Gypsies committed no sins; they were the servants of God. And God stood by the Gypsies, giving them food and everything that they needed.

Even though he had been responsible for the *gendarme*'s death, the old man was sad when he got word of what had happened. After all, the old man had helped to raise the boy. He decided that, as a mark of respect, he'd attend the *gendarme*'s funeral.

The Count, who was the *gendarme*'s grandfather, was at the funeral too. Learning that the old Gypsy couple had taken care of his grandson all those years before, the Count was really moved.

'If these Gypsies hadn't looked after my grandson when he ran away from home, surely the boy would have died!' the Count declared to everyone present. And the Count took the old man and the old woman and he had a house built for them as a token of his thanks. That's why Gypsies live in houses now instead of wandering from place to place with horses and carts as they used to. If it hadn't been for the Count, Gypsies wouldn't be living in houses to this day.

Even though Rózsi's story was almost certainly improvised, drawing liberally on the Biblical account of the Garden of Eden and on the plot of a Hungarian film, *Sitiprinc*, in which Rózsi had been given a small part,[5] the narrative is illuminating. Stories can be truthful precisely *because* they are fabricated; they reflect the tacit assumptions and values of those who conceive them. So what can we learn from Rózsi's tale?

WORK

Let's be blunt: the Gypsies in Rózsi's story weren't workaholics. They had a relaxed, carefree attitude to life. For the Gypsies who settled beside the forest, the conditions were paradisiacal. The forest offered firewood as well as water and all kinds of nourishment. There would have been rabbits, pheasants and partridges for the taking, as well as eggs and maybe the odd deer and wild boar. Aside from game, there would have been mushrooms and an abundance of berries and wild fruit. For the Gypsies, unlike the foolish peasants, there was no need to cultivate the land with back-breaking effort. The forest was bountiful and contained almost everything that a person needed. Those few necessities or luxuries that could not be found in the forest could always be obtained from the peasants or even from the Count's estate, whether by begging or stealing. Although this represented a happy and natural way of life for the Romani band in Rózsi's story, it would have been viewed rather differently by the peasants. As the latter would have seen it, their industry and virtue were constantly mocked and exploited by the Gypsies.[6]

In Rózsi's tale begging is freed from any shameful connotations. If you are poor then begging is a natural way to obtain what you need. Even theft is permissible provided it's limited to carrying off a chicken or two to satisfy the hunger of your children. But there is nothing in the story that would justify more spectacular crimes, motivated by greed rather than necessity, such as stealing jewels or other items of great value. The purpose of stealing is not to acquire wealth but to allow you and your family to stay alive.

Rózsi's account is much more than just a story; it instructs as well as entertains. The notion that the good life is one in which a person lives well while apparently expending little effort is deeply ingrained in traditional Vlach Romani culture. Michael Stewart, a British anthropologist who lived amongst a community of Vlach Gypsies in Hungary, in the mid 1980s, observed that they tended to value forms of economic activity which prioritise quick wittedness, even cunning, over laborious and time-consuming work, particularly wage labour.[7] The latter is seen as *pares*, a Romani term meaning 'heavy', in contrast to authentic Gypsy work, or *romani butji*, which should be *lases*, that is 'light' or 'easy'.

Rózsi's story exemplifies traditional Vlach Romani beliefs about appropriate ways of supporting yourself and your family. Such methods may include living off the land, commerce of various kinds or begging from Gadje. If food is scarce, or as proof of native cunning, pilfering the odd chicken or goose from peasants is acceptable.[8]

But there is no reason to believe that such values, which emerged in a particular rural environment and within a specific Gypsy community, are common to all Gypsies everywhere – or that they are not susceptible to change. Romania's Gábor Gypsies, for example, are widely admired for their thrift, honesty, commercial acumen and hard work. As they became more integrated, Hungary's Romungro or 'Musician' Gypsies, who make up over 70 per cent of all Gypsies in the country, lost not only their forefathers' Romani language but also much sense of a distinct cultural identity. In practice, many Vlach Gypsies, though paying lip service to the ideal of getting by with little effort, actually lead lives of conspicuous industry. For example, Rózsi told me that, after leaving her husband because of his persistently violent behaviour, she worked as a labourer at the local TSZ, or agricultural co-operative, by day, while building a simple house for herself and her three children at night. 'I did it, with my own two hands, I built it', she told me. 'But at night, by lamp light...when I became too tired I lay down on the straw and snoozed. Then I got up and went to work in the TSZ.'[9]

Even within a single family of Vlach Gypsies there are often huge variations of attitude and modes of life. Bőske, an elderly Vlach Gypsy whom I visited at her home, runs a successful smallholding with two of her sisters in south-eastern Hungary, some miles from the nearest village. Bőske, a cantankerous and frugal workaholic, has adopted the values and lifestyle of the Hungarian peasants. One of her brothers and his wife own a similar smallholding nearby. Another brother, a comfortably off horse-coper with a large house in a village, has a son who graduated from teachers' training college. The son has become a successful businessman and lives in a provincial town. Bőske's two remaining brothers, lacking ambition or enterprise, became alcoholics in later life. One of them held down a succession of manual jobs during the Communist era but struggled to make ends meet after he was made redundant in the early 1990s. The other brother, strikingly handsome in his youth, was jailed several times for theft. He settled down with a Gadjo woman whose family severed all ties with her when she declared her intention of living with a Gypsy. To ascribe a single, unchanging mentality to all members of a family, let alone to an entire ethnic group, is unsustainable; it is prejudice masquerading as truth.

PROPERTY

Rózsi's story also tells us something about traditional Vlach Gypsies' notions of property. There is no mention in her tale of who owned the forest and everything that it contained. For the Gypsies the firewood and the game were there for anyone to take who had the skill or the inclination to do so. But, although this band of Gypsies may have chosen to disregard nineteenth-century principles of property law, as they applied in the Austro-Hungarian monarchy, the forest and its riches must have been privately owned. My guess is that they belonged to the Count whose fugitive grandson was cared for by the old couple.

Of course, the Gypsies knew full well that, under the law, the chickens and geese that they took from the farms belonged to the peasants. That's why the Gypsies crept out at night to seize them when the peasants were fast asleep. But the Gypsies in Rózsi's tale had their own notions of property. The Gypsies treated the chickens and geese that they appropriated as rightfully theirs because, in the first place, they had won them with their cunning and daring and, no less importantly, because their families were hungry and needed to eat.[10]

But again a word of caution is in order. Rózsi never intended that the Gypsy band in her narrative should be seen as representative of *all* Gypsies. Or, to put it another way, Rózsi's understanding of who constitutes a Gypsy is much narrower than most Gadje might suppose. For her, the circle of authentic Gypsies is limited to her fellow Vlach Roma. At bottom, Rózsi's story only tells us about traditional Vlach

Romani attitudes towards stealing, particularly from Gadje.[11] But even the celebration of petty theft in Rózsi's story is deceptive. While it may evoke ancient Vlach Romani values it bears little correspondence to Rózsi's life. In her daily transactions with her neighbours, including elderly peasants, Rózsi is a model citizen who commands widespread affection and respect. Though she may invent stories about raids on peasant farms by wily Gypsies, when she needs something herself – cigarettes, a loaf of bread, coffee – she'll send her daughter or a niece to buy it at a nearby shop.[12]

GADJE

In Rózsi's story the Gypsies, though poor, were trusting and shared what little they had with those in need. They welcomed the lost Gadjo boy and treated him as one of their own. The Gypsies revealed all their secrets to the boy, holding nothing back. Yet the Gadjo betrayed their kindness twice over. As a child he behaved with unpardonable vulgarity, deliberately looking up the old woman's skirts. As a man, he betrayed them a second time by becoming a hated *gendarme*, the very symbol of authority and oppression, and assaulting the old couple who had looked after him.

Yet the Count was also a Gadjo and he was both kind and generous as well as forgiving (after all, the old Gypsy brought down the curse which killed the Count's grandson). The Count became the benefactor of the old Romani couple and, by extension, of the entire Romani people. In Rózsi's story the Count gave the elderly couple a house in which to live out their days so they no longer had to endure the discomfort and uncertainty of a nomadic existence. The old couple are a metaphor for the Romani people whose settlement after centuries of perilous wandering is due, at least in Rózsi's account, to the warmth and goodness of the Count.

Rózsi's story nicely captures the ambivalence in traditional Vlach Romani attitudes towards Gadje. While Gadje can be brutal and oppressive in their treatment of Gypsies, or crassly vulgar, they can also be unexpectedly generous. Gadje, with their industry and passion for farming, are also an essential source of food, as well as customers for a range of Gypsy crafts and services. Without the willingness of Gadje to pay for Gypsy artefacts and services, to cultivate their fields and to raise livestock, it's doubtful whether Gypsies could even exist. As Judith Okely has pointed out:[13]

Gypsies…have never been self-sufficient. They are dependent the larger economy, within which they took possession of or created their distinct niche. The Gypsies can only survive as a group within the context of a larger economy and society, within which they circulate supplying occasional goods and services, and exploiting geographical mobility and a multiplicity of occupations.

GOD'S SERVANTS

In Rózsi's story the Gypsies were powerful. While they were poor and apparently reliant on the charity of Gadje, from whom they begged or occasionally stole, the Gypsies had hidden powers bestowed on them by God. Although the Gadje were unaware of it the Gypsies cast spells with deadly effect. Rózsi's tale, though comforting to Gypsies who are marginalised and vulnerable wherever they find themselves, is an inversion of reality. A people without a land of their own, Gypsies have never been powerful except in their stories about themselves.

Rózsi's tale is reminiscent of the story of Adam and Eve. Like that Biblical couple, the Roma were living in paradise. The forest, with its plentiful firewood, water and foodstuffs was almost, but not quite, the Garden of Eden (unlike the Gypsies, Adam and Eve didn't have to beg or steal from peasants in order to supplement their diet). According to Rózsi, God looked after the Gypsies while they remained in a state of innocence. Stealing the odd chicken or goose from the peasants clearly didn't amount to a crime in the eyes of God (or in the eyes of the Gypsies), although the peasants would have viewed such acts of larceny in a different light! But Rózsi doesn't explain how the Roma came to fall from this state of grace. What sin did they commit which led them to be cast out of paradise and stripped of their magical powers?

SEDENTARISATION

Rózsi's tale offers an explanation of how Gypsies, particularly in parts of Central and Eastern Europe, came to abandon their nomadic way of life. That the story is fiction without any grounding in fact didn't concern her. What mattered to Rózsi and to her daughter, Ilona, who was spellbound by her mother's artful narrative, was that the tale explained how the Roma came to live in houses. It was a story they could believe in, independently of whether it was true.

In Rózsi's account, the old Romani couple were happy to forsake their nomadic way of life when the Count had a house built for them.

In reality, Gypsies in Central and Eastern Europe often gave up their nomadic habits because of coercion rather than consent. Sedentari-sation came in phases; though in part voluntary and representing a natural process of adaptation, at times it was the outcome of high-handed state policy. A succession of energetic and ruthlessly intolerant regimes in the region have compelled nomadic bands of Gypsies to adopt a more orderly, European mode of existence. In the mid eighteenth century, Habsburg Empress Maria Theresa issued a decree ordering Hungary's Gypsies to remain in fixed locations. Gypsies were no longer permitted to move outside their immediate locality without prior authorisation; they were even prohibited from owning horses or carts.[14] Eerily anticipating and even surpassing the assimilationist policies pursued by Communist regimes towards the region's Gypsies, some two hundred years later, use of the word 'Gypsy' was banned. It was replaced by such euphemisms as 'new peasant', 'new Hungarian' and 'new resident'.[15]

The efforts of Maria Theresa and of her successor, Joseph II, to sedentarise the Roma and to transform them into productive subjects met with only partial success. Yet the 1893 census of Hungarian Gypsies, mentioned in Chapter 1, found that only 3.3 per cent of all Gypsies were still fully nomadic while more than 89 per cent had become entirely settled.[16] Even so, the lingering traces of nomadism were viewed as a menace to civilisation. In a report evaluating the findings of the 1893 census a leading ethnologist of the day and academic expert on 'the Gypsy question', Dr Antal Herrmann, described nomadic Gypsies as living as freely as 'wild animals'.[17] He hailed the ending of Gypsy nomadism as 'a political as well as a humanitarian duty' that would safeguard society, while the abandonment of a nomadic lifestyle was described by the learned scholar as nothing less than 'the foundation of cultural development'.[18]

Dr Herrmann's policy recommendations were, to say the least, thorough and far-reaching. Arguing that it may be necessary to 'commit a little cruelty in the name of humanity', he advocated the founding of educational establishments around the country. These were to be used for the 'internment' and education of the children of any nomadic Gypsies unwilling or unable to send their children to school, in compliance with the law. By invoking the threat of removing their children, opined Dr Herrmann, 'it would be possible to have a greater influence on the parents through their children, than vice versa.'[19]

A PEOPLE WITHOUT A HISTORY AND HISTORY WITHOUT A PEOPLE

One of the things that we can learn from Rózsi's fable is that she and her daughter are almost completely ignorant about Roma history. Rózsi was compelled to make up a story in order to provide herself and her audience with an instant, improvised history. Whether she or Ilona actually cared about the authenticity of this narrative is doubtful.

Amongst younger, better-educated Roma such casual unconcern about the past has begun to fade. As noted above, a Romani intelligentsia, though comparatively small in size, is emerging.[20] Yet an indifference to their history and origins has been identified as a feature of traditional Romani culture.[21] Most Gypsies, it is said, live in the present.

Strangely, a lack of curiosity about Roma history extends to many professional historians writing about Central and Eastern Europe. Their books are often silent about the Gypsies even though Gypsies have lived in the region, in significant numbers, since the Middle Ages. The historians' lack of interest in the Gypsies can be attributed to the fact that the latter scarcely participated in most of the major economic, political, cultural and social developments that took place around them. Historians have reflected the Gypsies' absence from these events by omitting *them*, consciously or unconsciously, from their narratives.

Although the question may not excite the curiosity of Rózsi (or of most hidebound historians), I will pose it anyway: where did her ancestors come from? The strong affinities between Romani and various Indic languages – as well as the physical appearance of many Roma – suggest that the Roma are not indigenous to Europe. It is widely accepted by scholars that the Roma originated in northern India.[22] The reasons that prompted the Gypsies' ancestors to leave India remain subject to speculation. According to some theories, the Roma left because of the growing menace posed by Islamic warriors. However, it's clear that the Roma stayed long enough in Persia to absorb many local words into their language before groups of them continued onwards to Europe.[23] There is evidence to suggest that Romani bands appeared in modern-day Romania in the eleventh century. By the fourteenth century, Gypsies are reported to have settled in parts of the Kingdom of Hungary.[24]

So the Roma are relative latecomers to Central and Eastern Europe, arriving many centuries after the Dacians, Slavs and Magyars (Hungarians). Unlike many of the peoples who preceded them, the Roma were too few in numbers and too divided amongst themselves to entertain thoughts of military conquest, of becoming masters in a land of their own. In choosing to make a home for themselves in Europe the

Roma, like the Jews, understood they would remain a minority, always at the mercy of others.

In the early eighteenth century, Gypsies were hunted down like wild animals in Holland and in parts of Germany, while being a Gypsy was in itself a crime in much of Europe.[25] In the seventeenth and eighteenth centuries, Gypsies were variously branded, flogged, sent to the galleys, imprisoned for life or summarily executed simply for being themselves. Not uncommonly, children were taken away from their parents in order to give them a proper 'Christian' upbringing, a measure that has certain parallels with the experience of numbers of Jewish children in parts of Europe and Russia as late as the middle of the nineteenth century.[26]

Beyond Transylvania, in the Romanian provinces of Wallachia and Moldavia, Gypsies were kept as slaves from as early as the fourteenth century, often in the most wretched conditions, until finally emancipated in the 1850s and 1860s.[27] In his memoirs, published in 1837, Mihail Kogălniceanu, a leading Romanian writer, social commentator and political activist, recalled scenes involving Gypsy slaves that he had witnessed in his youth:[28]

I saw human beings wearing chains on their arms and legs, others with iron clamps around their foreheads, and still others with metal collars about their necks. Cruel beatings, and other punishments such as starvation, being hung over smoking fires, solitary imprisonment and being thrown naked into the snow or the frozen rivers, such was the fate of the wretched Gypsy.

Monasteries and religious foundations, as well as noblemen, owned copious numbers of Gypsy slaves, taking advantage of their skills and freely contributed labour. Such slaves often performed a variety of tasks – as cooks, bakers, gardeners, blacksmiths, musicians, household servants and so on – enabling their masters to concentrate on their religious devotions as well as other, more secular pursuits. Emancipation triggered a wave of Romani migration westwards. The living conditions of those Roma who remained behind were often desperate, forcing many of them to seek employment or aid from their former owners.[29]

GOOD MANNERS

According to most anthropologists, Gypsies are prudish, abhorring any mention of sexual organs or of bodily functions.[30] Yet Rózsi's tale, which she was happy to recount to a Gadjo and to her own daughter, is about a little boy who peers at an old woman's genitals. When Ilona and I proved obtuse, unable to figure out what the 'hairy thing' was that had so fascinated the little boy, Rózsi used a supposedly taboo word, 'pina', which means 'cunt' in Hungarian. Without a trace of embarrassment, Ilona immediately asked me what was the English word for 'pina'. Rózsi didn't reproach her daughter for asking such a lewd question.

Michael Stewart suggests that such 'irreverent sexual banter', although it would not be condoned in exchanges with other Roma, is not uncommon in relations with Gadje. The latter are seen as morally loose by the Roma and as having uncontrollable sexual appetites. Stewart argues that, accordingly, the Roma feel they can behave more freely with Gadje than with their own kind.[31] Yet, on earlier visits to Rózsi's home, when I had asked her about her recollections of the War, she was notably coy in her references to the sexually predatory behaviour of the Soviet soldiers who had occupied her village.[32] Rózsi had initially declined to use words such as 'rape', 'sexual intercourse', or their synonyms, preferring various euphemisms. Like an elderly Romani woman in Transylvania, who had recounted her wartime experiences to me, Rózsi had been straight-laced, almost Victorian, in her avoidance of sexually explicit language. My conversations with Rózsi about the War had taken place during the first year or so that we had known one another. Perhaps, over time, Rózsi grew more relaxed in my company and increasingly willing to reveal her earthy sense of humour. To typecast Gypsies as custodians of a strictly-defined – and unchanging – culture, bound up with notions of 'pollution' or 'shame', would be misconceived.[33] In her stubborn individuality, Rózsi transcends such rigid theorising.

3
The Devouring

I was introduced to Florin and his family in a run-down tenement occupied by Romani squatters on Byron Street, in the Transylvanian city of Cluj. As we sipped coffee and cola in the family's apartment, our conversation eventually touched on the treatment of the Roma during the War. Although Florin was born several years after the end of World War II he proved unexpectedly knowledgeable. His parents had been lucky; unlike Gypsies in some parts of Romania they hadn't been interned in a camp, forcibly resettled in territory captured from the Soviet Union without even minimal food and shelter, or harmed in any way. But everything else that Florin told me about the War and about the persecution of the Roma, including the fact that more than 20,000 Gypsies were killed in a camp at a place called 'Birkenau', was based on a book that he'd read.[1] With his curiosity about Roma history, his political activism and his penchant for reading, Florin isn't typical of the Gypsies in the Byron Street tenement. Unusually, he still has a full-time job at the local garbage dump. Florin is looked up to by the other Gypsies who've appointed him leader of an unofficial residents' association.

An elderly neighbour of Florin's had been present throughout my visit. She had spotted me earlier that morning when I arrived at the settlement accompanied by Eugen, a young Romani activist based in Cluj. Intrigued by the presence of a Gadjo with a camera and a cassette recorder, she had engaged us in conversation and had followed us into Florin's apartment. Although uninvited, her presence was accepted by Florin and his family as perfectly natural. As I was to observe elsewhere, privacy does not feature as an important value amongst traditionally-minded Roma. Receiving neighbours, friends or family in your home, at almost any time of the day, is viewed as a social obligation.[2]

Having listened to my questions about the War and the Holocaust, the old woman spoke out. 'I know,' she said, 'Because I lived through the War.' As a young girl, in 1944, she had stood at the side of the road and watched as a seemingly endless column of Jews, each with a yellow star sewn onto their outer clothing, was led towards the brick factory. I

3   A village war memorial in Hungary

could confirm this part of her story from what I already knew. During the War, a ghetto for the local Jews had been established at the brick factory at Iris, a suburb in the north of Cluj. Up to 18,000 Jews were herded into the ghetto where there was only limited access to water.[3] From the ghetto, the Jews were sent on by rail to the Nazi camps where over 90 per cent perished. By a strange coincidence, Byron Street is also in the suburb of Iris. As we talked, in Florin's apartment, we could not have been more than a few streets away from the former ghetto.

'We Gypsies watched the Jews being led off to the ghetto with great sadness', the old woman told me. 'The Jews aren't bad people', she added, as if rebutting a common presumption. 'They really suffered.'

The Roma had suffered too. The old woman recalled with particular bitterness the behaviour of some of the German troops towards the Romani girls. Rape was commonplace, although the old woman didn't use such sexually explicit language. She talked, instead, of how the Germans had 'grabbed' the girls and forcibly 'kissed' them. In one case, she said, three or four German soldiers had taken it in turns to abuse a Romani woman while her husband looked on, helplessly, a pistol pointed at his head.

But, miraculously, the Roma had survived. As the old woman remembered it, the Gypsy families in Cluj had been told to pack their things and to prepare for a journey the next day. The Jews had already been taken away by this time, and the Roma expected to have to follow them.

The next morning, their bags packed, the Roma waited. But, instead of the Germans or their Hungarian accomplices (Cluj and the whole of northern Transylvania had been annexed by Hungary in August, 1940), it was the Russians who came.[4] The Russian soldiers had entered Cluj mounted on horses, the old woman said, and they sang as they rode into the city. At the very last moment, as they stood on the brink of an abyss, the Gypsies had been saved.

Miraculous escapes and last minute reprieves are commonplace in Gypsy stories about the Roma Holocaust or Porajmos.[5] Whatever the facts, the Roma like to think of themselves as lucky.[6]

Rózsi is the oldest of the Roma I have come to know in Patakrét. At the end of the War she was eight years of age. I felt sure that she would have retained clear memories of that period and of what had happened to the Gypsies in the village. But, when I asked her about the War and the Holocaust, her first and most vivid memories were not of German soldiers or Hungarian *gendarmes*, but of the Soviet troops who had briefly occupied the village towards the end of the War.

'The Russians came', said Rózsi. 'They did horrible things to the women, they raped them.' *Rape* is a word I had suggested, although Rózsi adopted it. She was coy in her references to sexual behaviour, like the old woman in the tenement in Byron Street.

'Almost 50 of them did it to Zsófi, one of the women in the neighbouring house', Rózsi continued. Fifty sounds a lot. But stories of mass rape by drunken Soviet troops, as they 'liberated' swathes of Central and Eastern Europe, are legion. Elderly Roma living in a village to the east of the Hungarian city of Debrecen recall Soviet troops, stationed nearby in the closing stages of the War, slaughtering pigs with their machine guns whenever they fancied some good food and entertainment. Women from the nearby Romani settlement were called upon to cook the meat, while the settlement's Romani musicians were hired to play for the soldiers. After the impromptu meal had been served, the Romani women did their best to hide as the Soviet troops regarded the sexual molestation of any females who were present as an integral part of the evening's entertainment.[7] An elderly Jewish woman told me a similar story about her wartime experiences. As a teenager she lay concealed for most of a night beneath a blanket in the freezing cellar of a Budapest tenement, with her mother sitting on top of her, while Soviet troops scoured the building for serviceable women.

Rózsi recalled that Zsófi's elderly mother, who was approaching 70 at the time, had hurried over to their house for help. But Rózsi's family were powerless to intervene; the Soviet soldiers were armed and determined. Some of the troops even pursued the old woman to Rózsi's home, prompting Rózsi's elder sister to hide in the unlit oven. Rózsi's mother, who was no more than 40 or so and still handsome, grew alarmed that she too would be raped. Rózsi recalls that, in her despair, her mother had cried out in Romani, '[m]y God, what will happen to us?'

Whether Rózsi's account of what occurred next is true, or whether it is an exercise in embellishment or wishful thinking, I cannot say. Like a couple of other stories that she told me soon afterwards, it sounds too good to be true; but I would like to believe it, if only because such stories offer hope, and perhaps a sense that there is a benign and providential force watching over us.

As Rózsi tells it, when her mother cried out in Romani one of the Soviet soldiers who had entered her house pricked up his ears. It transpired that he was a Russian Gypsy. He replied to her in Romani saying, '[d]on't be afraid, I am your brother. I will speak to the other soldiers and make sure you come to no harm.' Apparently, he was true to his word. For as long as the Soviet troops remained in the village, the Gypsy soldier watched over Rózsi's home, going to sleep each night in their hallway, right by the front door. Rózsi's family were spared further molestation by their Soviet liberators.

But Rózsi began to grumble about something else that the Soviets had done. She recalled that they had positioned a big field gun in the yard of her family's house. The soldiers busied themselves, preparing the gun for use. Rózsi's parents grew worried that, if the artillery piece were fired, this would only incite any German or Hungarian forces remaining in the area to rain shells on them, almost certainly destroying the family's home in the process.

Again there was a near miraculous intervention that averted disaster. A small Soviet spotter plane appeared overhead, swooping low over the field gun. The pilot, a woman, gestured impatiently to the soldiers to pack up and move westwards, towards the receding front line. Rózsi's family and her home were spared; there was to be no more fighting in the village.

In her relief, which was still tinged with fear, Rózsi's mother cooked a meal for the departing Soviet troops. She baked *cigány bokoli*, a type of flat bread, which she served with bacon, fried meat and pancakes. She gave all the food to the soldiers. 'Let them satisfy their hunger and go, just so they don't kill us', she said to her family, who were horrified by her prodigal hospitality at a time of such scarcity.

'She was a *buta cigány*,' Rózsi says ruefully of her mother, 'a stupid Gypsy'. Her mother had been afraid of the Soviet troops even though they had not harmed her or her family. In fact, the soldiers had given the children some of their own food, exclaiming good naturedly, '*Tsigánka, Tsigánka!*', or 'little Gypsy girl!', whenever Rózsi passed by.

I asked Rózsi if German or Hungarian forces had mistreated any of the Roma in the village during the War. She said that the Soviet troops had arrived in Patakrét before the Hungarian *gendarmes* had had time to round up the Gypsies, although she'd heard that that was already in preparation. Rózsi assured me that the *gendarmes* had killed the Gypsies in a neighbouring village, throwing the corpses into pits where they were covered with quicklime.

Rózsi reserved her most memorable, if incredible, story for this part of her reminiscences. But, although unbelievable, the story may still be true. As Rózsi tells it, a heavily pregnant Gypsy woman was taken before the highest ranking *gendarme* in a village just a few miles from Patakrét. The officer was sitting behind his desk when she was brought to him. He rose from his chair and, without any preliminaries, the *gendarme* shot her in the head with his pistol, killing the woman instantly.

Somehow, and *this* is the incredible part – not the fact that a *gendarme* in wartime Europe should have shot a pregnant Gypsy – the woman's husband heard of what had happened and reached his wife's body within minutes of her death. Miraculously, the corpse had not been disposed of and was left unattended. According to Rózsi, the husband had brought his cut-throat razor with him. Without a moment's hesitation, the man sliced open his wife's belly and carefully removed the living foetus from her womb. Rózsi assured me that the baby thrived and that it had grown up into a healthy woman who was alive to this day, with a large family of her own.

For a long time I wondered how to treat Rózsi's 'recollections' of the War. At one level they can be enjoyed as stories, wonderfully crafted narratives expertly told, full of danger and excitement and with reassuringly happy endings. But, at another level, Rózsi's reminiscences offer genuine insights into the experiences of the village's Roma during the War, even if the stories have been embellished at the edges. Whatever the truth about the Soviet Gypsy soldier, or the Gypsy who saved his daughter by pulling the foetus out of his dead wife's womb, there is no doubt that Rózsi's first and most vivid memories of the War concern the deplorable behaviour of the Soviet troops. That simple fact tells us that the persecution of the Roma, at least in this corner of Europe, was less urgent and systematic than the campaign against the Jews. There were no pockets of relative safety in rural Hungary where Jews could live out the war unscathed. While Rózsi and the other Roma in Patakrét went about their business, almost unaffected by the hostilities raging around them, the Jews of the village, as the war memorial in the centre of the village poignantly reminds us, were rounded up and sent to their deaths.

Scanning the columns of names inscribed on the memorial, it soon became apparent that the list of those from the village who had died in World War II was not confined to soldiers or airmen killed on active service (Hungary had no navy to speak of). The names include the 'Khon family', 'Mr and Mrs Gelber', 'Mr and Mrs Freisinger' and several women including Mrs Czigler, Erzsébet Czigler, Mrs Herman Kramer, Mrs Sándor Kramer and Mrs Timár. For some reason, Mr Czigler, Mr Herman Kramer, Mr Sándor Kramer and Dr Károly Timár are recorded separately from their wives, while the Gelbers and the Freisingers are described as married couples. Although ages are not given, this list within a list must have included children (members of the Khon family, at least, as well as Erzsébet Czigler) and, more than likely, several who were elderly or infirm.

These people had not borne arms either for or against Hungary. They had been victims of another, parallel war that was fought over much of Europe alongside the war between states. The Khon family, Mr and Mrs Gelber, Mr and Mrs Freisinger, Mrs Czigler, Erzsébet Czigler, Mrs Herman Kramer, Mrs Sándor Kramer and Mrs Timár, as well as Mr Czigler, Mr Herman Kramer, Mr Sándor Kramer and Dr Károly Timár, had died in the Nazi war against the Jews.[8] They had been victims of a policy of 'ethnic cleansing' before that term had even been coined.

Of course, if the Soviets had not occupied Patakrét when they did, forcing the Germans and their Hungarian allies to retreat, Rózsi and all her family would have become increasingly vulnerable as the persecution of the region's Roma spread.[9] It could only have been a matter of time before Patakrét's Gypsies shared the fate of the Roma in much of the rest of wartime Europe. They too might have been interned in local camps without proper food or medical provision, killed indiscriminately by troops or *gendarmes*, deported in freight wagons to Auschwitz-Birkenau or to one of the other Nazi death camps, or forcibly sterilized.

THE PERSECUTION OF THE ROMA BY THE NAZIS
AND THEIR ALLIES DURING WORLD WAR II

The historical evidence suggests that the Nazi persecution of the Gypsies was almost an afterthought. Gypsies are not even mentioned in Hitler's rambling and incoherent political manifesto, *Mein Kampf*, indicating that the Roma were peripheral to his central ideas and preoccupations. During the entire period that Hitler was in power he is only known to have referred to Gypsies twice.[10] Unlike the Jews, Gypsies were a numerically insignificant minority in Germany when Hitler became Chancellor in 1933, accounting for only 26,000 persons. Frequently itinerant, mostly poor, these Roma were 'a strictly marginal element' in German society.[11] Yet, Gypsies like Jews came to be seen by the Nazis as less than human. Nazi ideology regarded Jews *and* Gypsies as virulent microbes capable of infecting the Aryan race.[12]

In the first volume of his masterly biography of Hitler, covering the years 1889–1936, Ian Kershaw argues that the targeting of Gypsies, along with certain other groups, probably originated with Nazi ideologues and over-zealous German police officers eager to elaborate the vision of the Führer by uncovering 'new internal "enemies" to combat'. These freshly discovered 'enemies' were mostly 'weak, unpopular and marginalized social groups such as gypsies, homosexuals, beggars, "antisocials", "work-shy", and "habitual criminals"'.[13] So Gypsies, it seems, were just an addendum to the Nazi roll call of those targeted for persecution and possible destruction.

But if the Nazis hated Gypsies less intensely than Jews, and certainly feared them less, Gypsies shared much the same fate as Jews in many parts of Europe. The severity of the persecution of the Roma during the Holocaust varied, often depending on local factors. In Hungary, anti-Roma policies were introduced later and applied more selectively, sometimes even arbitrarily, than the battery of legislative and other measures constricting the country's Jews.[14] Estimates of the numbers of Hungarian Gypsies killed in the Porajmos vary from as little as a few hundred to as many as 32,000, although the true figure cannot be calculated with any degree of accuracy.[15] By contrast, over 400,000 Hungarian Jews perished at Auschwitz-Birkenau alone.[16]

But, at its worst, the persecution of the Roma was scarcely distinguishable from that of the Jews. In the German Protectorate of Bohemia and Moravia itinerant Gypsies were interned in labour camps, such as Lety and Hodonin, where the guards were Czechs, not Germans.[17] In overcrowded and insanitary conditions, weakened by lack of food, hundreds of internees died of contagious diseases such as typhus. Survivors, along with the bulk of all the Gypsies remaining in Bohemia and Moravia, were deported to Auschwitz, where all but a few hundred perished.[18] In Jasenovac, a notorious death camp in the wartime Fascist state of Croatia, Ustasa guards butchered Gypsies, Jews and Serbs indiscriminately, in what was widely seen as a 'holy war' against the country's ethnic and religious minorities.[19] Reportedly, even German military personnel who visited the camp were appalled. Out of an estimated 28,500 Roma in Croatia in 1941, between 26,000 and 28,000 are thought to have died in the Porajmos.[20] In Romania, a close ally of Nazi Germany for part of World War II, over 13,000 sedentary Gypsies were rounded up and sent by train to Transnistria during September and October 1942.[21] Transnistria, formerly Soviet territory, had been occupied by Axis forces and placed under a Romanian administration. Many of the settled Roma deported to the region were given no opportunity to collect warm clothes, blankets or cooking utensils before their departure. Around 11,500 nomadic Gypsies from Romania had already been forcibly resettled in Transnistria by the end of August, while the territory had also become a dumping ground for Romania's Jews. A total of 180,000 Romanian Jews were deported to Transnistria between 1941 and 1944. Amidst terrible conditions, which resulted from a combination of malice and incompetence on the part of the Romanian authorities, Gypsies and Jews succumbed to typhus, starvation and to random persecution by *gendarmes*. According to a report compiled by Romanian officials in December 1942, in the Oceacov region of Transnistria, Gypsies were 'insufficiently fed being given only 400 grams of bread for those capable of working and just 200 grams for the old people and children'. This meagre diet was supplemented with 'a few potatoes and very rarely salted fish…in extremely small quantities'. The report went on to note that, in the Oceacov area, '[i]n recent days…as many as ten or fifteen [Gypsies] have died daily' and that the corpses were 'full of parasites'. Despite the severe cold in winter, the Gypsies were 'naked without any clothes, and clothing and heating materials are completely lacking'.[22] Of almost 25,000 Romanian Gypsies deported to Transnistria in 1942, only 6,000 are thought to have survived.[23]

Beginning in the spring of 1941, German *Einsatzgruppen*, augmented by thousands of locally recruited auxiliaries, followed in the wake of the Wehrmacht as it swept across the Soviet Union. The *Einsatzgruppen* focused most of their energies on killing Jews and Bolsheviks, categories that were seen by the Nazis as largely interchangeable.[24] But

Gypsies, particularly nomadic bands who were suspected of espionage and of aiding Soviet partisans, were routinely targeted for execution.[25] As one text dryly notes, '[t]he killing of Gypsy women and children was standard practice'.[26] Even in the Netherlands, long a byword for liberalism and tolerance, the Dutch police and *gendarmerie* diligently rounded up Gypsies in the spring of 1944, screening out Dutch nationals who were not ethnically Romani and handing over the 'real' Gypsies for deportation to Auschwitz.[27] Of these, less than 10 per cent remained alive at the end of the War.

In Germany, tens of thousands of Gypsies, the chronically sick and others deemed 'unworthy of life' were gassed in euthanasia programmes between the beginning of 1940 and August 1941.[28] By the end of the War, more than half of Germany's former Gypsy population had perished.[29] At the village of Chelmno, in a zone of Poland that had been annexed by the Reich in 1939, almost 5,000 German Roma were gassed in the back of specially constructed trucks, in January 1942, as a precautionary measure.[30] Typhus had broken out at the camp where the Gypsies had been interned. The same trucks had been used to gas Jews for at least a month. Approximately half of Germany's Romani population, over 13,000 Gypsies, were sent to Auschwitz during 1943, in accordance with a decree issued by Himmler which nominally exempted 'pure Sinti and Lalleri Gypsies'.[31] As a historian of the period has noted, '[m]any of those exempt from deportation were made subject to compulsory sterilization'.[32] Inside Auschwitz, where the Roma were kept in a specially constructed family camp, Gypsy children, along with Jews, were subjected to bizarre and medically worthless experiments by Josef Mengele, in a brutal parody of scientific inquiry.[33] Gypsies were also experimented on at Natzweiler, Dachau, Sachsenhausen and Ravensbrück. Within the space of four months, at the beginning of 1945, 15,000 Gypsies died of starvation and disease at the German concentration camp of Mauthausen.[34] While large numbers of Gypsies were interned in various concentration camps, including Mauthausen, Dachau, Sachsenhausen, Buchenwald, Bergen-Belsen and Ravensbrück, others were sent to specially constructed extermination camps – Birkenau (Auschwitz II), Belzec, Chelmno, Maidanek, Sobibór and Treblinka. If fewer Gypsies than Jews died in the Holocaust, the persecution and prolonged torment of a large proportion of Europe's Gypsies was real enough.

Even if the alleged intention of the Nazis – to kill every single Gypsy in Europe – remains unproven, the scale of the atrocities committed against the Roma during the War and the classification of the entire race as a threat to the German people place Gypsies in close proximity to Jews as fellow victims of the Holocaust.[35] History, it seems, does not provide us with grounds for dismissing the Porajmos as a sideshow.

While acknowledging the suffering of the Roma, some historians have expressed doubts as to whether the persecution of the Gypsies should be characterised as genocide. There was no *intent* to destroy the Gypsies as an ethnic group, it has been argued, in contrast to the proven plan of the Nazis to wipe out all the Jews. If Gypsies died at the hands of the Germans and their allies, their deaths were frequently unintentional, the product of a startlingly callous indifference to their plight. Whatever name we choose to give it, so these historians contend, we should not confuse the frequently inhuman treatment of the Gypsies during World War II with cold-blooded genocide, the *intentional* destruction of a national, racial, ethnic or religious group.[36]

Though sincere and well intentioned such scholarly arguments are mistaken. The persecution of the Roma and that of the Jews in the Holocaust were, in many important respects, comparable. And, in many instances, they were carried out for comparable reasons. In viewing Jews and Gypsies as *innately* corrupt and corrupting, the Nazis singled out these two ethnic groups from every other people in Europe.[32] To be a Jew or a Gypsy meant that, by virtue of your racial heritage, you were deemed a threat to the German *Volk*. One of the Nuremberg Laws, hastily adopted by the German Reichstag in September 1935, under the watchful eye of the Führer, aptly illustrates this thinking. The Law for the Defense of German Blood and Honour, whose passage had been advocated by influential groups of German doctors,[*] prohibited marriage or sexual relations between Jews and Germans to ensure 'the purity of German blood'.[38] Within a couple of months the prohibition was extended to forbid Germans from marrying or engaging in sexual relations with Gypsies, or with others of 'alien blood' such as 'Negroes'.[39] In a subsequent decree, forbidding marriage between Germans and persons with even one Gypsy grandparent, Germany's Minister of the Interior declared, 'Gypsy blood endangered the purity of…German blood to a marked degree.'[40]

If many Romani fatalities during World War II were not consciously planned, mass fatalities were, at the very least, predictable. While the Nazis *may* have transported German, Austrian and Czech Gypsies to

---

[*] For example, a meeting of doctors in Nuremberg, held in December 1934, had demanded the criminalisation of sexual relations between German women and Jews, in order to prevent 'further Jewish-racial poisoning and pollution of German blood'. Quoted in Kershaw, *Hitler, 1889–1936*, p. 564.

Auschwitz without any clear intention of killing them, conditions in the camp – malnutrition, lack of hygiene, chronic overcrowding – ensured the spread of deadly diseases such as typhus.[41] Much the same is true of Romania's chaotic resettlement of tens of thousands of Gypsies in Transnistria. The moral and legal culpability of those responsible is all too clear.

In many instances, mass deaths amongst the Roma were not the product of administrative bungling or indifference. The systematic killing of nomadic Gypsies, including women and children, in areas of the Soviet Union occupied by German forces, represented deliberate policy. Much the same was true in the wartime state of Croatia. In Germany itself, sterilisation was proposed in 1943 for all Gypsies not deported to Auschwitz.[42] In theory, sterilisation could be declined by individual Gypsies. However, in practice, '[w]hen a person refused to be sterilized, the police would often threaten dispatch to a concentration camp, and this threat usually brought about the desired consent'.[43]

These policies of mass murder and forcible sterilisation were motivated by a cold-blooded intent to destroy at least a large part of the Romani people. The measures adopted by Nazi Germany and several of her allies would, in all probability, satisfy the definition of genocide or of complicity in genocide found in the Genocide Convention of 1948.[44] Article II of the Convention, which entered into force in 1951, defines genocide as:[45]

> any of the following acts, committed with intent to destroy, *in whole or in part*,
> a national, ethnical, racial or religious group, as such:
> Killing members of the group;
> Causing serious bodily or mental harm to members of the group;
> Deliberately inflicting on the group conditions of life calculated to bring about its physical destruction in whole or in part;
> Imposing measures intended to prevent births within the group;
> Forcibly transferring children of the group to another group.

At the very least, the persecution of the Roma constituted 'Crimes Against Humanity' and 'War Crimes' as understood by the Charter of the Nuremberg Tribunal.[46] Overall, the Nazi treatment of the Gypsies was not merely 'persecution', as some historians would have us believe. In many parts of Europe the Gypsy experience in World War II fully merits the label genocide, or even 'Holocaust'.

THE FORGOTTEN HOLOCAUST[47]

In view of the scale and severity of the wartime persecution of the Roma by Nazi Germany and some of her allies, it is remarkable that the Porajmos remained largely unacknowledged until comparatively recently. This lack of acknowledgement can tell us much about attitudes towards the Roma, but also something about the Roma themselves. Usually, it is the victims of any major human rights abuse who are the first and the loudest in articulating their anger and sense of injustice. For a long time, the silence of Gadje about the Nazi persecution of the Gypsies was very nearly matched by the silence of the Roma. For years, the Roma seemed almost to collude with the tacit consensus not to draw too much attention to this neglected aspect of the War. As Isabel Fonseca remarks, with perhaps a trace of exasperation, Gypsies have 'no tradition of commemoration, or even of discussion' of the Porajmos, '[i]t is a story that remains almost unknown – even to many Gypsies who survived it'.[48]

Many Roma may have chosen to remain silent about their sufferings during the War because of a deliberate decision to put the past behind them and to concentrate on the present. In part, though, the Roma were silent because they lacked a voice with which to command the attention of politicians, the media, or the public at large. Low levels of literacy have meant that most ordinary Roma lack the skills needed to communicate effectively with non-Roma society.[49] When I asked Rózsi how to spell the name of the street on which she lives – I had promised to send her some photographs – she became flustered and could not tell me. Bubi, who lived in the same village, was unable to write his own name when I asked him to sign a receipt for the money that I had paid him for his 'services' as a guide. Even János, Bubi's son and more than a generation younger than Rózsi and his father, had asked me to write out the word *Anglia*, which is Hungarian for 'England', so that he could send me a letter after my return to Britain. The letter never arrived. Until fairly recently there were comparatively few Roma who could write articles for highbrow newspapers, or Romani scholars who could produce monographs on the Roma Holocaust. Even now there are very few Romani lawyers who can take up claims on behalf of their people; I know of only one Romani film-maker, Tony Gatlif. Although his art-house films on Romani themes are much admired by the critics, they lack the wide commercial appeal and popular impact of those of Steven Spielberg. Poverty, social marginalisation, lack of education and, not infrequently, scant respect for formal education, as well as a widely-held suspicion of bureaucracies and officials, have kept the Roma mute. As János confided to me the first time we met, '[education] isn't very popular with Gypsies, that's the problem'.

Unlike a number of other diasporic communities the Roma have very little clout.[50] Although there is a sizeable Romani population scattered around the world it lacks the political cohesion, intellectual resources or economic 'muscle' wielded by several other diasporic groups.[51] Gypsies, whether in Central and Eastern Europe or elsewhere, are overwhelmingly poor.[52] There are few, if any, Romani investors whom governments in Prague, Bucharest or Bratislava would wish to court. Politically, the Roma have relatively little influence, even in countries where they constitute a significant demographic element. There is no Romani state to represent Romani interests much as Israel, somewhat erratically, has championed the cause of vulnerable Jewish minorities in various continents.[53] Apart from occasional and limited help from India, the Roma stand alone.[54]

But even this isn't the whole story. In all my interviews with Roma in Central and Eastern Europe, I never heard a single spontaneous comment about the Porajmos. I always had to coax some recollection out of those of my interviewees who had lived through the War. It seemed to me that it was not fear or innate reserve that prevented these Roma from volunteering their memories of that period. The same people complained readily enough about the prejudice or obstructiveness that they encountered in their dealings with local officials, police officers or aid agencies. They spoke at length about the hardships that they have to endure each day in the course of their ordinary lives. If many Roma choose not to speak unprompted about the War perhaps it is because – with the exception of a small educated elite – they tend to live overwhelmingly in the present, rather than in the past or in the future.[55] As I was told repeatedly by social workers and others employed by aid agencies, chronically poor Roma – which is most Roma in the CEE states – are preoccupied with immediate needs and concerns, whether feeding and clothing themselves and their families, ensuring that their homes are habitable, or dealing with public authorities. The past, including the War years, when many Roma faced terrible persecution, or the imminent threat of persecution, has somehow lost its importance for most of them.[56] It can be recalled, in order to satisfy the curiosity of a Gadjo questioner, but the exercise is artificial.

4
Maybe Tomorrow there
Won't even be Bread

CHILDHOOD

András was born in 1940 in the Slovak town of Košice that Hungarians call Kassa. 'When the Germans started to deport the Jews and the Gypsies from Kassa and the surrounding area,' he says, 'I was spirited away by relatives to safety in Sátoralujhely. I had grandparents living there.'[1] Although András is comparatively light-skinned and could easily pass for a Slovak or a Hungarian, he and his family are Gypsies.

Today, Kassa and Sátoralujhely are separated by the border dividing Slovakia and Hungary. But in 1944, when four-year-old András fled for his life, Kassa belonged to Hungary. The area, known as the Felvidék by Hungarians, was considered an integral part of the historic Kingdom of Hungary. In the political settlement following World War I, Slovakia had been incorporated in the new state of Czechoslovakia, uniting the predominantly rural and conservative Slovaks with the more progressive, industrialised Czechs. However, during the previous half century, Slovakia had been governed from Budapest.[2] In November 1938, a southern strip of Slovakia, including Kassa and several other towns, were restored to Hungarian rule as a result of intervention by Germany and Italy, anxious to satisfy the revisionist aspirations of the pro-Axis Hungarian government.[3] Following World War II, the territory reverted to Czechoslovakia until the eventual dissolution of that country and the creation of two fully sovereign Czech and Slovak states in January 1993.

András doesn't know what became of his parents, whether they survived the War or whether they were rounded up and killed along with hundreds of thousands of Roma in parts of Europe controlled by Nazi Germany and its allies.[4] He has received no news of his parents since his hasty departure from Kassa. He can only speculate as to what may have happened to them.

For a while András lived with his grandparents in Sátoralujhely, a small town in north-eastern Hungary. 'We were very poor', he says.

4   András Balogh Balázs in his apartment in Salgótarján, Hungary

'Mostly, we survived on boiled potatoes but often there wasn't enough to go round. We hardly ever ate real bread. Sometimes, if my grandmother managed to get hold of a little flour, she'd make *bodak*, a type of flat bread that's popular amongst Gypsies.'[5] After his grandmother died, the boy was looked after by his grandfather until the old man fell ill. At this point, András was placed in an orphanage by his relatives.

András is a neat looking man, balding and in his early sixties. His large hands and muscular shoulders hint at a life of manual labour. For as long as he talks about his childhood he never smiles. Later, András says to me, 'it's better if I forget it [my childhood], but I can't erase it from inside me'.

András can remember passing through ten or more orphanages as a
child and being sent to live with various foster families. In return for
looking after the boy his foster parents received a small sum of money
each week for his keep. 'They pocketed the money', András says.
'None of them ever spent a penny of it on feeding or clothing me!'

If the foster family were peasants he was made to clean out the barns
where they kept their animals – pigs, cows, and maybe a few horses.
During the day it was his job to take the animals out to pasture. András
says that he rarely had the opportunity to attend school. 'The teachers
were glad if the Gypsy kids stayed away from classes', he says. In
those days, the authorities hardly bothered about Gypsies playing
truant. 'At night', says András, 'I had to sleep with the animals in the
barn, even in winter. None of the peasants ever let me sleep inside the
house with them.'

Interestingly, András says that he fared no better when he was
fostered by Gypsy families. 'They sent me out to beg in the streets
with a wicker basket tied to my back, or a bundle made out of an old
blanket that was knotted at either end and slung across my shoulders,'
he recalls. People, feeling sorry for him, would give him money or
maybe a little food. 'If the Gypsy family I was living with weren't
satisfied with what I'd collected during the day, they'd beat me when I
returned to their place at night. They'd slap me across the face or kick
me. I can't abide the sight of a bundle to this day.'

While András talks about his childhood he continues painting. The
title of the picture he's working on, an oil, is *Maybe Tomorrow there
won't even be Bread*. 'That's the position they're in right now', says
András, referring to his fellow Roma.

Many of András' paintings have wistful, evocative titles. He's called
another picture, depicting a ragged Gypsy couple walking towards
an uncertain future, *The Sun will not Rise again for them*. In András'
paintings the background is always black, even if the sun can be seen
clearly overhead.

Maybe Tomorrow there won't even be Bread depicts a Gypsy sitting
cross-legged in front of some ramshackle houses. With a long knife he's
cutting slices of bread from a loaf that he's cradling in his arms. The
village in the painting is based on a settlement in the Great Hungarian
Plain, where András was fostered for a while by a Gypsy family.

'No-one today would believe what these houses were like', he says.
A single room was hacked out of the bare earth and a simple roof was
placed directly over it. You entered by a door and went down some
steps to get into the only room. There were no beds. Instead, the family,

including András, slept side by side on piles of straw that they covered with old clothes.

'We stole the straw from the peasants', says András, rather sheepishly. He's clearly embarrassed by this admission but determined, at all costs, to tell the truth. A morally upright man, András is critical of younger Roma who steal or rob even though he concedes that, 'it's more and more difficult just to survive if you're a Gypsy. The trouble is there are people in this society who treat Gypsies as if they're all the same rather than in accordance with their individual merits.'

Throughout their long and troubled history in Europe stereotyping has been the curse of Gypsies, reducing them to a few clichéd images as thieves, vagabonds, idlers and, on occasion, extravagantly talented musicians. András, with an exemplary work record, a gleaming apartment and a passion for painting in oils doesn't fit these stereotypes.

One of András' foster families lived in the medieval town of Eger in northern Hungary. For Hungarians, the town of Eger has strong historic associations. It was the scene of a famous siege by the Turkish Ottoman army in 1551. Although the defenders were heavily outnumbered and outgunned they held off the Ottoman forces who eventually gave up, returning to their strongholds in the east. It's chronicled that, in this epic struggle, Hungarian women fought alongside their menfolk on the battlements of Eger's castle.*

For András, Eger has less happy associations despite the fact that it's the place where he met his present wife, Jolán Oláh. 'When I was a child, the man in the family I was sent to live with in Eger was a homosexual. In other words, he was ill.' András says that the man sexually abused him over a long period. 'When I was 13 or 14 I was finally strong enough to resist him.'

András left the foster family in Eger and struck out on his own, wandering from town to town. Eventually, by the age of 16 or 17, he wound up in Budapest. Like many Gypsies who had had little formal education, the only work that András was able to find was as a labourer.

'I only completed one and a half years of school', András says. 'In the summer, the orphanage sent me to school half-naked and without shoes. The floorboards in the classroom were oiled and the oil stuck to the soles of my feet.' In winter, he can remember attending school with rags tied round his feet in place of shoes. 'I wasn't the only one',

---

* Although Hungarians don't like to be reminded of the fact, the Ottoman army, commanded by Sultan Mehmed III, returned to Eger in 1596 and took the castle. The Turks remained in Eger until 1687.

he says. 'Even some of the Gypsy kids who lived at home with their parents went to school with rags on their feet.'

ADULTHOOD

András didn't take up painting until much later in life. For years he worked in Budapest, first as a labourer, later delivering sacks of coal to apartment buildings. For a while he dug ditches and helped to lay pipes. In the meantime he got married and had a couple of children.

In 1962, on a visit to friends in Eger, he met Jolán. They fell in love almost immediately and decided to set up house together. Jolán was living in Salgótarján at the time, a sprawling industrial and mining town in northern Hungary, close to the border with Slovakia. They agreed that András should join her there. Moving house wasn't a complicated affair. 'I only had one pair of trousers, one pair of shoes and one shirt. That was all!' he chuckles.

After settling in Salgótarján, András did various jobs. At first he worked in a foundry, then in a steel mill. For five years he toiled as a miner in the local coal mines. Throughout the last 22 years of his working life, until he was forced to take early retirement in 1992, András was employed by the Nógrád County Waterworks. 'I did everything connected with pipes', he says. 'I laid new pipes and repaired any of the old ones that were broken or cracked.' In contrast to the widely held view in Central and Eastern Europe that Gypsies are work-shy, András was energetic and conscientious. Twice, during the Communist era, he was designated a *kiváló dolgozó*, or 'outstanding worker'. András has kept the certificates he was given in a drawer and offers to show them to me.

When András moved to Salgótarján to live with Jolán, they set up house together in the town's notorious Gypsy settlement. However, despite the lack of even basic amenities in the settlement, the couple have fond memories of this period of their lives.

'There was a real sense of community', says András. 'No-one called you names for being a Gypsy. If you ran out of coffee, or anything, you could always borrow some from a neighbour.'

'Couldn't you do that here?' I ask. For years, he and Jolán have lived in a modern apartment block, close to the centre of town.

'I've never tried', András confesses. The idea of asking one of his Hungarian neighbours if he could borrow something clearly strikes him as outlandish.

But, for all its warmth and sense of comradeship, the former Gyps‚ settlement in Salgótarján had numerous drawbacks. Water had to be brought by hand from a public well at the bottom of a hill, almost half a kilometre away. Until the mid 1960s, when the authorities finally installed some communal toilets, there weren't even any lavatories in the settlement. The Roma were forced to relieve themselves in a nearby wood.[6]

'The house we lived in was built right up against the side of a hill', says András. 'When it rained, the water poured down the hill and straight onto the roof.' Over time, much of the roof rotted away so that the rain began to seep through in several places and into the rooms below. In winter, it was unbearably cold as the house lacked proper insulation. In these unhealthy and insalubrious conditions, their few pieces of furniture soon started to spoil, growing mouldy.

As early as 1961, Salgótarján's town council had decided to tear down the Gypsy settlement on public health grounds. Gradually, Romani settlements in other towns were dismantled and their occupants resettled. This was not just a matter of improving the quality of the housing stock available to Gypsies so as to achieve greater parity between Roma and Hungarian living conditions. Eliminating the Romani settlements also represented a means of removing one of the most important physical barriers impeding the integration of Roma within the broader society. Nevertheless, by 1967, there were still upwards of 60 houses on the Romani settlement in Salgótarján, each of which was occupied by a Romani family. It wasn't until the early 1970s that the last remaining houses were demolished.

The Romani families uprooted from the settlement were given the choice of a modern apartment in the town, or of financial assistance towards the cost of building a house for themselves nearby. András and Jolán opted for a brand new one-and-a-half-room apartment. They moved to their present home, comprising two rooms, kitchen and bathroom, a couple of years later. When the opportunity arose, they bought their apartment outright.

In 1992, two years after the defeat of the incumbent Communists in Hungary's first genuinely democratic elections in over 40 years, András was presented with a stark choice by his employers, the County Waterworks. At the time, Hungary was taking its first faltering steps towards establishing a market economy. In the process, hundreds of thousands of jobs were lost as state-owned enterprises were closed down, restructured, or sold off to private bidders who quickly streamlined their operations.[7]

53

could either volunteer for early retirement or face
~~dismi~~irás recalls. A proud man, András decided to accept
~~al~~ although he knew it would be a struggle to get by
~~on a pe~~ _nsion, particularly at a time of mounting inflation.
~~And~~ ~~ras~~' wife, Jolán, had already been forced to retire as a result of ill
health. For years she'd worked on the surface at one of the local coal
mines. Together with several other women she had stood all day beside
a wide belt on which the coal was carried along. With little in the way
of protection from the dust and filth, the women had to pick out stones
and other debris that had got tangled up with the coal. It was dirty and
unhealthy work, exacerbating Joláns' health problems.

András and Jolán have two children of their own, a son and a daughter
now in their thirties. Their son completed eight years of education, the
statutory minimum in Hungary. He's employed as a labourer by the
waterworks, like his father before him. Their daughter, who is married
and has two children of her own, stays home to look after her family.

THE IMPACT OF COMMUNISM ON THE ROMA
OF CENTRAL AND EASTERN EUROPE

If it were not for the fact that András took up drawing and painting in
his spare time, his story would be typical enough of an entire generation
of Gypsies in Central and Eastern Europe, particularly in the 1950s
and 1960s. With little formal education and high levels of illiteracy
amongst the Roma of the region, the Communist authorities forcibly
integrated Gypsies into the various national economies as unskilled or
semi-skilled workers, whether in factories, in construction and road
building projects, or in the newly formed agricultural co-operatives.
The working life of Lajós, a Romungro Gypsy living in Cluj in western
Romania, which I describe in Chapter 6, was strikingly similar to that
of András in neighbouring Hungary. During the first two decades of
Communism, policies concerning the Roma were broadly comparable
throughout the region. Urban Gypsies like András and Lajós – as well
as Vlach Roma in villages such as Patakrét – were expected to become
workers in a great new socialist experiment. They were to become
proletarians and, at least nominally, equal citizens, shedding much or
all of their Gypsy identities along the way.[8]

In Hungary, for example, the Political Committee of the Communist
Party adopted a key decision, in June 1961, on 'The Improvement of
the Situation of the Gypsy Population'.[9] It called, in effect, for the
assimilation of the country's various distinct Romani communities

within Hungarian society.[10] Although the term 'assimilation' – found in all of the preparatory documents leading up to the adoption of the Committee's decision – was dropped in favour of the more diplomatic term 'integration', this was just a euphemism.[11]

The Party's decision emphatically rejected the proposition that Gypsies constitute a distinct national or ethnic group within Hungary. It also expressed unequivocal opposition to any measures that might impede or delay the vital 'integration' – that is, assimilation – of the country's Gypsies:[12]

> There are still some erroneous views in circulation regarding the solution of the Gypsy question. Many treat it as if it were a nationalities issue and recommend the development of the 'Gypsy language', the establishment of Gypsy-language schools, colleges and of separate agricultural co-operatives for Gypsies, etc. Such ideas are not only wrong they are positively harmful as they preserve the isolation of Gypsies and slow down their integration within society.

An unashamedly assimilationist approach to the Gypsy 'problem' was pursued by both Bulgaria and the former Czechoslovakia right up until the final collapse of Communist rule in 1989.[13] In the case of Czechoslovakia, this was combined with a campaign encouraging the sterilisation of Romani women. From 1986, sterilisation was available to women of 18 and above in Czechoslovakia, including those who had not yet had children. A substantial financial incentive was paid to volunteers. Although the sterilisation programme was not explicitly confined to Gypsies, it was widely recognised that it was intended 'primarily to slow the rapid growth of the Romani population'.[14]

Elsewhere in Central and Eastern Europe greater tolerance was shown over time towards Romani minorities and their distinctive cultures. For example, beginning in the early 1970s, the Hungarian authorities gradually rejected assimilation as an appropriate goal – having embraced it in 1961 – finally recognising the Roma as a distinct ethnic minority in 1984.[15] In other states in the region, notably Poland and Romania, assimilationist campaigns were fitful at best. For much of the time, particularly after the mid 1970s (in Romania) and after the mid 1960s (in Poland) the Roma were ignored.[16]

As an exercise in social engineering the assimilationist phase of the Communist project for the Romani peoples of Central and Eastern Europe had glaring faults – at least in retrospect. It wilfully ignored the customs and values that many Gypsies had preserved to some degree, particularly those living in comparative isolation in Romani settlements. Communist officials examining the 'Gypsy question', especially in the 1950s and 1960s, saw only poverty, social neglect, ignorance and chronic health problems – as well as a stubborn refusal to conform – rather than authentic minority cultures. In a heavy-handed way, they assigned Gypsies to jobs in factories, mines, agricultural co-operatives or on building sites that, in many cases, were artificially created and had no long-term (that is to say, post-Communist) future.[17] And in executing this policy, the Communists didn't spare a thought for the skills, occupational habits, lifestyles or values of those affected. For example, Hungary's Vlach Romani community favour forms of economic activity that prioritise quick wittedness, even cunning, over laborious and time-consuming work, particularly wage labour.[18] Traditionally, they have chosen, wherever possible, to engage in commerce or trade as a way of earning a living. Such personal or cultural preferences were casually ignored in a process that saw Hungary's Vlach Roma assigned to jobs offering them little in the way of personal satisfaction.[19] Similarly, forcibly sedentarising bands of nomadic Gypsies (in fact, a small fraction of the region's Romani population by this time) was seen unequivocally as a progressive, emancipatory measure. By taking away nomadic Gypsies' horses and carts, Communist authorities in Central and Eastern Europe believed that they were contributing to the creation of healthier and more orderly societies.

However, hundreds of thousands of Roma, like András and Lajós, grew up with little sense of a distinct cultural heritage and in conditions of acute poverty. For them, the Communists offered a secure way of life, freedom from hunger and want. In contrast to the quaint stereotype of Gypsy bands leading their colourful wagons from place to place, the great majority of Gypsies in Central and Eastern Europe had given up a nomadic way of life several generations earlier. As noted above, according to a census of Hungary's Gypsy population conducted in 1893, over 89 per cent of Gypsies were fully sedentarised. A further 7.5 per cent were semi-nomadic and only 3.3 per cent of Gypsies remained entirely nomadic by this date. Of the sedentarised Gypsies, 40 per cent lived together with non-Gypsies rather than in isolated settlements.[20]

Many Roma, particularly those living in mixed communities, had embarked on a slow process of integration,[21] acquiring more and more of the habits, lifestyle and ways of thinking of the peasants or industrial workers around them. Except in their physical appearance, they were less and less like the 'authentic' Gypsies of popular imagination.

Even members of comparatively traditional Gypsy communities who had resisted integration, such as Hungary's Vlach Roma, often welcomed the relief from hunger and squalid living conditions that the Communists brought. Vlach Gypsies may have chafed at the monotonous and tiring work that they were obliged to perform in factories and agricultural co-operatives.[22] But, nonetheless they were often keenly aware of the dramatic improvement in their living standards as a result of having a regular wage packet.

'Kádár was good for the Gypsies; perhaps for the Hungarians as well', Rózsi confided to me. Kádár, Hungary's astute and widely respected Communist leader, held power for over three decades until 1988. 'There was work', Rózsi added. 'While Kádár was around everything was good.'

Bubi, a middle-aged Vlach Gypsy, living just a few streets away from Rózsi, told me much the same thing as we chatted in the front room of his brick-built house, erected during the Communist years with a low-interest loan. 'When Kádár was alive, there was work. But now a man who needs work can't even get a job sweeping the streets. Now there is nothing.'

Unsurprisingly, the Communist vision of equal citizenship for Central and Eastern Europe's Gypsies was imperfectly implemented. Long-standing prejudices didn't disappear overnight as a result of the radical transformation of the institutions and norms governing the newly socialist societies. In their innermost convictions, many people – including the managers of agricultural co-operatives and factory foremen – remained largely unreconstructed.

'Gypsies always got the dirtiest jobs', recalls András Balogh Balázs. 'A Gypsy had to work three times as hard as a Hungarian to stand any chance of being promoted.'

Nevertheless, like most other working-class Gypsies, whether in Hungary, Romania or elsewhere in Central and Eastern Europe, András is wistful when he talks about the Communist years. 'The basic necessities of life were guaranteed', he says. 'That's what we need now. There should be work for able-bodied Roma so they can earn wages and look after their families. That's better than having to rely on charity, as they do now.'

It has become customary to regard the Communist era in Central and Eastern Europe as embodying the denial of elementary rights. Even though some Communist societies, including Hungary, succeeded in satisfying a number of basic consumer demands, the preponderant view is that such material rewards could not possibly compensate for the loss of fundamental freedoms:[23]

> A consumer society – though a third-rate one – had developed under 'Kádárism'...Large sections of the population rose from the level of proletariat in the classic sense to become petit bourgeois. Hungary was in the process of becoming a middle-class society...A Trabant or a house was no substitute for freedom; it only made non-freedom more tolerable and the soft banality that had replaced hard-line dictatorship less suffocating.

However, such views mainly reflect the thinking of the region's intelligentsia and sections of the middle classes. To a demographically significant part of Central and East European society – one that included but was by no means confined to most Roma – the reformist and egalitarian thrust of Communist policy was profoundly emancipatory. Formerly marginalised and chronically impoverished social strata in the CEE states, whether in the cities or the countryside, were given unprecedented opportunities under the new Communist order, as well as material support to pursue education up to university level. Some went on to enjoy careers, whether as teachers, engineers, administrators or doctors, that would have been inconceivable to their parents and grandparents. As noted by the distinguished economic historian Ivan Berend:[24]

> Hundreds of thousands of young people from worker and peasant families were enrolled into the universities...During the prewar decades, only 1–2 percent of university students came from workers and peasant families in Czechoslovakia; their percentage increased to 51 percent in 1975–6.

All sections of society were freed from basic material concerns; no-one, not even a Gypsy, had to worry any longer about feeding and clothing themselves or their family. Unprecedented levels of social provision for Central and Eastern Europe's Gypsies, including access to health care, education and, over time, decent housing, represented a basic tenet of Communist policy.[25] Since 1990, in the bumpy transition to democracy and market economics in the region, that reassuring safety net has been abruptly removed.

As suggested above, the deficiencies of Communist policy towards the Roma – including 'the creation of phantasmagorical "socialist" jobs for the Gypsies' and the failure to raise Romani educational standards sufficiently – have undoubtedly contributed to the minority's problems during the post-Communist transition.[26] Moreover, the social and economic benefits that were instituted under Communism cannot be equated, in every sense, with 'rights' as understood in liberal, democratic Western states. Notions of judicial review were largely alien and material privileges – access to university, foreign travel, well-paid or stimulating employment – could be withdrawn or withheld, notably from political dissidents or their families.[27] Under Communism, citizens enjoyed privileges rather than rights in a system that was characterised by the state's virtual monopoly of power.

However, there were few, if any, political dissidents amongst the Roma of Central and Eastern Europe. For the most part, they were either quiescent – embarked on a slow process of social integration – or they succeeded in maintaining a more traditional Romani life for themselves, outside the stifling, bureaucratic controls and petty intrusions of the Communist state. But, whatever their individual choices, the Roma were not revolutionaries – they had no interest in overthrowing the Communist regimes or in challenging their authority. As a result, though the Roma were viewed as a social or humanitarian problem by the Communists, they were never perceived as a threat.

VISUAL ARTS AND THE ROMA

If the Roma are associated with a single art form it's music. The exuberance, flair and virtuosity of Romani musicians has long been recognised around the world. Whether it's flamenco guitarists in Andalucía, Turkish-influenced brass bands in the Balkans or Gypsy violinists in Hungary and Romania, the Roma are acknowledged as gifted, intuitive musicians.[28] Amongst the Roma, professional musicians tend to form a caste. Skills are handed down within families, from one generation to the next. When András decided to take up a hobby in his spare time, he chose drawing. 'At school, I got a "5" for drawing, the top mark. Everything else, I failed', he recalls. András says that for years he'd return home from work in Salgótarján, eat a meal prepared by his wife, and collapse, dog-tired, in an armchair. Gradually, to amuse himself, he took up drawing. 'At first, I bought pencils and sketch pads', he says.

When András started to draw the family were living in the cramped, one-and-a-half-room apartment that they'd been assigned after leaving Salgótarján's doomed Gypsy settlement. András would sit at their only table for hours, absorbed in drawing. If a picture pleased him, maybe a landscape or a portrait of someone he knew, he'd hang it on the wall.

Over time András began to experiment, doing some larger drawings and trying his hand at watercolours. Becoming more and more engrossed in his new hobby, András started to paint on canvas using oils. But he is strangely incurious about the work of other artists, despite the availability of art galleries in Budapest and in the major provincial cities. András says that, up to the present day, he's only ever visited an art gallery if he's been invited to attend the opening of an exhibition featuring the work of Romani painters.

András was not the first Gypsy in Hungary to make something of a name for himself with his painting. János Balázs had already achieved a measure of public recognition for his paintings in the 1970s. Born in 1905, Balázs wound up in Salgótarján as a child after the death of his parents. Entirely self-taught as an artist, like András, he only took up painting when he was already retired and in his sixties. Although both men would probably have resisted labels (János Balázs died in 1977), they can fairly be described as naïve artists; that is, they're untutored, lack an understanding of perspective and other conventional artistic techniques, but have an intuitive grasp of colour and composition.

Living in the same town, András knew János Balázs but the two men had never been more than acquaintances. After some of András' paintings began to appear at exhibitions around the country he recalls János saying to him, 'it's the end for me'. Jealous of András' reputation, Balázs could not bear the thought that he was no longer Hungary's sole acknowledged Gypsy artist.

András works slowly, taking weeks or even months to finish a single painting. Using only the tip of his brush he applies repeated small dabs of paint to the canvas in contrast to the broad, impatient brushstrokes of Jolán, who took up painting some time after her husband. Far more prolific than András, she stores her numerous canvases haphazardly in a room in the basement of their apartment building.

'We sell maybe a couple of paintings a year', says András. Some of their pictures have been bought by major public institutions, including Budapest's prestigious Museum of Ethnography. Others are sold to private collectors. But the couple's earnings, as artists, aren't always enough even to cover the cost of materials, let alone augment their meagre pensions.

'Earlier this year the town council gave me some financial help for the first time', András says. 'I went to them because I'd no money to buy paint or canvases.' The council awarded András the equivalent of $140.

Before I left Salgótarján, taking the long-distance bus back to Budapest, I asked András Balogh Balázs how he chose the themes of his paintings. 'They're based on my experiences as a child', he said.

In fact, András' pictures are a form of visual history, an attempt to preserve some record of the Roma way of life that he witnessed in the years following the War. 'There are Gypsy kids here in Salgótarján who can't believe that, as recently as the 1940s, Gypsies lived underground in rooms dug out of the earth.'

The title of one of his paintings is *The Chimney isn't Smoking*. András explains that, in Romani, this expression means that 'there's nothing to eat'. He recalls that, as a child, he heard Gypsies in one of the settlements where he lived for a while baiting one another with the words 'isn't your chimney smoking?'

'It was the greatest source of shame for a Gypsy not to have any food', András says. The image of Gypsies taunting the poorest, most wretched members of their community, though harsh, has the unmistakeable ring of truth. It is sharply at odds with the sentimental picture sometimes presented by Gadje of Gypsy solidarity and fellow feeling. Such portrayals have tended to idealise and misrepresent the Roma rather like the eighteenth- and nineteenth-century Rousseauesque myths of the 'noble savage', an absurdly romantic and wilfully inaccurate product of the European imagination.

If András picks the themes of his pictures from a conscious desire to construct a pictoral memory of Romani social history, his choice of colours is dictated by an intuitive sense of what they represent. For András, blue signifies 'a purer inner world' while lilac expresses poverty; black is the colour of bitterness. Out of this palate of conflicting emotions, black always predominates. Despite occasional splashes of colour in his paintings, yellow, lilac, white, brown, blue and green, the black and the sense of bitterness are enveloping.

Some days later, back in Budapest, I met the film director Edit Kőszegi. She has made a series of documentaries about Hungary's Roma as well as the film *Sitiprinc*. *Sitiprinc* features several Hungarian Roma from the village of Patakrét as extras or as actors in supporting roles. In Transylvania, where part of the film was shot, a band of nomadic Gypsies were hired as extras.

Over the years, Edit Kőszegi has become knowledgeable about Romani art. The walls of her apartment, in the heart of Budapest, are hung with paintings by András Balogh Balázs and Jolán Oláh, as well as by other Romani artists including Márta Bada and Teréz Orsós.

'Many Romani artists are extremely poor', Edit says. 'Some time ago I learnt that one particular painter needed money urgently so I took several of her canvases round some of the private galleries in Budapest to see if I could sell them.' Edit's efforts had been in vain. 'One gallery owner said that if he were to exhibit artworks by Gypsies many of his regular customers would desert him.' In the decade or so since the collapse of Communism anti-Gypsy prejudice, always pervasive in Central and Eastern Europe, has intensified alarmingly.[29]

5

The Czardas*

My phone call took him by surprise. For a moment or two he was angry. 'What do you mean you found my name in a book about Gypsies? Who gave them permission to write about me?'

I had come across a reference to Miklós Rácz (not his real name) some days earlier, while browsing in a bookshop in Budapest. A slim volume about Hungarian Gypsies, published several months previously, contained an appendix listing famous Hungarian Roma, past and present. In a section on Romani musicians, Miklós Rácz was described in the following terms: 'Miklós Rácz (1931–), concert pianist and Professor of Piano Studies at the Music Conservatory in Cluj, Romania.' Known as Kolozsvár by Hungarians and as Klauszenburg by Germans, Cluj has a richly multicultural heritage. With theatres, opera companies (one Romanian, one Hungarian), a clutch of universities and over 30,000 students, it's the intellectual and cultural capital of Transylvanian Romania.

I tried to calm Professor Rácz as best I could. 'I'm visiting from Britain', I said. 'I'm writing a book about the Roma of this region and I'd like to say something about their contribution to music.' I hesitated. 'I was wondering if you'd be willing to talk to me?'

To my surprise, he consented. We agreed to meet the next day, at noon, in the bar of my hotel in the centre of town. 'I have to give a lesson at the Conservatory at 1.00,' he said, 'so we can talk for half an hour.'

Miklós Rácz did not look or move like a man in his seventieth year. Spry and a little below average height, he was casually but smartly dressed in a well-cut leather jacket and neatly pressed dark trousers. His shoes looked expensive. Smiling broadly as he shook my hand, Miklós exuded a very Central European air of shrewdness allied to charm.

---

* The czardas, spelt *csárdás* in Hungarian, is the national dance of Hungary and is often associated with Gypsy orchestras. The nineteenth-century composer Franz Liszt, who had steeped himself in the playing of Gypsy musicians in Hungary and Transylvania, drew on the Czardas in composing the Hungarian Rhapsodies.

5   Romani musicians performing outside Budapest's Keleti Railway Station

'So tell me about this book in which you read about me', he said, after some pleasantries. 'Where was it published? Who's the author?' I mumbled the name of a distinguished Hungarian sociologist, István Kemény, who had edited the volume and who has devoted much of his career to studying the conditions of the Roma of Central and Eastern Europe.[1]

'I'm giving a series of concerts in Hungary in a few months' time', said Professor Rácz. 'I'll look him up.' Somehow, I didn't think the encounter would be pleasant.

'It's true that my father was a Gypsy but my mother's name was Weisz. She was Jewish. My parents' marriage caused quite a stir in her family.'

Professor Rácz seemed anxious to tell me that his mother was Jewish, as though to dilute his Romani ancestry. For him, it was evidently better to be thought part-Jewish than wholy Roma. Ironically, many Jews in Central and Eastern Europe, particularly from the generation who lived through the War, often go to considerable lengths to disguise their Jewish origins.

Miklós told me that his father had been a well-known Gypsy violinist and band leader in the Transylvanian town of Baia Mare, which Miklós referred to by its Hungarian name of Nagybánya. Miklós' parents had been keen for their son to train as a classical musician, even though it had entailed many financial sacrifices for the family. In the autumn of 1945, at the age of 14, Miklós was sent to Cluj to study at the Sigismund Toduta music school, boarding in the school's dormitories. Previously, in Baia Mare, he had attended a school run by priests. At 18, on graduating from the *liceu de muzica*, Miklós enrolled at Cluj's Music Conservatory.

At 69 years of age Miklós had enjoyed a distinguished career as a concert pianist, with regular engagements at home and abroad. A popular and much respected figure in Cluj, which he had made his home, he also held a prestigious teaching position at the Conservatory. Married to an ethnic Hungarian, Miklós was admired by the people of his adoptive city. At some point in his busy life, he had shed any lingering reminders of his Romani origins like a shabby or ill-fitting suit of clothes. 'My parents never showed much interest in matters of national identity', he said, in response to my questions about how he viewed himself.

Romanian acquaintances had told me that there are Gypsies who have become teachers, lawyers, doctors and engineers. Almost invariably, it was said, these Gypsies had chosen to draw a veil over their ethnicity, severing all links with their ancestral community. Whether out of embarrassment or careerism, these successful, educated Gypsies had refashioned themselves as Romanians. In Transylvania, with a Hungarian minority of approximately 1.7 million people, some middle-class Roma, fluent Hungarian speakers, had chosen to assimilate with the Hungarians. As a result, I was told, the bulk of the country's Gypsies, who subsist at the margins of Romanian society, have few role models to emulate. Miklós, or Mihai as he is known to his Romanian concert audiences, was the first such 'closet' Roma I had met.

THE ROMA CONTRIBUTION TO MUSIC
IN CENTRAL AND EASTERN EUROPE

Of all the art forms, music is the one in which Gypsies have excelled. For a people who were nomadic throughout much of their history, music represented a practical means of entertainment and self-expression. For some, music also became a means of earning a living. Unlike painting or sculpture, which would have involved the transportation of bulky objects, music-making required no more than a few simple instruments, or just the unaccompanied human voice. Even the Gypsies' instruments were often improvised, with the use of everyday objects such as *kancsós* or water jugs, spoons, pots and lids as means of rhythmic expression.

'Gypsies were mostly poor', Kálmán, a Romani folk musician and amateur musicologist told me, when we met in Cluj. 'For a long time they couldn't afford proper instruments. That's why they used whatever came to hand for rhythm to accompany their singing.'

The men would strive to imitate musical instruments such as the double bass or the drums with their voices. They would compete with one another in bravura displays of virtuosity. The tradition survives and has occasionally fused with other musical idioms. Not long ago, in Budapest's fashionable Jazz Garden Restaurant, I saw a roomful of diners fall silent, spellbound by the violently percussive 'scat', or vocal improvisations, of a burly young Gypsy in a jazz ensemble.

Storytelling has also occupied an important place in the lives of Gypsies down the centuries. However, stories are generally told for the amusement of the Roma themselves rather than as a means of entertaining Gadje for profit. Only recently have Romani poets and writers, such as the Hungarians József Choli Daróczi, György Rostás-Farkas and Béla Osztojkán, begun to make a mark in the wider society.[2] Even now, the publication of poems, stories and novels by Romani authors frequently relies on subsidies from government ministries or charitable foundations keen to promote a more positive image of the Romani people.

When making music for themselves, rather than for Gadje, the Roma of Hungary and Romania traditionally sang unaccompanied.[3] The songs, which can be slow or fast, solemn or joyous, formed an integral part of important family and community occasions such as weddings and funerals. In recent years, some younger Romani musicians have begun to adapt this authentic Gypsy music for wider audiences, adding instruments such as guitars to the vocalists. Hungarian groups including Kalyi Jag (a Romani expression meaning 'Black Fire') and Ando Drom ('On the Road') have achieved notable success, touring widely abroad and recording numerous CDs.

By contrast, much of the so-called 'Gypsy' music found in parts of Central and Eastern Europe contains little, if anything, that is truly Roma. For example, Hungarian 'Gypsy' music, of the type performed by costumed ensembles – comprising a violin, a viola, a double bass, a *cimbalom* or hammer dulcimer and maybe a clarinet – actually consists of well-known songs of the pre-War era and pieces from the light classical repertoire. Gypsy 'salon' music of this kind owes more to composers, such as Brahms and Liszt, than to authentic Romani music of the kind that has been kept alive in Hungary by Beás and Oláh (that is, Vlach) Gypsies.[4]

However, even when playing frothy classical pieces or pre-War popular songs, Romani musicians have invariably managed to add certain elements uniquely their own. Instrumental virtuosity, improvisation, elaborate ornamentation – as well as a taste for *rubato*, or subtle variations of rhythm – have been the hallmarks of Romani musicianship. But the melodies and choice of instruments have generally been dictated by the surroundings and by the tastes of Gadje audiences. As Rhoda Dullea puts it, in an article in the *Central European Review*, Gypsy musicians' 'performance style featured a unique ability to adapt to indigenous local forms, styles and repertoires, while simultaneously maintaining and projecting their own identity through certain idiosyncrasies in performance that served as ethnic markers'.[5]

I had rather expected Miklós Rácz to disdain Gypsy 'salon' music of the type that, though less popular than even a few decades ago, is still widely performed in restaurants across Hungary, particularly those catering to foreign tourists. I thought he would deem it vulgar and unsophisticated, an unwelcome reminder of his modest Romani origins. But, to my surprise, he was effusive in his praise. He said that, like many classical soloists, when in Hungary, he liked to go to a restaurant after a concert where he could be sure of catching a fine Gypsy ensemble. Miklós reeled off a list of some of the twentieth century's greatest violin and cello virtuosi – Joachim, Haifetz, Menuhin, Casals, Kreizler. 'I know for a fact that if they were performing in Hungary each one of them loved to go and hear a good Gypsy band after their concert was over!' His face lit up at the prospect. 'To hear a talented Gypsy violinist is like listening to an organ. They weave their harmonies so wonderfully!'

Although aspiring Romani musicians have to work hard to perfect their technique, mere application is never enough. 'It's something you're born with', says Miklós, referring to the Gypsies' innate sense of harmony. 'This is how they come into the world', adds Márta, who has has played the viola for many years in one of Hungary's top symphony orchestras. Kálmán, the Romani folk musician whom I met several times on visits to Cluj, echoes their remarks. 'Gypsies have an intuitive feel for harmony', he says. In London I was introduced to Krysztof, a classical chamber musician who plays the viola in a much lauded string quartet. A Gadjo and a graduate of Warsaw's music conservatory, Krysztof expressed unstinting admiration for the brilliance of Gypsy violinists. 'Some of them can play things that are so complex you couldn't express them in musical notation. They can imitate the sounds of birds with their instruments, achieving incredible feats of virtuosity.'

In recent times, the popularity of Gypsy 'salon' music has declined sharply amongst Hungarians, forcing many Romani musicians to look for other types of work, notably in commerce.[6] Substantial numbers of Romani musicians and their families, who formerly constituted an elite amongst Hungary's Gypsies, have been compelled to give up their traditional way of life as Hungary's musical tastes have undergone a major change.

Beginning in the 1970s, growing numbers of mainly educated young Hungarians, many living in the cities, became increasingly interested in their musical 'roots', that is, in traditional Hungarian folk music and in the accompanying dances. In part, this represented a calculated reaction to the efforts of the Communist authorities in Hungary, as elsewhere in Central and Eastern Europe, to dictate the cultural tastes as well as political opinions of the people. Cultivating an interest in Hungarian folk music, which was heavily associated with Transylvania where the tradition had been kept alive, also represented an act of solidarity with Romania's beleaguered Hungarian minority. Under Ceauşescu, in the 1970s and the 1980s, the Romanian authorities pursued an energetic policy of 'Romanisation' to the alarm of ethnic Hungarians in Transylvania and public opinion within Hungary.[7]

Hungary's Tánchaz, literally 'Dance House', movement, with its commitment to the preservation of Hungary's folk music tradition, remains popular up to the present day.[8] Hungarians, many between 18 and 40 years of age, some dressed in folk costumes, gather weekly to perform the dances of their peasant forbears. The accompanying music, earthy, rhythmic and repetitive, is provided by earnest young musicians on the violin, the kontra, a stringed instrument developed in Transylvania, and a bowed double bass. There is no place for Hungary's traditional Gypsy ensembles, with their polished, cosmopolitan repertoire, in these celebrations of an almost extinct Hungarian rural life.

Ironically, the quintessentially Hungarian music celebrated by the Tánchaz movement, much of which originates in Transylvanian Romania, was kept alive over the centuries by a caste of professional and semi-professional Gypsy musicians, hired to play at weddings and at other important occasions.[9] So, the preservation and transmission of this important strand of Hungarian culture has relied on Gypsies rather than Hungarians.

At one time, many villages in Transylvania had one or more Gypsy bands. In Tismana, a straggling village some 30 kilometres north of

Cluj, in Transylvanian Romania, I met one of the daughters of the last Gypsy band leader in the village. Since her father's death, some years before, the village has not had a regular band, although formerly Tismana could boast two popular and successful Gypsy ensembles. One of these had been known as the Kolbász or 'Sausage' Band.

In another Transylvanian village, Almás, I was introduced to an elderly Romani man, Jancsi. Once there were 46 Romani musicians in the village, he told me, proudly.[10] Jancsi's father had been a violinist and Gypsy band leader. Jancsi used to accompany him on the accordion while his wife played the drums.

But demand for their style of music had died out, Jancsi said. Now people owned music centres; they played CDs or cassettes at family celebrations. 'But there was a time when not a Saturday or Sunday would go by when we didn't go to a *lakadalom*, or wedding reception, hereabouts.' Often, they would take other musicians along with them to create a fuller sound, usually a second harmonica, a *kontra* and a double bass. If the wedding party were ethnic Romanians, the band would play Romanian songs. If they were Magyar, or Hungarian, the musicians would perform the *csárdás* and other Hungarian favourites. With equal facility, the band could play traditional Gypsy pieces for a Romani wedding in one of the surrounding villages. In multicultural Transylvania, Romani musicians had to be versatile if they wanted to make a decent living.

Miklós Rácz grimaced when I mentioned the Táncház movement. 'The music's primitive; fit only for the village!' he said. 'Young people like it because it's simple.'

Miklós' explanation – that it was the simplicity of the music that appealed to young Hungarians – did not altogether convince me. Music is rarely just a matter of aesthetics or personal taste. Hungary's folk music revival can be seen as part of a wider, regional phenomenon with nationalistic overtones. The celebration of national cultures, including the rediscovery of a long-neglected authentic folk music tradition, is part of a process of cultural reassertion. Originally an act of defiance against Communist authoritarianism and its denial of cultural pluralism, the Táncház movement has become one facet of a broader exploration of national identity. The thousands of young Hungarians pouring into sweaty dance halls to dance the *verbunkos* or the *csárdás*, on Friday and Saturday nights, are not just celebrating an arcane art form but also a sense of their Hungarianness.[11] Since the collapse of Communist rule, over a decade ago, every nation in the region – Poles, Czechs, Slovaks, Slovenians, Ukrainians, Romanians and others – has been engaged in much the same sort of exercise, testifying to a region-wide shift, in political and intellectual discourse, to questions of ethnicity, culture and religion.[12]

Yet, in summing up the Romani contribution to music in much of Central and Eastern Europe, one would have to conclude that it has been pervasive. The Roma occupy a key role in popular and folk music traditions. In addition, small but growing numbers of Roma have become classical musicians, joining orchestras and chamber groups, particularly since 1945. The greater availability of music scholarships during the Communist era – and the generally reformist, egalitarian ethos of the new socialist regimes – created a climate in which it became significantly easier for talented young Romani musicians, like Miklós Rácz, to study at music conservatories and to pursue careers in classical music. The concert pianist György Cziffra, who spent the latter part of his life in France, and Endre Banda, cellist in the Budapest-based Tatrai String Quartet, were both of Romani origin, as is the young violin soloist József Lendvai. Banda's grandfather had been a well-known *cigány primás*, or Gypsy band leader, while Lendvai's father played both Gypsy 'salon' music and jazz. But, like Miklós Rácz, many of those who have become successful and respected classical musicians have chosen not to advertise their Romani origins. The sense of shame, or at least of discomfort, has rarely been entirely absent, notwithstanding the widely-held belief that, as compared with many other sectors of society, 'music is very democratic'.[13]

Unsurprisingly, talented Romani musicians, with their characteristic virtuosity and skill at improvisation, have been extremely successful in jazz. According to one recent book, 'Gypsy musicians preside over Hungarian jazz.'[14] In the realm of pop music, a style known as 'Romapop', with an insistent, pounding rhythm, has attracted many followers in Romania and Hungary. Romani musicians in Central and Eastern Europe have made a notable – though sometimes self-effacing – contribution to almost every musical genre.

ROMANI FOLK MUSIC TRADITIONS
IN TRANSYLVANIA AND BEYOND

I was given an introduction to Kálmán Urszui, a successful and energetic Romani folk musician, by Bianca, the administrator of the Transylvanian Symphonic Society. Based in Cluj, Kálmán is a member of the 16-strong folk ensemble that, together with the Transylvanian Symphony Orchestra, is jointly administered by the Symphonic Society.

In addition to his work with the folk ensemble, Kálmán regularly tours abroad, sometimes with a small group of Romanian folk musicians. He has recorded several CDs, most recently a ravishing album entitled *Te Djiewiss* with the Netherlands-based Romani violinist Nello Mirando.[15] At weekends, if he is home, Kálmán earns a little extra money by playing with a local band at weddings in the villages around Cluj. 'We leave Cluj in the afternoon and don't return till the following morning', he tells me.

In his spare time, Kálmán has become an enthusiastic musicologist, with a particular interest in the contribution that Romani musicians have made to traditional music, in all its forms, in Transylvania. He has amassed a substantial collection of recordings by Romani artists from the various corners of this large and, in places, inaccessible region with its poorly maintained roads and limited infrastructure. Along with others, Kálmán is convinced that an era is drawing to a close and that, in a generation or so, there will no longer be enough Romani musicians left in Transylvania to preserve the region's rich and diverse tradition of folk music.

Travel books published in Western Europe and North America continue to write lyrically about the talented Romani bands who can be heard in the simplest village bars across Transylvania. But when I ask Kálmán whether I should try to catch one of these bands, he smiles ruefully. The custom of regular live gigs died out several years ago in the villages around Cluj.

According to some accounts, the disappearance of many of the village bands, such as those that flourished in the village of Tismana until comparatively recently, can be ascribed to the peasants' increasing poverty. Since the dissolution of the agricultural co-operatives established under Communism many peasants, lacking either capital or machinery, struggle to farm tiny and uneconomic strips of land, relying on horses, water buffalo, or just themselves.[16] These peasants can no longer afford to hire a Gypsy band to play at a wedding.

However, Kálmán offers another explanation. 'Amongst Hungarian Gypsies, the older musicians died and the next generation mostly chose other occupations', he says. 'They want to be modern; they don't want to do the same things as their fathers.' Kálmán tells me that, in the days when his father played in a band, Gypsy musicians were treated badly by the villagers. 'When the Romanians got drunk they often abused the musicians', he says. 'But the Gypsies had to put up with it; it was how they earned a living.'

The Romani bands that could once be found all over Transylvania were very different to the sophisticated Gypsy ensembles that flourished in capital cities such as Budapest. In their heyday, a successful Gypsy orchestra in Budapest or in one of the larger provincial cities might boast a line-up of first and second violin, viola, *cimbalom* or hammer dulcimer, an instrument which the Gypsies may have brought with them from Persia, double bass, clarinet and, at one time, even a cello. By contrast, the Transylvanian Gypsy bands, who played at weddings and at other festivities in the region's villages, barely earnt enough to support three musicians. For the most part, these bands consisted of just a violin, a *kontra* and a double-bass.

'The *kontra* was only found in Transylvania', Kálmán says. Kálmán is convinced that the *kontra*, which can be adapted from either the violin or the viola, was invented by Romani musicians. Instead of having a rounded bridge, which is characteristic of string instruments that are bowed rather than plucked, the *kontra* has a flat bridge. Consequently, you can draw the bow across three strings at once. Not only does this allow the performer to play a complete chord, the sound produced by the *kontra* is also significantly louder than that of a conventional stringed instrument. 'That was important in the days when there wasn't any amplification', Kálmán explains. 'Two or three musicians had to play for a crowd of anything from two to three hundred!'

In Transylvania, Romani musicians were often so poor that they couldn't afford professionally made strings for their instruments. 'At first they used lengths of wire instead of catgut', Kálmán says. With the exception of the lead instrument, the violin, the quality of the sound that the musicians produced was considered of secondary importance. What mattered most of all was that the band could be heard above a noisy and rumbustious crowd of wedding guests.

Gradually, says Kálmán, the Gypsy musicians began to experiment. 'They went to the slaugher houses and bought lengths of gut for next to nothing', he tells me. They stretched strands of gut tightly between nails on the walls of their houses and left them to dry. From time to time, the musicians would rub these drying lengths of gut with garlic and other substances to make them supple as well as durable. Although serviceable and cheap, these home-made strings produced an inferior sound to that of proper, shop-bought catgut. They could be used on the *kontra* and the double bass, which mainly provided rhythmic accompaniment, but they were less suitable for the lead instrument, the violin, which had to carry the melody. In even the humblest of Gypsy bands, the violin had to have sweetness of tone.

Today, a number of Gypsy bands, drawn from various parts of Central and Eastern Europe, have become famous.[17] But it is no longer the elaborately costumed Hungarian Gypsy ensembles, with their sophisticated, semi-classical 'salon' music, who are in demand. With the current vogue for 'world music', embracing the musical traditions of formerly neglected peoples and cultures, Romani bands of a very different stamp are attracting a global audience. Variations of the homespun Gypsy groups, which were once a common feature of the Transylvanian villages, continue to flourish in Wallachia and in other regions of Romania, as well as across much of the Balkans. These Romani ensembles vary significantly in terms of instrumentation and repertoire. At one extreme, they encompass raucous and anarchic Gypsy brass bands in Macedonia and Serbia, a legacy of the Ottoman military bands of the nineteenth century. They include, in addition, the violins, accordions and double bass of the Gypsy *taraf*, or band, in Wallachia. While often retaining their popular base at home, where they are much in demand at weddings and at other celebrations, such bands offer the sort of 'authentic' musical experience that foreign audiences crave, particularly in Western Europe and North America. As for the traditional folk music of Transylvania, Kálmán says that there's more of a demand for it in Budapest, Paris or Amsterdam than in Cluj.

The pre-eminent Romani band on the 'world music' scene is Taraf de Haidouks. Based at their home village of Clejani in Wallachia, not far from the Romanian capital, Bucharest, the band comprises an assortment of musicians ranging from some who are well above pensionable age to others who are teenagers. The band has attracted a formidable reputation around the world for its fast-paced virtuosity, verve and eclectic repertoire, while somehow remaining close to its musical roots. Featured in Tony Gatlif's award-winning film about the Romani diaspora, *Latcho Drom*, the group has also recorded a CD with the Kronos Quartet, more usually noted for their performances of contemporary chamber music. Other Romani bands who are attracting an international following include the Hungarian group Kalyi Jag, who mostly sing in Romani and who focus on the music which the Roma traditionally made amongst themselves, albeit adapted for modern, non-Romani audiences through the addition of instruments such as guitars to the vocal line-up. Representing an altogether different Romani musical tradition, the Kočani Orkestar, from the town of Kočani in Macedonia, offer a characteristically exuberant example of a brass-dominated Gypsy ensemble from the Balkans.[18] The band comprises two trumpets, three tubas, saxophone, clarinet, *zurla* (traditional oboe), accordion and percussion.

THE FEAR OF BEING EXPOSED

During one of our meetings in Cluj, Kálmán told me about a friend of his, István. A successful Romani folk musician, István is married to an ethnic Hungarian. They live in a comfortable apartment in a smart suburb of Cluj and have two children, a boy and a girl, now in their teens. 'István told me that he's never discussed his ethnicity with his kids', Kálmán said. 'He doesn't even know if they realise that their father is a Gypsy.' Like Miklós Rácz, the concert pianist whom I'd met on another visit to Transylvania, István is acutely sensitive about his ethnic origins. Having achieved a comfortable, middle-class lifestyle he rarely meets Gypsies, apart from a handful who are educated and assimilated musicians like himself. His neighbours, in-laws, most of his colleagues and his children's schoolfriends are ordinary, middle-class Romanians and Hungarians. Because of the low esteem in which Gypsies are widely held in Romania, István was too embarrassed to discuss his ethnicity with his children. He feared that, if they didn't already realise that their father is a Gypsy, the news might come as a shock to them; it was a subject best avoided.

Like Miklós Rácz, István leads a busy, successful life in Romania. Yet, each of them is convinced that the price of their professional and social acceptance is a sharp distancing from their Romani selves. If these talented musicians had openly acknowledged their Romani identity, it's conceivable that they might have served as examples to younger Roma, and a source of pride for the minority as a whole.

All too often, the available role models for Romani kids in Central and Eastern Europe, growing up on miserable settlements or in semi-derelict tenements, are bleakly negative and discouraging. As noted above, a large proportion of the Roma lost their jobs in the region's often painful and faltering transition to market economies in the 1990s.[19] With limited education and little prospect of alternative employment in increasingly sophisticated, skill-driven economies, many Roma have come to subsist on casual work of various kinds, state handouts (where available) and, in some instances, occasional petty crime. The intermittently homeless, middle-aged Romani couple, whose lives I describe in Chapter 6 are fairly typical examples of this process of unrelenting social and economic marginalisation.

However, it may be unrealistic to imagine that educated musicians, like István or Miklós, could serve as role models for the mass of desperately poor and demotivated Roma in Romania, or elsewhere in the region. It's a common mistake, on the part of Gadje, to assume that Gypsies represent a single culture or people, roughly comparable to the long established 'nations' of Europe. Although there have been recent efforts by Romani activists and intellectuals to construct a sense of Romani nationhood, this project is still a long way from being realised, as noted in Chapter 1. Identity, amongst the Roma, is generally construed much more narrowly. Traditionally, the various groups classified as 'Gypsies' by outsiders comprised a kalaidescope of different communities and subcultures who often had little contact with one another and who frequently spoke various languages or dialects amongst themselves. Occupational specialisation was a prominent feature of these essentially inward-looking groups, with parents handing on their skills and know-how – whether as musicians, menders of copper pots, still makers, wooden spoon or wooden trough carvers, brick makers, horse-copers, silver workers and so on – to their children. Having little or no sense of a shared culture, history or identity, each 'Romani' community tended to cherish its sense of separateness from other so-called Gypsy groups.[21]

Hungarian 'musician' Gypsies in Transylvania, like István and Miklós, grew up in a very different environment, with markedly different values and expectations, to many of the region's other Gypsy communities. The gulf separating these urbane, integrated musician Gypsies from the bulk of Central and Eastern Europe's Roma may well be unbridgeable. Elsewhere in Romania, much the same phenomenon has been observed. Wallachia's *lăutari*, professional Romani musicians, consciously distance themselves from other Romani groups whom they regard as culturally different and generally inferior.[22]

Talking to Kálmán, it was clear that what he saw as the passivity of many Roma and their tendency to live spontaneously, rarely putting money aside for the future, were well nigh incomprehensible. 'They don't bother about tomorrow', he said to me with a shrug, echoing the remarks of a social worker I knew in Cluj. To Kálmán and Miklós, the frequently illiterate and fatalistic Roma – living in squalid settlements, in abandoned buildings, or in the 'Gypsy quarters' of villages – are profoundly alien. With their education, Hungarian mother tongue, middle class lifestyle and musical vocation, Kálmán and Miklós are every bit as foreign to most Roma in the region, such as the former agricultural workers I met at Pata Rât.[23]

The visceral fear of being exposed as a Gypsy that I sensed in Miklós Rácz, along with István's inability even to broach the subject of his ethnicity with his teenage children, suggest how little the Roma believe they are accepted, either socially or professionally, in Romania. Anti-Roma prejudice remains commonplace, even virulent, in much of Central and Eastern Europe. Since the end of Communist rule, the Roma of the region have been subject to widespread physical assaults as well as increased levels of social exclusion. Gypsies have been regularly villified in the media and by right-wing politicians anxious to appeal to populist sentiments in the electorate. In addition, the Roma have experienced severe economic marginalisation and curbs on access to public services.[24]

For all their faults, the former Communist regimes were ruthlessly efficient in maintaining public order while their approach to the Roma, though paternalistic and often heavy-handed, was broadly inclusive. As indicated in Chapter 4, Communist strategy was generally aimed at integrating (or in some instances assimilating) the Roma, both socially and economically. In some Central and East European states, notably Bulgaria and the former Czechoslovakia, a vigorous policy of assimilation was maintained until the very end of Communist rule. This strategy even extended to matters of culture and language. In his recent and detailed analysis of the treatment of the Roma in Central and Eastern Europe, Professor Barany observes: 'Bulgaria and Czechoslovakia actively discouraged objective scholarly research on Romani life, culture, and language in order to erode Gypsy identity. The writings of Milena Hübschmannová and of the few other independent Romanologists of the region were heavily censored.'[25] The negative stereotypes of Gypsies, that are virtually omnipresent in Central and Eastern Europe, can only encourage successful, upwardly mobile Roma to abandon any public links to their ancestral community. In social and professional terms there is little, if anything, to be gained – and often much to be lost – by 'coming out' as a Gypsy. In many cases, successful, integrated Roma, like Miklós or István, prefer to blend into the wider society in a process that, superficially, may be characterised as voluntary assimilation.

However, the chronically fractured nature of Romani identity and culture is also an impediment to the construction of a more positive Romani self-image. Successful Roma – whether businesspeople, musicians or professionals – are often seen as fundamentally 'different' or 'alien' by the mass of downwardly-mobile Roma, in Central and

Eastern Europe, who often belong to other Romani subgroups. To put it another way, many potential Romani role models are not recognised by other Roma as constituting part of a collective 'self'. Gábor Roma in north-western Romania, for example, with their smart, broad-brimmed hats, social cohesion and distinctive customs, are as far removed from the life experience of most Roma living in the settlements of Romania and Slovakia as any Gadjo.

THE ROMA AND THE RECOGNITION OF MINORITY RIGHTS

In many ways, the failure of post-Communist societies to come to terms with their Romani minorities – which represents a failure to come to terms with their 'true' selves – is grimly ironic. Since the collapse of Communist rule, Central and Eastern Europe has undergone a human rights revolution. As part of the process of democratisation, every state in the region has adopted binding constitutional guarantees for the protection of individual rights.[26] For example, Chapter II of Title II of Romania's 1991 Constitution, is entitled 'Fundamental Rights and Liberties'. It contains a long and detailed catalogue of human rights that are guaranteed to the country's citizens.[27]

Often, the new or revised constitutions in the region also contain provisions recognising the rights of national and ethnic minorities. Article 68 of the revised Hungarian Constitution is widely regarded as particularly generous in this respect:[28]

(1) The national and ethnic minorities living in the Republic of Hungary share the power of the people; they are constituent factors in the State.

(2) The Republic of Hungary grants protection to national and ethnic minorities, it ensures the possibilities for their collective participation in public life, and enables them to foster their own culture, use the mother tongue, receive school instruction in the mother tongue, and freedom to use their names as spelled and pronounced in their own language.

(3) The laws of the Republic of Hungary ensure representation for the national and ethnic minorities living in the territory of the country.

(4) National and ethnic minorities may set up their own local and national government organizations.

The provisions concerning national minorities in the Romanian Constitution, though more limited and circumspect, are illustrative of the same process. Article 6 of Title I provides:

> (1) The State recognizes and guarantees the right of persons belonging to national minorities, to the preservation, development, and expression of their ethnic, cultural, linguistic, and religious identity.
> (2) The protecting measures taken by the Romanian State for the preservation, development, and expression of identity of the persons belonging to national minorities shall conform to the principles of equality and nondiscrimination in relation to the other Romanian citizens.

At the international level, the post-Communist states are parties to a broad range of human rights instruments. These include the European Convention on Human Rights and Fundamental Freedoms as well as the Council of Europe's Framework Convention for the Protection of National Minorities, which entered into force in 1998.[29] The obligations assumed under these and other treaties, such as the UN's Convention on the Elimination of all Forms of Racial Discrimination or the International Covenant on Civil and Political Rights,[30] are complemented and reinforced by a series of 'political commitments' that these states have accepted as members of the OSCE.[31]

In theory, if not yet in practice, the peoples of Central and Eastern Europe are finally living in an age when everyone is free to celebrate both their individuality and their ancestral culture as citizens of modern, democratic societies. As Europe's leaders declared in the Charter of Paris for a new Europe, which was adopted in November 1990 at a summit meeting of the OSCE, '[h]uman rights and fundamental freedoms are the birthright of all human beings' while '[t]heir protection and promotion is the first responsibility of government'.[32] The Charter went on to affirm the rights of national minorities, including 'the right freely to express, preserve and develop that identity without any discrimination and in full equality before the law'. It also declared the commitment of Europe's leaders to democracy 'as the only system of government of our nations'.

The Council of Europe's Framework Convention, referred to above, goes further. The Preamble redefines the very notion of what it means to be 'a pluralist and genuinely democratic society' where national minorities are located on the territory of a state:

a pluralist and genuinely democratic society should not only respect the ethnic, cultural, linguistic and religious identity of each person belonging to a national minority, but also create appropriate conditions enabling them to express, preserve and develop this identity.

The Preamble also states that 'the creation of a climate of tolerance and dialogue is necessary to enable cultural diversity to be a source and a factor, not of division, but of enrichment for each society'. According to this morally enlightened view, minorities, such as the Roma, are to be welcomed for the skills, qualities or aptitudes that they contribute to the societies in which they find themselves.[33] All too often, in Central and Eastern Europe, national and ethnic minorities have been viewed as a threat to the 'purity', unity of purpose or historic mission of the state or the nation.

Unfortunately, the liberal, pluralist ideology which underpins modern international human rights instruments is difficult to reconcile with the nationalistic, exclusivist political and social currents that are to be found, to some degree, in every post-Communist state. A preoccupation with national cultures and national destinies and a lingering suspicion of rival nations and national minorities represent abiding, albeit sharply fluctuating, characteristics of most societies in the region.[34] Such nationalistic concerns can even be discerned in some of the region's constitutions. For example, the Preamble of the 1991 Slovak Constitution contains the following, disturbingly chauvinistic passage:[35]

> We, the Slovak nation, mindful of the political and cultural heritage of our forebears, and of the centuries of experience from the struggle for national existence and our own statehood, in the sense of the spiritual heritage of Cyril and Methodius and the historical legacy of the Great Moravian Empire, proceeding from the natural right of nations to self-determination, together with members of national minorities and ethnic groups living on the territory of the Slovak Republic...

The emotive characterisation of Slovakia as the realisation of long-cherished Slovak national aspirations for self-determination is striking. Yet, Slovakia contains substantial Hungarian and Romani minorities, accounting for well over 20 per cent of its total population. Though citizens of the Slovak state, members of the country's national minorities are excluded from the Slovak 'nation'. In political, if not legal, terms, this suggests that members of Slovakia's national minorities have an imperfect, secondary status. Minorities are, at best, marginal to the historic mission of the state.

Although such nationalistic tendencies in the region should not be exaggerated, neither should they be discounted.[36] They are part of the complex but all too palpable historical legacy that Central and Eastern Europe has to contend with.

If successful, integrated Roma, such as Miklós Rácz or Kálmán's friend István, prefer to draw a veil over their ethnicity, that is understandable. As yet, the rhetoric of human and minority rights has done little to alter popular prejudices and preconceptions about Gypsies in Romania or in the surrounding countries. In contrast to anti-Gypsy sentiment, which largely comes from 'below', that is from what ordinary people think privately, or say amongst family, workmates or friends, human rights initiatives, particularly those aimed at extending Roma rights, have mostly been imposed from 'above'. They represent progressive measures introduced by governments and bureaucrats which, at least in part, are intended to satisfy international treaty obligations or simply to curry favour with the west. At bottom, they are part of the price of admission to coveted western 'clubs' such as the Council of Europe, NATO and, ultimately, the European Union.[37] Human rights initiatives on behalf of the Roma almost invariably lack significant support from the general public.

One Sunday morning, a couple of years ago, I was sitting in a scruffy bar in the village of Patakrét. A middle-aged man entered and ordered a beer. Addressing no-one in particular, he declared with a chuckle that he'd just left another bar because he didn't care for the other customers. 'It was full of Gypsies', the man said. 'I was surrounded.' In Cluj, a balding, Hungarian taxi driver, with whom I struck up a conversation, declared that Hitler had the right idea about how to deal with 'primitive, uneducated Gypsies'. But the man conceded that the much smaller number of integrated, musician Gypsies, like Miklós Rácz, were a different matter entirely. It turned out that he knew all about Miklós, even the fact that he's half-Gypsy. Miklós, he said, was 'totally integrated. We're proud of him'. Transylvania's Hungarians were 'proud' to acknowledge Miklós Rácz – who had achieved distinction as a classical musician, and demonstrated by his lifestyle that he was culturally assimilated – as one of their own.

But casual conversations with taxi drivers, or with strangers in bars or on buses and trains, are not necessarily an accurate barometer of public opinion. Much more disturbing was an article published in *Szabadság*, a serious broadsheet and Cluj's leading Hungarian-language daily newspaper. The article concerned the theft of an elderly lady's wheelchair in the city. It seems that the wheelchair, on which the lady was dependant, had been stolen by Gypsies from whom it was eventually retrieved at a price. In addition to identifying the likely culprits as Gypsies, the journalist allowed herself to make the following blatantly racist remarks:[38]

> It's no disgrace to be of Gypsy extraction! But centuries of misbehaviour [by Gypsies] is a great problem for all of us. They used to say that Gypsies are forced to steal because otherwise they couldn't live. But how is it that Gypsies rarely feel constrained to do any work?

Comments of this sort, particularly if published in sober broadsheets like *Szabadság*, serve only to validate and reaffirm latent prejudices; they make racism, particularly directed against Romania's Gypsies, respectable.

The Framework Convention, discussed above, envisages that: '[e]very person belonging to a national minority shall have the right freely to choose to be treated or not to be treated as such and no disadvantage shall result from this choice'. As a statement of principle it is admirable. Individuals like Miklós Rácz or István should not feel bound to identify with – or be identified with – a particular ethnic group for their entire lives simply because of an accident of birth. In the Europe and North America of the late twentieth and early twenty-first centuries, identity has become much more fluid, multilayered and freely determined.[39] But, in the world in which Miklós, István and other Roma live, decisions regarding which national or ethnic group they choose to be identified with are hardly devoid of far-reaching consequences. While the Roma are despised, routinely discriminated against and subject to crude stereotyping in the media, Miklós and István can scarcely exercise a free choice.

Although they should not be discounted altogether, minority rights do not represent an instant panacea for the severe and wide-ranging problems experienced by the Roma of Central and Eastern Europe. With their emphasis on cultural and political rights, including the right to study in a minority language or to be taught it, the right to receive and impart information and ideas in minority languages, or the right to display signs and inscriptions in a minority language that are visible to the general public,[40] minority rights do not tackle the issues that are currently of greatest concern to the mass of the Roma of the region.

Lack of employment opportunities, a shortage of affordable housing, problems in gaining access to health care and to other public services, or difficulties in catching up with the levels of educational performance of other ethnic groups in the countries concerned, cannot be resolved by means of minority rights, at least as currently conceived. Many of the problems experienced by the Roma of Central and Eastern Europe, outlined above, cannot be alleviated in the forseeable future without a massive allocation of resources and a partial shift away from the liberal, market economy model that the CEE states have struggled to introduce since 1990. Yet such sweeping and financially burdensome changes are unlikely to happen.

However, it is at least possible that, over time, minority rights may play a small but significant part in improving the overall status and self-image of the Roma in societies that sometimes show little inclination to accommodate them. For too long, the label 'Gypsy' or 'Roma' has signified only poverty, helplessness and various social problems rather than a distinct culture or cultures, with values and attributes that are worthy of study, consideration and respect. One of the medium- to long-term effects of the new emphasis on minority rights may be educative, helping Roma and non-Roma alike to perceive 'Gypsies' in a more nuanced and positive light. This slow transformation of often negative social attitudes, towards national and ethnic minorities, is clearly one of the objects of minority rights instruments such as the Council of Europe's Framework Convention. Article 6(1) of the Framework Convention provides:[41]

> The Parties shall encourage a spirit of tolerance and intercultural dialogue and take effective measures to promote mutual respect and understanding and co-operation among all persons living on their territory, irrespective of those persons' ethnic, cultural, linguistic or religious identity, in particular in the fields of education, culture and the media.

However, there is no inevitability about this process. It is even conceivable that societies in Central and Eastern Europe may be alienated eventually by the new minority rights 'industry'. They may come to view it as cyncial, self-serving, an unwarranted use of scarce public resources, and as an attempt to 'brainwash' or hoodwink the general public. At present, there is evidence for each of these conflicting tendencies.

Proponents of minority rights regimes may wish to point to another advantage of such schemes. Minority rights instruments, whether international or national in character, almost invariably contain some mechanisms of scrutiny and review, however imperfect or rudimentary. Such mechanisms can help to draw much-needed attention to the problems experienced by vulnerable national or ethnic minorities, such as the Roma. Over time, well-publicised comments by independent experts, such as the advisory committee established under the Council of Europe's Framework Convention (Article 26), may encourage the mobilisation of greater institutional and financial resources to tackle the underlying problems experienced by the Roma. However, this is a strategy that demands considerable, perhaps excessive, patience.

6
Nomads

I was introduced to Eszti several years ago. A young Romani activist had offered to show me some of the Gypsy settlements that have grown up in and around Cluj. Thousands of Roma, or Gypsies, have drifted to these settlements in the decade or so since the fall of Communism, no longer able to afford the rent on an apartment. In some cases, Romani families sold off their apartments, which they'd managed to buy cheaply as long-standing tenants. Whether they did so out of necessity – often their men folk had been without regular work for several years – or from an ill-considered impulse, they were soon in difficulty once more. Moving to the settlements, they were penniless once again as soon as their modest windfall was spent.

For the most part, the apartment blocks that sprang up around Romanian cities such as Cluj are drab and poorly constructed. Designed without any concession to aesthetics, they were thrown up during the Ceauşescu years[*] to accommodate the tens of thousands of peasants who were encouraged to leave the countryside to become industrial workers in towns and cities. In the post-War era, Romania, along with the other 'Eastern bloc' countries, underwent a rapid and ideologically-driven process of industrialisation – one of the defining features of state socialism.[1] Between 1970 and 1988, industrial production in Romania rose by 500 per cent, one of the highest rates of increase in the region.[2]

If the apartment buildings that were constructed to accommodate the country's burgeoning urban proletariat were ugly and utilitarian, at least the apartments were affordable. Though Romania's Communist regime was notorious – even by the standards of the 'Eastern bloc' countries – for its systematic and ruthless denial of civil and political rights, it guaranteed low rents and cheap utilities for the country's

---

[*] Nicolae Ceauşescu was appointed General Secretary of Romania's Communist Party in July 1965, following the death of his predecessor Gheorghe Gheorghiu-Dej. Ceauşescu remained Romania's undisputed Communist leader until 22 December 1989 when he was toppled from power, following the defection of the army. With his wife, Elena, he was executed by a military firing squad on Christmas day, 1989.

6   The workmens' hut briefly occupied by Eszti and Lajós
in the Mărăsti district of Cluj

citizens as well as jobs for everyone, including the Roma. As Ivan
Berend has noted:[3]

> With all its [*sic*] shortcomings and distortions…the various
> welfare measures of the post-Stalinist countries assured, without
> discrimination, basic services for the entire population and offered
> at least minimal assistance…A premature welfare system became a
> significant characteristic of paternalistic post-Stalinist regimes.

The right to work was enshrined in the various Communist-era
constitutions that, in turn, were consciously modeled on the Soviet
Constitution of 1936.[4] For example, Hungary's 1949 Communist
Constitution stated: 'The Hungarian Peoples' Republic guarantees to
its citizens the right to work.'[5]

Since 1990, even modest apartments in towns and cities across
Romania have become too expensive for many Roma who were
disproportionately affected, as elsewhere in Central and Eastern Europe,
by a wave of large-scale redundancies as state-owned enterprises were
progressively closed, privatised, or compelled to reduce their workforce.
Now, many of Romania's Gypsies rely on casual work of various
kinds such as collecting scrap metal, cardboard or other materials for
recycling, on modest welfare handouts,[6] or simply on begging. Some,

though far fewer than popular opinion in Romania or in other Central and East European countries might suggest, resort to stealing.[7]

In certain respects, Lajós, Eszti's husband, can be cited as an example of this phenomenon of de-skilling and of economic marginalisation that has impacted so relentlessly on the mass of ordinary, poorly qualified Roma in the post-Communist states. For over 25 years, until he was made redundant in May 1992, Lajós worked for the Transylvanian Construction Company, rising over time to become a semi-skilled worker. Since then, with the aid of a little hand-drawn trolley, he has made a living collecting used cardboard for recycling. In a day he can expect to earn the equivalent of one US dollar, or maybe one dollar and 50 cents.

When I met Eszti at the Coastei Romani settlement in Cluj, she and her family no longer had an apartment of their own. They had been evicted for non-payment of rent from their one-room flat in a suburb of the city. Eszti says that they paid the rent without fail until their elder daughter drowned in a freak accident at a nearby river. Eszti and Lajós, her husband, became distraught. She says that they let things slide and didn't worry about the rent. Although Eszti doesn't mention it, the couple may also have lapsed into bouts of heavy drinking.

One day, says Eszti, a truck came. Their furniture and other possessions were piled into the back and she, Lajós, and their surviving daughter, Alina, were packed off to a wretched apartment in a village 20 or 30 kilometers from Cluj. 'We couldn't do anything out there', says Eszti. 'There was no way for us to earn a living.' Eventually, the family found temporary lodgings back in the city.

After some months, she and Lajós ended up living rough on the streets of Cluj. They put Alina into the care of a state-funded placement centre located in a small town, some 30 kilometers' distance from Cluj. Lajós had been born in the town and he'd worked there for a while before taking a job in Cluj with the Transylvanian Construction Company. One of Lajós's brothers still lives there, with his family, in an apartment that they've bought from the municipality.

'At least we knew Alina would be well cared for', says Eszti. As it happens, her confidence was well founded. Social workers have told me that the placement centre, which I've visited a number of times, is the best of its kind in the entire county. Clean, comfortable and well run, the centre has pot plants lining the wide steps that lead up to the girls' dormitories. With no more than five or six to a room, the dormitories are spacious. On the ground floor, in a room next to the dining hall, there's a large glass cabinet containing art works by some of the girls. Outside, there are pleasant, well-tended gardens.

'There are around 80 girls living in the centre right now', the director told me. Smartly dressed and efficient, the director is in her early thirties. 'We try to give them every opportunity to make a life for themselves. When they finish elementary school, the brighter ones have the chance to go on to high school, then college or maybe even university.' In Romania only the first eight years of schooling are compulsory. 'Alina's a very good pupil', the director said. 'She likes to study.'

When a girl from the placement centre approaches the end of her final year at elementary school, her teachers review her academic performance and potential and consider whether she's likely to be suitable for higher education. Girls judged capable of going on to college or to university are sent to one of two local high schools. However, most of the girls at the placement centre aren't particularly academic. They're sent to a trade school instead, where they learn practical skills such as sewing or cooking that will hopefully equip them for jobs and enable them to make an independent life for themselves. In 2001, the last year for which figures were available when I interviewed the director, 12 per cent of the girls living at the placement centre were studying at high school or at an institution of higher education.

When I asked her whether a smaller proportion of Romani children from the centre continue their studies at high school or at college, as compared with their non-Romani peers, the director admitted that that was probably correct. But she pointed out that it's impossible to provide accurate statistics. 'It's difficult to know who's Roma and who isn't. It's not the sort of thing that most parents talk about.'

While Alina was being looked after at the placement center, Eszti and Lajós remained in Cluj. They were spotted by Miklós, a Romani garbage collector, who was emptying bins on the street where the couple were living rough. 'Poor people', the garbage collector said to me, recalling the day that he first laid eyes on them. 'I brought them home with me.' Miklós didn't have a spare room in his modest house; his son, daughter-in-law and grandchildren were already living there, with him and his wife. So he gave Eszti and Lajós the shed out in the yard.

'Before, when I used to have more money, I'd buy a piglet, keep it in the shed and fatten it up', he said. 'When the pig was big enough, we'd slaughter it and keep the meat in the freezer. But I had to sell the freezer and the TV just to make ends meet, so the shed was lying empty.' Eszti's benefactor, Miklós, gestured at the bare sideboard where a TV once stood.

Miklós lives in Coastei, a sprawling Romani settlement that has
grown up on the crest of a hill overlooking Coastei Street in the Mărăsti
district of Cluj, just a couple of kilometers from the center of the city.
The flimsy houses on the settlement, hardly more than shacks, consist
of a couple of rooms with maybe a kitchen. Miklós pointed to the
ceiling in the room that serves as his sitting room, dining room and
bedroom. 'When it rains, the water pours in at several places. We have
to collect the water in buckets.'

There's a lot of redevelopment going on in the Mărăsti district right
now. A smart, new office block is being built at the foot of the hill on
which the Romani settlement is perched. A few hundred yards away,
immediately beneath the Gypsies' shacks, they're finishing work on an
Orthodox Church. The Romanians are a devout people; on Sundays,
the Orthodox churches are full to overflowing. Worshippers spill out
onto the street forming large, reverential crowds. The service is relayed
to those outside on loudspeakers.

While I was talking to Miklós, Eszti entered the room. Barely five
foot tall, she is slightly built. At the time, she was in her early fifties.
Neatly dressed in a white blouse and matching cardigan with a colourful
skirt and white, open-toed shoes, Eszti was immaculate. Her black hair
was tied back carefully in a bun. As Eszti began to talk to me I was
struck by the fastidious way in which she spoke Hungarian. Eszti and
her husband are Romungros, or Hungarian Gypsies. They are fluent in
both Hungarian and Romanian.

Eszti was keen to tell me her story. When she got to the end, I half-
expected a plea for money. 'Thank you for listening to me', was all
she said.

I asked Eszti if I could take a look at the shed, out in the yard, which
was now her home. The shed, next to the outside lavatory that served
the house, was about five metres square and built of stone. The roof
consisted of sheets of corrugated iron held in place by a few rocks.
When they moved there, the building had no windows or any means
of heating or lighting and the roof leaked. Eszti and Lajós had done
what they could with it, lining the inside walls with sheets of cardboard
for insulation. The couple had installed beds, electric lighting, a small
stove for cooking and a little table. Colourful rugs and a few posters
of pop idols and movie stars, including Madonna and Patrick Swayze,
decorated the walls. The posters belonged to Alina, who came from the
placement center to visit her parents whenever she could. On the day I
happened to call, a Saturday, Alina was home for the weekend. Before I

left, I took a few photos of Eszti and her daughter standing, arm in arm, in front of the shed's open doorway.

NOMADS: FROM THE PIGSTY TO THE RAILWAYMEN'S PARK

I didn't see Eszti again for almost a year and a half. When I finally caught up with her, outside the little shed at Coastei, Lajós was with her. They were packing up the last of their belongings before leaving the settlement for good. Apart from some rubbish strewn on the floor, the hut was completely empty; it already felt abandoned. I looked at Eszti; her appearance had changed since we'd last met. Her hair was untidy and her face was smudged with dirt. There was a reddish-blue bruise under one eye; her clothes were grubby.

'How did you get that bruise?'

'I fell. I tripped on something inside the hut. It was dark.' A little later, Eszti added that she'd been drinking before she fell. 'I was miserable, so I drank.'

'They said they'd burn the hut down around our heads if we didn't leave', said Eszti, pointing angrily at the nearby house of her former landlord, Miklós. 'They want the shed to store some chemicals.' The garbage collector had become a self-employed pest-controller.

Eszti motioned to me to sit down on a large piece of wood outside the hut. Lajós, who was standing a little distance away from us, stared silently at the ground.

'Did you pay any rent for the hut?' I asked Eszti.

'They never asked for any. But she [Miklós' wife] would come into the hut from time to time and help herself to anything that took her fancy. I used to have some nice rugs but she took them all.'

The pest-controller's wife, the object of Eszti's wrath, was taking the air outside her house. She looked down over the rooftops of Mărăsti and chatted to neighbours, but kept well away from us.

'If Alina came to stay for a few days, then I'd give them some money for the cost of the extra water and electricity', Eszti adds.

'And where will you go?' It was already late September. Within a couple of months autumn would turn to winter. In this part of Romania, the winters are unforgiving. Every year, there are stories in the local newspapers of people dying of hypothermia in unheated homes, or on the streets.

'I've a cousin who's got a small apartment in town. He says we can spend the winter with him.' Eszti gave me the address of an apartment building on Republici Street, round the corner from my hotel. 'Come and see us before you leave Romania.'

I found Eszti and Lajós's new lodgings. They were at the top of an inside stairwell in an old building that had been crudely divided into apartments. The house, which abuts the mediaeval city walls, still has vestiges of its former grandeur. Constructed in the early nineteenth century, it had once belonged to a wealthy nobleman. On the first and second floors the apartments consist of two or three rooms each, with a kitchen and bathroom. The residents are ethnic Romanians and Hungarians. On the top floor, there's a long, windowless corridor with rooms leading off it on either side. Although it was the middle of the day when I called, the corridor was dark and gloomy. The electricity supply to this part of the building had been cut off some time ago for non-payment of bills. Near the stairwell, at one end of the corridor, there was a cold water tap and a couple of lavatories for the use of everyone on the landing. Most of the rooms along the corridor now accommodate an entire family. Up here, in this starkly segregated building, which is almost a metaphor for contemporary Romania, there are no ethnic Romanians or Hungarians, only Roma.

Eszti's cousin, Laci, rents one of the rooms on the top floor and a small kitchen across the corridor. A vigorous, handsome man in his mid thirties, he has a secure and comparatively well-paid job working nights as a street cleaner. Laci has a wife and six children but his wife left him, taking their two oldest children with her, just a few weeks before Eszti and Lajós got in touch with him. Laci needed someone to look after the younger children while he was out at work. Eszti had turned to him for help at just the right moment. While Eszti looked after the children, Lajós spent his days, as before, collecting scrap cardboard for recycling with the aid of his little trolley.

By the following Spring, Eszti and Lajós were forced to move on once more. Laci's wife had returned to the one-room apartment on Republici Street with the couple's two eldest children. There were now ten people living and sleeping in a single, medium-sized room. When I called at the little apartment on Republici Street, Laci told me that Eszti had already left. She and Lajós had moved into a disused workmens' hut on a piece of wasteland not far from the Romani settlement at Coastei where they had lived before.

The previous autumn, when I went to look for Eszti and Lajós at her cousin's flat on Republici Street, I had some trouble locating the stairs leading up to the apartment. A thin man in late middle age, who was locking an old bicycle to a railing in the courtyard, asked me who I was looking for. An ethnic Hungarian, Tivadar lives with his much younger Romanian wife and their eight-year-old son in an apartment on the first floor. Since retiring from his job as an engineer, when he reached the age of 60, Tivadar has been the building's janitor. He also does odd jobs, such as repairing typewriters, to supplement his modest pension. Tivadar showed me the way to the upper floor, where Eszti was living with her cousin, and invited me to visit him afterwards.

From then on I called on Tivadar whenever I was in Cluj. By a strange coincidence he had known Eszti, who is seven or eight years his junior, when they were both children. They had lived in neighbouring apartment houses. 'I recognised Eszti immediately', Tivadar told me. 'Her family were *úri cigányok*, or upper-class Gypsies.' Tivadar said that many of the men in her family had been successful musicians, including several violinists. 'They had a clean apartment', he recalled. Most of the other tenants in the building where Eszti spent her childhood were middle-class ethnic Hungarians and Romanians who had white-collar jobs in offices.

Unexpectedly brought together again, in middle age, Tivadar and Eszti would exchange a few words whenever they met in the courtyard of the apartment house or on the stairs. Tivadar's apartment is on the floor immediately below the corridor occupied by Eszti, Lajós and the other Gypsies.

'Lajós was drunk most days', said Tivadar. 'Sometimes, he could hardly get up the stairs. He spent most of the money that he earned from collecting cardboard on alcohol. Now and then Eszti was drunk too.'

Tivadar said that he happened to be in the courtyard just as Eszti and Lajós were about to leave the building for good. They had put all their possessions on the little hand-drawn trolley that Lajós uses to collect cardboard for recycling.

'Eszti looked sad', Tivadar recalled. 'But she said that she had to go from there because she wasn't respected.' Eszti told Tivadar that, since her cousin's wife and children had returned, her life had become intolerable. Eszti confided to Tivadar that her cousin had resumed sexual relations with his wife although they lay just a few centimetres away from her at night. 'Their behaviour disgusted Eszti', Tivadar said.

So Eszti and Lajós had decided to return to the Mărăsti district of Cluj. But they had not gone back to the Romani settlement, on the crest of the hill, where they had lived for a couple of years in the shed belonging to Miklós. Instead, they took up residence in a tiny hut, built of breeze blocks, on a piece of wasteland adjoining Dorobantilor Calea, a major road leading to the centre of town. The hut, which was demolished a few months later, was just a few metres away from several lanes of fast-moving traffic. Water had to be brought by hand from nearby shops, a church or a petrol station; many of the local people were helpful and let them use a water tap. Eszti and Lajós's new home had no electricity, plumbing, heating or cooking facilities, although Eszti had improvised a 'barbecue' outside the hut using three bricks.

I visited Eszti and Lajós several times at the workmens' hut on Dorobantilor Calea. On the first of these visits I'd already been with them for well over an hour before they mentioned what had happened the previous night. At around half past ten in the evening a crowd of youths, twelve or fifteen strong, had gathered outside the hut. They shouted abuse and threatened to douse the hut with petrol and set it on fire. It was just a couple of days after Easter and Alina was staying with her parents in the hut.

'Alina was crying; she was really frightened', said Eszti, who showed me the large hammer that she kept for protection just inside the door. 'If I have to, I'll use it.' But I took Eszti's words for bravado. If the youths had come again in the night they wouldn't have encountered much opposition. Apart from shouting, there's not much that Eszti and Lajós could have done.

A few months later I learnt through a Romani social worker, who kept in occasional contact with Eszti and Lajós, that the couple had been forced to vacate the hut and to find alternative accommodation. The owners of the building, the local electricity company, had ejected them on the grounds that they were about to demolish it. Whether the company had decided on this course of action because they'd been notified that a Romani couple were living there, or whether they'd done so because they no longer had any use for the hut, my informant couldn't say.

After some time back on the streets, Eszti and Lajós found refuge in a hostel for the homeless located in a run-down, industrial area of Cluj. The hostel, funded jointly by Dutch and British religious charities, operates in accordance with strict Christian principles, as I was subsequently told by its director. I heard that, for a while, the couple had flourished there. Eszti worked in the kitchens while Lajós was employed on a construction project that the hostel's foreign backers had started in a nearby village. It seemed as if Eszti and Lajós were slowly rehabilitating themselves and might some day be able to live as a normal family once again, together with their daughter. However, the hostel's director caught Lajós in a drunken state one day and the couple were ejected. The hostel maintains strict rules forbidding the consumption of alcohol. Residents have to promise that, for as long as they're living there, they won't even touch alcohol while they're off the premises. Following their eviction from the hostel, which happened in August, Eszti and Lajós mostly lived rough in the Parc Feroviarilor, or 'Railwaymen's Park', close to Cluj's largest slaughterhouse.

During my next visit to Cluj, just a few weeks after Eszti and Lajós had been evicted from the hostel, I traced them to a one-room, basement apartment in the city. The couple had spent the last three nights there together with the apartment's tenants, a Romani couple with four small children of their own.

Lajós was visibly weaker, more subdued than when I'd last seen him, the previous spring. There were cuts and bruises above one eye and on his forehead. Eszti, who confessed that she'd been drinking before I came, was agitated. She kept picking fights with Lajós who rarely responded. A few days earlier, while sleeping in the Parc Feroviarilor, they'd been set upon in the middle of the night 'by a gang of Gypsies', as Lajós put it.

Eszti showed me a small scar on her forearm, where one of their assailants had cut her with his knife. 'I got away,' she said, 'but Lajós was too drunk to move, so I left him there.' The gang had apparently kicked Lajós about the head and taken all the money that he had on him, as well as some other things. The couple's meagre stock of possessions had dwindled to almost nothing. Apart from what she wore, Eszti scarcely had any clothes left. She said that she'd sold most of her skirts, blouses and other garments soon after leaving the hostel because she had no money.

'I could have remained at the hostel even though Lajós was banned', Eszti told me. But she'd decided to stay with her husband of 34 years. Lajós protested that he was not the only hostel resident to have consumed alcohol. 'I was unlucky', he said. 'The director caught me the one time I got drunk.'

'Alina's furious with her father', Eszti said. 'A few weeks ago, when we were all together, she slapped her father about the head and spat at him. She said she wanted nothing more to do with him because of what he's done to me with his drinking.' Lajós seemed not to remember the incident. When Eszti jogged his memory he only smiled wanly, as if to signify that Alina hadn't really meant what she'd said.

Eszti recalled their time in the disused workmens' hut, in the Mărăsti district, with unexpected fondness. People in the neighbouring apartment blocks had been kind to them. 'From time to time, people would give us some food or a little money and we could always get water from one of the nearby shops, or even from the Orthodox Church across the road.' Eszti seemed to have forgotten the gang of youths who had gatherered outside the hut one night, jeering, throwing stones and threatening to immolate them.

'We're going to have to leave this apartment today or tomorrow', Eszti said. 'We can't stay here any longer; there's no room.' If this was a cue for me to offer them some money I didn't do so immediately, knowing that they would only spend it on alcohol.

A few days later, I heard a slightly different version of the events leading up to Eszti and Lajós's eviction from the hostel. I rang the hostel's director in the hope of persuading him to take the couple back. 'The hostel's run in accordance with Christian principles', the director told me. He spoke rapidly, in staccato bursts, like a man with a great deal to do and far too little time. 'Both Eszti and Lajós broke the rules several times. I had to expel them. They could have become a bad influence on the other residents.'

It seemed that, after all, Eszti had not been as innocent as she'd pretended. Eszti had not left the hostel voluntarily, as she'd told me, in order to remain with her husband. She'd been expelled along with him for repeated infraction of the hostel's rules. Maybe Eszti had managed to convince herself that Lajós was at the root of all her problems. In any case, while I was with them, Lajós didn't bother to contradict her version of events.

Shortly before I tracked down Eszti and Lajós to the little basement flat in Cluj, I visited the placement centre in which Alina had been living to ask the director some questions about the Romani girls in her care. While I was in her office, the director sent word to Alina to join us.

Slightly built, like her mother, Alina seemed too small and physically underdeveloped for an adolescent girl approaching 15. Later, an experienced social worker in Cluj told me that she'd seen quite a few similar cases amongst her clients. Poor diet in childhood could often stunt growth later on.

Alina asked me whether I'd seen her parents. 'Whenever we were together, during the summer, I tried to convince them that they're alcoholics and that they need treatment', she said. 'I borrowed a little money from some of the girls here and gave it to them.' Despite everything that Eszti had told me, Alina said nothing to indicate that she blamed her father for her mother's predicament. 'I worry about them,' she said, 'which makes it hard for me to concentrate on my studies.' In many ways, the roles of parent and child had been reversed.

RELUCTANT WORKERS: LAJÓS' EMPLOYMENT HISTORY

From the first time we met, Eszti and Lajós would tell me repeatedly that the Transylvanian Construction Company, for which Lajós had worked most of his adult life, made a mistake in calculating the number of years that he'd been with the company. Lajós had lost his *carnet de muncă*, a document issued to every worker in Romania with details of their employment history. When he went to the company's offices to have the *carnet* replaced they provided him with a substitute. However, Lajós is adamant that the new document does not record the full number of years that he actually worked for the company. The couple were worried that, as a result of this bureaucratic error, Lajós would lose his entitlement to a proper pension when he reached retirement age.

Eszti says that she went to the company's offices herself to ask how Lajós's employment record could be straightened out. 'They were rude and unhelpful', she told me. 'They wouldn't tell me what documents I needed or where I should go to get them. It's because I'm a Gypsy and a Hungarian Gypsy at that.' In Transylvania, with its mixed population of ethnic Hungarians and Romanians – and a long history of conflict between Romania and Hungary for ascendancy over the region – to be a Gypsy with a Hungarian name may represent a double misfortune.*

I promised Eszti and Lajós that I would look into whether the details recorded on Lajós's *carnet de muncă* could be amended if they should turn out to be inaccurate. Thanks to the persistence of my Romanian research assistant, Ela, and much to my surprise, the Personnel Office of the Transylvanian Construction Company agreed to talk to us.

In a cramped office heavy with dog-eared files, three middle-aged women and a man were working at their desks. After Ela and I introduced ourselves and explained how we came to be interested in Lajós Szilárd and his employment history with the company, one of the women said that she remembered him.

'He wasn't a good worker', she said. 'He was often drunk. He used to work for a while, but then he'd disappear. That was common enough amongst the Gypsies, even in the Communist era.'

---

* For all practical purposes, the historic conflict for control over Transylvania was ended by the 1920 Treaty of Trianon which awarded the region to Romania. Briefly, during World War II, Hungary regained control over northern Transylvania with German support. But, since the end of World War II, the whole of Transylvania has reverted to Romania.

The woman leafed through some files in a cabinet and produced Lajós's *adeverinta*, or employment record. Without my even asking for it, she made a photocopy and handed it to me. 'Lajós Szilárd was sacked during the Communist period, which was very unusual. In fact, he was sacked twice.'

According to the *adeverinta*, Lajós was sacked for the first time on 18 December 1976 for 'indiscipline', contrary to Article 130/I of the Labour Code. He was rehired the following May and then sacked a second time, for the same offence, on 21 December 1983. As a local lawyer later explained to me, 'indiscipline' was a common euphemism for drunkenness. Although Lajós was rehired a third time by the company in February 1990, he was made redundant in May 1992.

'Really, he should have been sacked', said the woman in the Personnel Office. 'But we felt sorry for him. By making him redundant at least he was entitled to some benefits.' Everyone in the Personnel Office took the view that it was impossible that a mistake could have been made in calculating the number of years that Lajós had worked for the company.

Later that day I went to see a legal counsellor at the local Pensions Office. She examined my photocopy of Lajós's *adeverinta* and quickly calculated that he had worked for the company for a total of 25 years, nine months and six days. From the date of his second sacking by the company, in December 1983, until he was rehired in 1990, there was a long and inexplicable gap in his employment record. Previously, Lajós had told me that he'd worked abroad for extended periods as an agricultural labourer, mainly in Hungary. On the last occasion he was caught by the Hungarian police and deported as an illegal alien. Lajós showed me the stamp in his passport that barred him from returning to Hungary for several years.

'When he reaches the age of 62 he'll get a small pension', the legal counsellor said to me.' 'Sixty two is now the minimum pensionable age for a man in Romania. But, as a man, he would have had to work for a minimum of 30 years to qualify for a full pension. What he'll get won't be enough to live on.' Lajós was born on 6 May 1943. Assuming he lives that long, he'll be 62 in May 2005.

It had become increasingly clear, from all the information that I had been able to obtain about the couple, that Lajós and Eszti were neither model citizens nor ideal parents. They were not a clear-cut example of the catastrophic and largely unavoidable effects of the transition process on the mass of ordinary Roma in Central and Eastern Europe. To some degree, Lajós and Eszti must bear responsibility for what has happened to them, although these days alcoholism is usually viewed as a disease rather than as a vice or moral shortcoming. If what I had been told about him by his former employer was broadly correct, then Lajós' bouts of drunkenness and occasional disappearances from work had contributed to the decision to make him redundant in 1992. Neither he nor Eszti appeared capable, at this point in their lives, of the sustained effort and self-control necessary to maintain jobs, look after children and run a home.

Nevertheless, in countless other cases, the working habits of individual Romanies in the region had not affected their prospects of retaining – or of finding – regular work. However diligent or even exemplary their record – for example András Balogh Balázs recounts in Chapter 4 that he received two official commendations during the Communist era from the Nógrád County Waterworks for being an outstanding worker – hundreds of thousands of Roma were made redundant or forced into premature retirement. The massive economic restructuring that occurred in Central and Eastern Europe in the final decade of the twentieth century – and the vulnerability of the mass of ordinary Roma because of their comparatively poor educational qualifications and their concentration in unproductive sectors earmarked for radical restructuring – virtually condemned the Gypsies to long-term unemployment. These factors have been compounded by widespread racism and stereotyping, which impose further and serious obstacles to Romani employment.

As suggested elsewhere in this book, social and economic integration is a slow, incremental process. It has to contend with other tendencies, including the fact that, traditionally, the Roma generally provided services of various kinds to the broader community while preserving a significant degree of autonomy.[8] Some Romani subgroups, such as Vlach Gypsies in Hungary or the Gábor Roma in north-western Romania, have partially succeded in maintaining a tradition of economic independence up to the present day.[9] Lajós' grudging acceptance of wage labour, and his apparent tendency to disappear for days at a time while employed by the Transylvanian Construction Company, were not necessarily evidence of incorrigible laziness, or of an incurable moral defect. His conduct can also be understood as stemming from a partial internalisation of the norms of the society in which he found himself and of a consequent distaste for the rigid structures and lack of autonomy that working for a company had entailed. Despite his protestations, and although he could no longer afford to rent even the tiniest of apartments, he seemed quite satisfied with his current, freelance work of collecting cardboard for recycling. In a sense, he had traded comfort and security for a kind of freedom. The rapid dismantling of the paternalistic and authoritarian Communist system, which both required Lajós and other Roma to accept jobs and at the same time provided them and their families with a reassuring safety net, has jeopardised this process of slow social and economic integration, throwing it into reverse.

NEW RIGHTS FOR OLD IN CENTRAL AND EASTERN EUROPE

On the day I met Eszti at the Coastei settlement, Miklós, her Romani landlord, told me that he'd been 'inside' a couple of times. 'I won't hide the truth from you', he said. 'I'm not ashamed of it.' Miklós' crime had been 'social parasitism'. Twice, during the Ceauşescu years, the police had arrested him for not being able to show that he had a job. Under the Communist order, work was both a right and a duty. The state guaranteed everyone a job of some kind. In return, every able-bodied person had to contribute his or her labour to the general good. These principles were enshrined, for example, in Hungary's 1949 Communist Constitution which guaranteed every citizen 'the right to work' and to be paid in accordance with 'the amount and the quality of the completed work', while emphasising 'the fundamental duty' of all citizens to contribute to the 'economic strength' of the state.[10] Much the same provision can be found in all the Communist-era constitutions that were adopted in Central and Eastern Europe.

During the Ceauşescu era, Gypsies were alloted jobs by the state. Many, like Miklós, worked as garbage collectors. Others, like Lajós, were employed in the construction industry, in factories or on co-operative farms. Under the paternalistic if heavy-handed Communist order, Gypsies were housed and given access to free education and health care. In the cities, Gypsy families were allocated apartments; in the villages, they were provided with houses or materials so that they could build houses for themselves. In Transylvania, much of the pre-War ethnic German population left for Germany, with the acquiescence of the Communist authorities who levied a 'tax' on these migrants.[11] Many of their abandoned village properties were assigned to Gypsies.

Since the end of Communist rule, ideas concerning the proper functions of the state have changed fundamentally in Romania and in the other countries of Central and Eastern Europe. Rights to work or to housing are no longer the constitutional entitlement of every citizen.[12] As in most western liberal democracies, the role of the state is now more modest. For the first time in well over two hundred years, there is an extraordinary degree of ideological convergence across Europe. In many respects, this new consensus was heralded by the Charter of Paris for a New Europe. Adopted by the continent's leaders in November 1990, the Charter emphasises that a commitment to human rights, democracy, at least minimal respect for the rights of national minorities and economic liberty are amongst the key foundational principles of the 'new' European order.[13] The Charter's understanding of the proper scope of 'human rights', a notoriously elastic concept, is unambiguous. The document affirms the core civil and political rights – including rights to freedom of thought, conscience and religion, freedom of expression, freedom of association and peaceful assembly, freedom from torture and so on – as the rights of *every* individual. By contrast, the Charter declares that everyone has the right 'to enjoy *his* economic, social and cultural rights'.[14] Whereas civil and political rights are *universal*, available to everyone, social and economic rights are *particular*, confined to those entitlements that have been legally recognised within specific jurisdictions. The distinction introduced by the Charter between these two types of rights – and regarding their respective degrees of importance within the new, pan-European constitutional order – is all too plain.

The tensions between the 'old' and the 'new' notions of what a state should deliver are reflected in many of the region's post-Communist constitutions.[15] Vestiges of the largely discredited socialist principle that the state should assure social and economic rights to its citizens can be found in most of these constitutional texts. For example, Article 1(3) of Title I of Romania's 1991 Constitution provides that, 'Romania is a democratic and social State governed by the rule of law.'[16] However, the nature of its 'social' character is not spelt out. After a long catalogue of civil and political rights, enumerated in Chapter II of Title II of the Constitution, there is a much more limited list of social and economic rights. Instead of a right to work, Article 38(1) merely recognises that '[t]he right to work cannot be restricted'. Most importantly, Article 43 provides that:

(1) The State shall be bound to take measures of economic development and social protection, of a nature to ensure a decent living standard for its citizens.
(2) Citizens have the right to pensions, paid maternity leave, medical care in public health establishments, unemployment benefits, and other forms of social care, as provided by law.

However, rights are only effective and meaningful if courts and tribunals are willing to enforce them and, where legal provisions lack clarity, to give them substance. As noted above, Article 1(3) of the Romanian Constitution, which provides that 'Romania is a democratic and *social* State', is opaque.[17] Exactly what the 'social' character of a state may entail, in terms of welfare and employment policies, is far from clear. However, rather than invest the term with meaning, 'a silent consensus has been reached to consider this provision merely as rhetorical, and to ignore it'.[18]

The situation is scarcely different in the Czech Republic. Although social and economic rights are included in the country's Charter of Rights and Freedoms, the Czech Constitutional Court has been reluctant to enforce them.[19] In Hungary, the Constitutional Court, while showing itself willing to annul measures that would have abruptly terminated long-standing schemes of social protection for families, did so on the basis of rule of law principles, particularly the principle of legal security.[20] It was the brutally sudden manner in which the established schemes of social assistance were withdrawn – and on which families had come to rely – that the Court held unconstitutional. While emphasising the right of the government and legislature to radically change the country's social welfare structures, the Court pointedly reminded them that they could not evade the duties derived from the Constitution concerning the protection of mothers, children and families.[21]

In general, Constitutional Courts in Central and Eastern Europe treat socio-economic rights that have been included in constitutions as of limited legal significance. As noted by the distinguished Polish scholar Wojciech Sadurski, socio-economic rights have largely been used by Constitutional Courts 'to challenge discriminatory or arbitrary distinctions in legislation and policy rather than to address more fundamentally the wisdom, or otherwise, of a government's socio-economic policies'.[22]

ARE HUMAN RIGHTS IRRELEVANT TO THE REGION'S ROMA?

It has become almost commonplace in academic circles to express scepticism about the use or even the utility of rights as a means of creating more just and fundamentally decent societies. As human rights have become increasingly mainstream and 'respectable', part of the legitimating language of governments and international organisations, growing numbers of scholars have begun to question the abuse of human rights discourse. For example, while upholding the political and philosophical importance of the concept of human rights for sections of humanity who are weak, exploited or powerless, Professor Baxi has drawn attention to the way in which human rights are in danger of being hijacked by elements with a very different, indeed exploitative, agenda: [23]

> the paradigm of the Universal Declaration of Human Rights...is being steadily, but surely, *supplanted* by that of trade-related, market-friendly human rights. This new paradigm seeks to reverse the notion that universal human rights are designed for the attainment of dignity and well-being of human beings and for enhancing the security and well-being of socially, economically and civilizationally vulnerable peoples and communities. The emergent paradigm insists upon the promotion and the protection of the collective human rights of global capital in ways that 'justify' corporate well-being and dignity even when it entails gross and flagrant violation of human rights of actually existing human beings and communities.

Others go much further, casting doubt on even the potential relevance or importance of human rights discourse in what amounts to a modern form of apostasy.[24] There is considerable irony in this turn of events. In the seventeenth, eighteenth and nineteenth centuries – and more recently – human rights were generally seen as radical and subversive in intent, a challenge to self-perpetuating political elites and to entrenched social and economic hierarchies.[25] However, the apparent triumph of human rights at the start of the twenty-first century – human rights are included, in some form, in almost every modern constitution as well as in a host of multilateral treaties including the Charter of the United Nations – has been accompanied by increasing rights scepticism amongst scholars.

At least three distinct criticisms of rights are commonly advanced.[26] First, the ideology of human rights, particularly when enshrined in law, is accused of being: 'insufficiently sensitive to the hegemonic power of its own discourse. Rights are an incredibly powerful rhetorical tool, and they get everywhere, strangling other devices, stymieing alternative developments.'[27]

Second, the content of human rights instruments, such as the European Convention on Human Rights, are seen as partial and selective, representing 'a particular political – and party-political – vision of what it is that society should privilege and prioritize'.[28] Third, the role of judges and of courts as the ultimate arbiters of our rights has been called into question. As Adam Tomkins puts it, 'locating the task of enforcing rights in the courts can lead to the suffocating of alternative avenues for dispute resolution', while: '[b]y inflating the power and responsibility of the judiciary, the influence and contribution which could be offered from other less well-dressed, but perhaps better-suited, institutions has been sidelined and overlooked.'[29]

Each of these arguments has undoubted force. As suggested above, the deliberate refocusing of rights that has occurred in the post-Communist states, with the displacement and gradual erosion of social and economic rights in favour of a western, liberal conception of the centrality of civil and political rights, has been damaging for socially and economically vulnerable groups such as the Roma. The factors (political and economic) that led to this reconfiguration of rights in Central and Eastern Europe are readily apparent.

However, discarding the very notion of rights because human rights instruments are a product of political processes seems to be a clear case of 'throwing out the baby with the bathwater'. On the whole, and until a better vision of human dignity comes along, it is a 'baby' worth keeping and even nurturing. If human rights texts emerge from intense political debate (and other processes) then those with a concern for the marginalised and the undeprivileged should be ready to engage in tough and protracted political advocacy. This is, in broad terms, the position of the distinguished sociologist and legal scholar Boaventura de Sousa Santos, who has emphasised the 'emancipatory potential' of human rights discourse and who has called for a cross-cultural reconstruction of human rights'.[30]

If the mass of ordinary Roma in Central and Eastern Europe were consulted they would plead for the restoration of the social and economic rights that they enjoyed under Communism – which assured them a degree of material security – rather than embrace some new, socio-political experiment. Almost without exception, the numerous working-class Gypsies whom I interviewed in Romania and Hungary recalled the Communist era in the fondest, most positive terms because of the ready availability of jobs, subsidised housing and cheap food. Increasingly, many Roma now also recognise the importance of the civil and political rights with which they have been invested more recently – although the latter remain vastly less crucial to their well-being than the former.

The role of courts and tribunals in the enforcement and interpretation of rights clearly depends on the quality, integrity, social understanding and vision of those appointed as judges or as members of tribunals.

Such agencies can never be a guarantor of wise or progressive decision-making. However, the judicialisation of rights represents a radical departure from the bureaucratisation and politicisation of rights that existed under Communism. As noted elsewhere in this book, under Communism, socio-economic rights were often treated as privileges that could be abruptly withdrawn or withheld from an individual (or from an entire family) in the event of political dissent. The judicial enforcement of rights – in a system governed by the separation of powers and the rule of law – is surely preferable.

The judicial interpretation of rights, as every lawyer knows, can amount to a form of (tacit) judicial law-making. By its very nature it is both profoundly undemocratic and unpredictable. To me, at least, this suggests a need to ensure that the selection and training of judges is as transparent and well conceived as is humanly possible, rather than grounds for replacing the judicial element in our constitutions by other, more overtly political processes. Who today would advocate disbanding the European Court of Human Rights or the US Supreme Court, however much one might disagree with individual decisions? Courts have an important role to play in any modern constitutional settlement although the contribution of other agencies, in elaborating and safeguarding rights, is at least as crucial. To advocate abandoning courts, notwithstanding all their imperfections, in favour of some radical (and untested) new constitutional mechanism is a utopian prescription.

Rights, as suggested above, are 'an incredibly powerful rhetorical tool'; that really is the point of them. The emancipatory and egalitarian vision of rights remains highly relevant, even essential, particularly in societies where they represent a comparative novelty and where the Roma (or other national or ethnic groups) are often seen as less than fully human. In the history of Central and Eastern Europe – as in the history of much of the rest of the world – religion, ethnicity and, more recently, class, have often determined an individual's life choices or, in some cases, even labelled them as unworthy to live.[31] Mankind is still a long way away from being able to declare that notions of rights have become an anachronism.

7
Anikó

I first saw Anikó on a fine spring morning. She was sashaying down the street, a half tumbler of *pálinka* in her hand. The *pálinka*, or fruit brandy, was not for herself. Anikó never touches liquor of any kind. She had bought it at a nearby bar for the workmen who were refitting the bathroom in her house. In Patakrét, as in many villages in Central and Eastern Europe, it has long been the custom for men to start each working day (and often weekends as well) with a generous shot of *pálinka*. Notionally, the alcohol is intended to fortify them against the elements. In practice, it is also habitually drunk by men who hardly venture out of doors. In adopting this happy custom Gypsies have simply followed the example of Gadje amongst whom they settled.

I was accompanying the Hungarian film director Edit Kőszegi, the Budapest-based ethnologist Péter Szuhay and their cameraman, Gyuszi. We were heading for Anikó's house which is situated in the heart of the village. We were still some distance away when Gyuszi caught sight of Anikó walking by the side of the road. Anikó's long black hair was tied back, while she wore a loose flowing skirt topped by a suede jerkin trimmed with wool. Her figure was full, voluptuous even, but not stout like those of many middle-aged Romani women. When the car drew level and stopped, Anikó bent down and appraised us through the open window. Although Anikó's face was lined and she wore no make-up she was strikingly handsome. Until a few years ago she must have been beautiful.

'I expected you yesterday', she said, a trace of annoyance in her voice.

Communicating with Anikó, as with the other Roma in the village, can be difficult as very few of them can afford a telephone. Even in the age of the mobile phone they mostly rely on other means to keep in touch. Many of the older folk have never learnt to read or write, so letters are of little use.[1] Occasionally, if the matter is urgent, Anikó will call Edit from a public telephone, or Edit might leave a message for Anikó with a Hungarian neighbour who has a landline. But, most of

7   Hungarian Vlach Romani woman with her children

the time, neither phones nor letters play much part in the lives of the village's Roma.

Anikó was the principal reason we had come to Patakrét. Edit and Péter were making a documentary about Anikó and a number of scenes were to be shot during this brief visit. An additional reason for the trip had been to screen Edit's recently completed movie, *Sitiprinc*, in the village culture house. As described above, numerous Roma from the village had been cast in the film, mainly as extras, though the leading roles were taken by professional actors. Anikó and her husband had been given small parts in the movie. They play a childless Romani couple who raise an orphaned Gadjo boy, the eponymous hero of the film, as their own son.

Anikó is a talented as well as photogenic actress, who has mastered the art of behaving naturally before a camera. But it was not her qualities as an actress that had prompted Edit to devote a documentary to her.[2] Edit, who has made a series of films about Hungary's Gypsies and who has resolutely espoused their cause, was drawn to one strikingly unusual feature of Anikó's life. In ethnic terms, she is only half-Gypsy. Anikó's father, János, is a darkly handsome Vlach Romani, but her mother, Kati, was an ethnic Hungarian.

The couple had met and fallen in love in Dunaujváros, a new industrial town founded in 1949 by Hungary's Communist rulers. János was employed as a labourer in the construction industry, like many other Roma at that time. As described elsewhere, the newly installed Communist regimes in Central and Eastern Europe made a concerted effort, particularly in the early years, to integrate the Roma, both economically and socially, within the new socialist societies.[3] Because of their generally low level of formal education – a high proportion of Roma in the region remained semi or fully illiterate in the 1940s and 1950s – many Gypsies were assigned routine jobs in factories, as labourers on the newly created agricultural cooperatives, or as workers in the construction industry.[4] Originally, Dunaujváros had been called Sztálinváros, or 'Stalin Town' in homage to the Soviet leader of the time. But, with the demise and subsequent discrediting of Stalin, on account of his brutal excesses, the town was given a new, less politically troublesome name.[5]

By 1959, Kati and János were living together in Patakrét. Marriages or long-term relationships between Gypsies and non-Gypsies remain comparatively unusual and were much rarer still in the 1950s.[6] Unsurprisingly, Kati's family had bitterly opposed the union. They saw it as bringing shame and dishonour on them all because of the low esteem in which Gypsies are held. When Kati's brother, then a police officer based in Budapest, learnt that his sister had set up house with a Gypsy, he travelled to Patakrét in a vain effort to persuade her to return with him. But Kati refused to leave the village and her Romani lover; her brother went back to Budapest, angry and alone. From that moment, Kati's family severed all ties with her. Kati was left to become a Gypsy by degrees settling, as best she could, amongst Patakrét's Vlach Roma.

However, Edit disabused me of any sentimental notions I might have had that Anikó's mother was welcomed with open arms by her common-law husband's family. It should come as no surprise that Gypsies can be every bit as narrow-minded and intolerant as Gadje.[7] Kati remained an object of mistrust, Edit said, subject to predatory sexual advances by some of the Romani men in the village whenever her partner was away for any length of time. Many Roma assumed that Anikó's mother was promiscuous, a common Romani perception of Gadje women.[8] By contrast, Vlach Gypsy women, particularly those of child-bearing age, are expected to behave with conspicuous modesty and to remain virgins until they marry; Vlach Romani women who commit adultery are subject to major social sanctions.[9] For the remainder of her unhappy life, Kati was suspended between two mutually suspicious and uncomprehending worlds.

Unlike her mother, Anikó was accepted unreservedly by her father's family and by the Vlach Romani community of the village. Because of the periodic absences of one or both of her parents – Anikó's mother fled Patakrét from time to time when she could no longer endure her life there – Anikó spent much of her childhood with three aunts, sisters of her father. The aunts own a *tanya*, or smallholding, some kilometres from the nearest road. The aunts were still there, although grown old, when I visited them accompanied by Anikó. As in the years when Anikó lived with them, all the key decisions about the running of the *tanya* are taken by Bőske. As shrewd and industrious as János and another of her brothers are feckless, Bőske has run the smallholding profitably for many years. She also owns a house in Patakrét but rarely uses it because of what she described as 'the noise and bustle of the village', things that she abhors. As a child, Anikó spent several years on the *tanya*, helping her aunts to look after the livestock – chickens, geese, ducks, as well as a few cows, horses and some pigs. She relished the atmosphere of peace and tranquillity on the smallholding that contrasted so forcibly with the strife and dissension in her parents' home in the village.

For many years Anikó remained uncurious about her Gadje relatives, people her mother occasionally spoke of but whom she had never met. In her teens, Anikó married a wiry, good-looking man with a characteristically Vlach Romani passion for horses. For the Vlach Gypsies of Patakrét, 'the meaning and the purpose of a Rom's life is horses. The man who does not have a horse is perhaps no longer a Romani.'[10]

The couple had two sons, handsome, dark-haired boys who look much like their father. But the birth of her third child, Csilla, abruptly reminded Anikó of her mother's Gadjo origins. To the consternation of many of the Roma in the village, Csilla is pale-skinned and red-haired.

She doesn't remotely resemble the popular stereotype of a Gypsy. Rumours began to circulate amongst the local Roma that the little girl had to be the product of an illicit liaison between Anikó and a Gadjo lover.

Anikó says that it was the death of her mother, in 1993, that finally prompted her to look for her Gadje relatives. This was a quest that immediately excited Edit too. It would make an excellent subject for a documentary. There was a distinct possibility that, even if Anikó succeeded in making contact with her estranged Gadje relations, they would rebuff her, exposing the strong current of anti-Gypsy sentiment in Hungarian society, something that had actually increased in the transition from Communism to democracy.[11] If, however, Anikó's relatives turned out to be friendly and welcoming the documentary would serve as a timely and heart-warming example, to Hungarians and Roma alike, of the possibilities of mutual respect and harmonious co-existence between the two peoples.

When Edit explained her project to me, long before I met Anikó, I became uneasy. 'What if she finds her Hungarian relatives only for them to snub her because she's a Gypsy?' I asked. I had a sudden vision of Anikó, tearful and disconsolate, a door having been literally, as well as metaphorically, slammed shut in her face.

For an instant, the look in Edit's eyes became uncharacteristically hard. 'Either way, whether her relatives accept her or not, it'll make a good ending!'

But I need not have worried about Anikó's bruised feelings. As I quickly came to realise, Anikó is not as naïve or thin-skinned as I had feared. If Edit was using Anikó to make a documentary about Hungarian racism and the need for Magyar–Roma understanding, Anikó was using Edit to achieve several ends of her own. Not only did Anikó insist on being paid handsomely for her services (although she always grumbled that the money wasn't nearly enough and that it was far less than a professional actress would have received), she also acquired valuable and cost-free assistance in tracing her relatives. Without Edit and Péter to root out telephone numbers and to do battle with unhelpful local government officials, it is unlikely that Anikó would have had the resources or the determination to undertake the work. And Anikó, as I saw for myself, was having a great deal of fun; she was being filmed in various locations around the village by people who'd come all the way from Budapest just to be with her. This was an experience that would boost her standing in Patakrét, amongst Gypsies and smallholders alike. There was also the prospect of an all-expenses-paid trip to Szabolcs-Szatmár county, in north-eastern Hungary, an area that she had never seen. Anikó's mother came from this region that lies close to the Ukrainian border. Some of her relatives were likely to be living there to this day. By any form of reckoning, Anikó was way ahead.

Unlike most of the Roma in Patakrét, who live in the distant and unfashionable *uj falu*, or 'new village', Anikó lives in a house which lies in the heart of the older and more established portion of the village. Her neighbours are smallholders. Living in the main part of Patakrét, among peasants rather than Gypsies, confers an added status on Anikó, setting her apart from most of the other Roma. But her house is modest enough. A single-storey affair, set in a small plot of land, it comprises three rooms, with a stable at the back. The stable is an extension of the house, allowing the animals (invariably horses) to enjoy some of the warmth generated by the wood-burning stove in the sitting room.

Edit and Péter were impatient to begin shooting a couple of scenes for the documentary so Anikó, having dropped off the *pálinka* at her house, accompanied them to the centre of the village. The short scenes that Edit wanted to shoot that day were set in the post office and at a nearby phone booth. In the documentary Anikó is shown taking the initiative in the search for her Gadje relatives. According to the script, Anikó enters the phone booth and calls a local government official in a distant town who has information about the whereabouts of some of her relatives. On being told that she must submit her request in writing, Anikó strides into the post office, little Csilla in her arms, and enquires at one of the counters about sending a fax. In reality, of course, Anikó had not taken the initiative at all. Step by step, she was doing exactly as she was told by Edit and Péter. But documentaries, as I quickly discovered, employ many little fictions in order to convey some larger truths.

FINDING ANIKÓ'S GADJE RELATIVES

Several months later, in the autumn, I was with Péter, Edit, Gyuszi and Miklós, a film producer from Budapest, when they arrived outside Anikó's house at 5.45 one morning. Before setting off that day in quest of Anikó's Gadje relatives, a journey on which they would be accompanied by Anikó and two of her children, Csilla and Gábor, Edit wanted to film the family's departure from Patakrét. The two versions do not correspond exactly. In the documentary, Anikó and Csilla are seen getting into a gleaming, almost new Opel, with Gábor, a young man of eighteen or so, at the wheel. We are led to believe that Gábor drives his mother and sister all the way to Szabolcs-Szatmár county. In reality, the family's only car is a decrepit Lada. As soon as Gyuszi, the cameraman, had filmed them setting off in the Opel, the car reversed and came to a stop. Anikó and Gábor climbed into the back of the car, joining Csilla, while I took the front passenger seat. The Opel belonged to Miklós, the producer of the documentary, who had come down from Budapest for a couple of days to see how filming was progressing. He insisted on driving the car himself. Edit, Péter and another colleague of theirs, together with all of the sound and camera equipment, were in a second vehicle. Bald, bespectacled and soberly dressed, Miklós has the manner of a pedantic schoolteacher.

In the documentary, Anikó is eager to make contact with her mother's family. She is consumed by the quest for her Gadje relatives whom she has never met. After all, little Csilla, with her pale skin and curly red hair, is a constant reminder of the family Anikó has 'lost'. Sometimes, though, I could not help wondering how authentic Anikó's curiosity really was. Before we set off that morning, Anikó and Edit had an argument. Anikó kept insisting that she wanted to return home the same day while Edit pointed out, rather crossly, that it might take two or three days to track down her mother's relatives. It was largely a matter of luck. 'That's the whole point of this, isn't it?' Edit impatiently reminded her, 'To find your relatives?'

Maybe Anikó had a point or two of her own. Before setting off from Patakrét that morning Anikó had importuned Miklós. 'Give me some money that I can leave with my family', she said, extending the palm of her hand. 'You can see we're poor.' Miklós took out his wallet and handed over two 1,000 Forint notes, a tidy sum. 'You'll be paid your fee when the documentary is finished', he reminded her, sounding particularly schoolmasterly. Later, and despite his own behaviour, Miklós gave me some advice. 'You mustn't give any money to Gypsies', he cautioned. 'They think every Hungarian is stupid.'

But, whether Anikó was merely acting, or whether her interest in finding her relatives was genuine, she played her part well. Dressed in an immaculate white blouse and a long, fashionably cut skirt, she looked elegant and, at the same time, faintly exotic. Anikó's thick, black hair was swept back, revealing large gold earrings. Despite the differences in their backgrounds (Edit once told me that her own father had grown up in a castle that belonged to his family), Anikó rivalled Edit in her disdain for authority. 'Anikó's like a queen!' Edit remarked admiringly, more than once.

Our journey that day took us first to Nagykálló, a small town in Szabolcs-Szatmár. Enquiries at the town hall revealed that no-one called 'Göszi' – Anikó's mother's maiden name – still lived in Nagykálló. So we headed for Nyíregyháza, the county town. We were already on the outskirts of Nyíregyháza when, while manoeuvring to turn into a side street, we collided with an old Lada. Miklós' Opel was wrecked although none of us was injured.

Leaving Miklós to wait for a tow truck, the crumpled Opel having been pushed up onto the kerb, the rest of us headed on foot to Nyíregyháza's town hall to enquire whether anyone called Göszi was known to be living in the area. But there was no trace of Anikó's relatives in Nyíregyháza.

As a result of the collision we were left with only one serviceable car. Due to lack of space, at least one of us would have to remain behind with Miklós. Reluctantly, I conceded that it ought to be me.

I learnt about the rest of Anikó's quest for her Gadje relatives a few weeks before Christmas, on my next visit to Hungary. As with other events that took place while I was in Britain, such as the funeral of a Gypsy I'd known in Patakrét, I relied in part on what people were able to tell me. In Budapest, I spoke to Edit, Péter and Gyuszi about the latter stages of their search for Anikó's relations. In Patakrét, I heard about them from Anikó herself as well as from her son, Gábor. But, as with the Romani funeral, I had an additional source of information which was to prove invaluable. Gyuszi had shot several hours of film, covering every stage of their picaresque journey in Szabolcs-Szatmár. Sitting in his well-appointed studio, high up in Budapest's Ethnographic Museum, I could watch and listen to what had happened for myself.

After leaving us at the roadside, Péter and the others head east for Orsos, a small town that has become a virtual suburb of Nyíregyháza. Anikó recalled her mother saying that her family had lived in Orsos for a while before settling in Nyíregyháza. Finding a gaunt, elderly man in overalls, working in his garden, Anikó asks him whether he has heard of her grandfather, János Göszi.

'Of course!' says the old man, with a chuckle. 'János Göszi was a miller. He bought the mill from a Jew.' If I had been present I would have wanted to ask the old man about the date of that transaction. During World War II, Hungary enacted a series of anti-Jewish laws that gradually excluded the country's Jews from most sectors of commerce and industry, forcing them to relinquish their property for little or no compensation.[12] At the same time, Jews in professional or white-collar employment were progressively dismissed from their jobs, while able-bodied Jewish males were conscripted into labour battalions attached to the Hungarian army.[13] Many of the latter were treated with conspicuous brutality and sadism. Perhaps János Göszi was one of those 'lucky' Hungarians who had profited from the misfortunes of the Jews, acquiring property for only a fraction of its true value.

At another house in Orsos, to which they're directed, Anikó introduces herself to an old woman. The woman says she remembers János Göszi well. 'He was a small, handsome man', she tells Anikó. 'Dark and rather fleshy.' The Göszi family had prospered until, after the War, the mill was nationalised by the Communists.[14] 'After that', says the old woman, 'the family packed up and moved to Nyíregyháza.' She gazes fondly at Anikó, calling her *kedves* or 'dear'.

Anikó's manner with the old woman is tender and solicitous. As Anikó gets up to leave she tells her softly, '[d]on't be angry with me for disturbing you'. But it is clear that Anikó's visit, with the attendant film crew, has made the old lady's day.

Watching the rushes, I was continually impressed by Anikó. Her questioning of the old man in his garden and of the old woman, with her memories of the portly János Göszi, is adroit. Anikó has an evident flair for the craft of interviewing. Her gently insistent manner and low-pitched, soothing voice encourage the interviewees to dig deep into their memories. And Anikó always seems to know exactly how to follow up one question with another. Gradually, in watching the rushes, I shed my former cynicism about her motives. When Anikó finally meets one of her cousins, she is visibly moved.

A fit looking man in early middle age, wearing a faded T-shirt, he is standing in his front garden, painting his house. His surname is Göszi, he tells Anikó, although he says he has lost touch with his father's side of the family. He was only a child when his father died. After talking to one another for a little while, Anikó and the man realise that they are cousins.

Anikó cries as she tells him about her mother's death, in 1993. 'That's when I began to look for my mother's relatives', she says. 'My parents set up house together in 1959. Jancsi, my mother's brother, came down to fetch her home before it was too late. But my mother wouldn't go with him.'

'The men in the Göszi family generally had enormous moustaches', Anikó's cousin recalls. 'The moustaches were so long that they tied the ends together behind their heads.' He tells Anikó about another member of the Göszi family, István Göszi. But he warns her that he has not had any contact with István for some years. Maybe the family has moved away. The address is in Tiszavasvári, a small town just a few miles west of Nyíregyháza.

Mrs Göszi is at home when Anikó calls, unannounced, at the house. A sturdy woman, in her early sixties, she is standing in the front garden chatting to a neighbour. Anikó introduces herself and shows the two women photographs of her late mother. Mrs Göszi, friendly and smiling, invites everyone into the house. Recently widowed, she lives there with her son and teenage granddaughter.

As they look through family photographs, Mrs Göszi mentions to Anikó that another of her relatives lives near by. She's an aunt of Anikó's mother and, almost certainly, Anikó's oldest surviving relative on her mother's side. Arms casually draped around one other's shoulders, as if they have known each other all their lives, Anikó and Mrs Göszi set off to walk the short distance to the old woman's house.

Anikó's great aunt, tiny and bent, opens the front door when they knock. Mrs István Göszi explains to the old lady who Anikó is and why she has come. The old woman beams at them. 'Come in!' she exclaims.

Dressed in dark clothes and a kerchief that she wears even indoors, the old woman has hardly any teeth. Well into her nineties, she tells Anikó that she started work at the age of eleven as a *napszámos*, or day labourer, on local farms. That must have been in the early 1920s. When the Communists took over after the War and collectivised agriculture 'everyone was forced to join the co-operatives', the old lady says. 'I was doing heavy manual work until I retired from the co-operative at the age of 60.'

The old woman, who is an aunt of Anikó's mother on her father's side, is plainly delighted to meet her great niece. With difficulty, she sits down next to Anikó, telling her in a wavering voice, '[t]his is where you belong – amongst the Göszis!' If Anikó's mother was cast out for marrying a Gypsy, Anikó has now been accepted back into the fold.

'I wondered what became of your mother?' the old woman says. But her own relations with her family had been strained. Raised as a Catholic she had become a Jehovah's Witness in her youth. 'My brother didn't like the fact that I'd become so religious.'

In her long life the old woman has experienced much hardship. Marrying a fellow member of her church, they went on to have seven children. But the Communists imprisoned her husband 'because he was a believer'. Released from a prison camp, in 1956, he died just three years later. Such stories are not uncommon. Many adherents of fundamentalist religious sects, Seventh Day Adventists, Pentecostals,

Nazarenes, Baptists and Jehovah's Witnesses, were sentenced to periods of forced labour by the Communists in Hungary, as in the other Communist states, in the early 1950s.[15] After years spent toiling in inhuman conditions, the health of such men was often ruined by the time they were set free and allowed to rejoin their families. Of the old woman's seven children, three have predeceased her. But, despite a lifetime of adversity and suffering, Anikó's great aunt is quietly triumphant. Her faith has consoled her into extreme old age. 'Everything written in the Bible is coming true!' she pipes.

Anikó's final encounter in Tiszavasvári is with Guszti, Mrs István Göszi's daughter. Guszti is about the same age as Anikó, with teenage sons and a married daughter all living at home. Guszti is a big woman, like her mother, but sloppier. Dressed in a shapeless floral dress, her brown hair tied back in a bun, Guszti seems unconcerned about her appearance. Like many middle-aged and elderly women thereabouts, she is missing several teeth. Guszti clasps Anikó to her bosom in a spontaneous gesture of affection as soon as they meet; she does not know whether to laugh or cry. They sit side by side in Guszti's garishly decorated sitting room, smoking cigarettes and looking at family photographs. Every now and again, Guszti gives her cousin another hug.

'We don't own a car, so we couldn't come to look for you', Guszti says, in a hoarse voice. 'How do you live?'

'We're poor', Anikó tells her.

'And what do you think we are? We're poor too!'

At Guszti's insistence her visitors stay for a hurried meal. Pieces of chicken, fried in breadcrumbs, are placed between thick slabs of white bread. The food is washed down with glasses of sickly-sweet King Cola. Guszti and Anikó, sitting at a table in the kitchen, give every appearance of having become firm friends; Guszti happily accepts an invitation to visit her cousin at her home in Patakrét. Even Gábor, Anikó's son, is looking cheerful. He is talking animatedly with one of Guszti's sons, a tough-looking youth in a floral patterned shirt that's unbuttoned to the waist. When Péter takes a group photograph, before their departure, Guszti rests her head playfully on Anikó's shoulder. With her head tilted sideways, Guszti grins at the camera. The visit seems to have been a great success.

Some months later, as promised, Guszti and her family came to spend a few days with Anikó in Patakrét. Their rail fares were paid for by the film company. But the return visit had not passed off as smoothly. Anikó told me afterwards that she had gone to a great deal of trouble and expense, preparing a number of tasty dishes for her guests and inviting several relatives from the village to meet them. To her dismay, Guszti had declined to touch any of the food that Anikó had cooked. Although she had very little money, Guszti went to a nearby corner shop and bought bread and cold cuts of meat. For the duration of their short stay in Patakrét, Guszti and her children only consumed food that they bought and prepared themselves. Understandably, their behaviour had caused great offence to their hosts, although Guszti's husband had redeemed himself by sampling all of Anikó's dishes with evident appetite and enjoyment.

For a long time afterwards Anikó tried to make sense of Guszti's baffling conduct. After the spontaneous warmth and good humour that Guszti had exhibited, on meeting Anikó for the first time in Tiszavasvári, why had she been so anxious and uncomfortable during her short stay in Patakrét? Anikó could think of only one explanation. 'Do you think that, when she first met me, Guszti didn't realise that we're Gypsies?' she asked.

ROMANI CULTURE AND WOMEN

Every relationship, certainly every marriage, has its own dynamic. Anikó, with her forceful personality and refusal to conform to the expectations of others, challenges many assumptions about the meekness and subservience of Romani, especially Vlach Romani, women. As Edit had remarked to me, Aniko's bearing could often be proud, almost regal. Striking good looks, a sharp intelligence, as well as an ingrained sense of superiority to most of the other Vlach Roma in her village – possibly because her mother had been a Gadjo – no doubt contributed to Anikó's considerable sense of self-worth and to the way that she was perceived and treated by others.[16] Anikó's husband was known to be ambivalent, at best, about his wife's search for her Gadje relatives. But he didn't oppose her efforts to make contact with them, nor the visit by Guszti and her family to his home.[17]

In many respects, Anikó is an emancipated Romani woman, although the term 'feminist' would have little meaning for her. Traditionally, Romani women have been treated as 'second class' within Romani culture. However, broad generalisations have to be set against the sheer diversity of Romani practice arising from the existence of a plurality of distinct Romani subgroups, each with its own set of occupational specialisms, values and customs. Even within a particular Romani community, as Anikó has shown, strength of personality or other factors may go a long way to counteracting the effect of cultural norms. For the most part, though, Romani women continue to live more circumscribed lives than their menfolk, often work much longer hours, enjoy less standing within the family and the community, and are expected to defer to men. Instances of domestic violence, in my experience at least, are depressingly common. It is almost as if the rigid social hierarchies that have confined most Roma to a lower social status than almost all non-Roma, in Central and Eastern Europe, have been mirrored by the gender-based stratification characteristic of Romani culture(s).

In his study of a Vlach Romani community in Hungary, in the mid 1980s, Michael Stewart noted that, '[b]oys learned early in life to expect pre-eminence and priority over girls in all matters', while '[a]t home, men ate first, washed first, and were given priority in most affairs'.[18] At the same time, women bore responsibility for the housework and child rearing while men, when not at work, often did nothing: '[q]uite often I caught myself wondering, in a slightly puritanical spirit, how men could spend so much time happily sitting around "without doing anything"'.[19] In the same Vlach Romani community, men enjoyed considerable sexual freedom, including liberty to seek sexual partners before marriage or to engage in adulterous affairs. By contrast, Vlach Romani women were subject to far-reaching restrictions on the expression of their sexuality:[20]

Young Gypsy men said they would sleep with women when and as they felt fit; women, by contrast, had to wait until they were married and then have sex only with their husbands. Girls, too concurred in this...Many parents were supportive of a son's sexual exploits... in cases of suspected adultery...a public expression of anger was most likely to be directed against the other female party rather than the man, who was not expected to control his desire and whose transgressions were not constructed as threatening the social order.

Stewart concludes that while the status of women is higher in some other Romani communities, generally as a result of different economic or political circumstances, all Romani groups are characterised, at bottom, by 'a radical, gendered division of social affairs'.[21] Other accounts of the responsibilities and restrictions imposed on Romani women – and of their subordinate status – are strikingly similar.[22] Isabel Fonseca, who lived for a while with an extended Mechkari Romani family in Albania, notes that the younger wives were expected to rise at 5.30 each morning, long before the men or the children, to begin their seemingly endless round of household chores.[23]

However, Fonseca suggests that the women were content with their lives and that they were actually better off than their menfolk:[24]

> Nobody, and certainly not the women, considered it remotely unfair that they did all the work. In addition to their regular tasks, all through the day they had to fit in those that the men continually made for them – for example, by using the floor as an ashtray. Nor in this closed world did they feel themselves to be victims. Quite the opposite: they had the comfort of having a clear role in a world of unemployment without end. It was the men, jobless and bored, who looked the worse off.

Fonseca's breezy view that the young women in the Albanian household were 'happy' with this unequal and frankly exploitative state of affairs is perhaps a little naïve. The ready acceptance of their fate no doubt reflected an awareness of the social and other sanctions that would be applied if they showed resistance. Their acquiescence probably stemmed, in addition, from an inability even to conceive of a different state of affairs. Living in such a tight-knit community, or 'closed world' as Fonseca describes it, the young women would have had little, if any, exposure to an alternative way of doing things. Unremitting drudgery from before daybreak till late at night would seem entirely 'natural' to them.

The nature and extent of the restrictions placed on Romani women depend, to some degree, on the particular community that they belong to. Amongst the Gábor Roma of north-western Romania, for example, it's generally considered that two or three years of schooling are quite sufficient for girls, equipping them with basic numeracy and literacy skills.[25] By contrast, Gábor boys are expected to remain in full-time education for eight years until they complete elementary school. Recently, so I was told, a Gábor girl who was top of her class and who was keen to continue her studies was taken out of school by her parents, despite the entreaties of the village's Presbyterian pastor. From the parents' point of view, an over-educated daughter might have difficulties in being accepted by other members of the community and could face problems in finding a suitable marriage partner. In keeping her at school beyond the age of puberty, there was also the risk that she might be accused doing something 'shameful', which would have reflected badly on the entire family.[26] For the Gábor Roma, women have no right to determine the course of their own lives in accordance with their personal tastes or preferences.[27] Their role, first and foremost, is to become wives and mothers. In case of need, they may be expected to supplement the family income by small acts of commerce such as hawking goods – sets of knives are a favourite item – in local towns.

Surprisingly, perhaps, even well-educated Romani women from comparatively integrated, urban backgrounds often retain a residual belief in the innate 'superiority' of men and in their ultimate right to dictate a couple's affairs. Ági, a bright young Romungro woman brought up in Budapest, whose late father had been a professional musician and whose mother worked in the catering industry, was completing her studies at a teachers' training college when I met her in Budapest. Her comments confirm that attitudes regarding relations between the sexes are beginning to change amongst the Roma, particularly amongst younger, educated Roma. However, her views are, at the same time, strikingly (and unselfconsciously) ambivalent. All traces of the traditional Romani belief in the subordination of women have not yet disappeared, it seems, even amongst educated young Romani women such as Ági:[28]

> *Ági*: Amongst those of Gypsy extraction, relations between men and women are quite distinctive; women are subordinated to men. But when a woman studies, if she's clever, then she can break out of these Gypsy traditions. Then these old traditions, expectations, viewpoints are overturned; they no longer apply. The new generation has a new viewpoint. We [the Gypsies] are also undergoing modernisation, we're obliged to. There is democracy between men and women, there's no subordination [of women]. Of course, as it's written in the Bible, Eve was made out of Adam's rib. That still holds good because men, irrespective of whether they're Gypsies or Hungarians, are stronger.
> *Me*: Physically, but not mentally!
> *Ági*: A man has to be stronger mentally as well, more protective...For example, in relations between a man and a woman, the man has to take the lead. Even if the woman is more highly educated she has to accept subordination [to her partner] because this is an ancient law. The man is the leader.

The subordination of women, which has characterised Romani culture, appears to have resulted in a fairly high incidence of domestic violence. However, this remains something of a taboo subject in much of the literature on the Roma, possibly because of a desire to present the Roma – and their traditions – in a positive light after centuries of incomprehension and villification. However, in the course of my fieldwork, I came across repeated instances of violence directed against women, or plausible allegations that women were being physically abused. In Patakrét, where I regularly visited a number of Vlach Romani families, a middle-aged woman told me that her son-in-law was 'a good boy', but that she wished he wouldn't beat his wife, my interviewee's daughter. The girl in question, in her mid twenties, had a haunted, furtive look. There were always dark circles around her eyes.

Rózsi, also living in Patakrét, told me that, much earlier in life, she had left her husband after 15 years of abuse at his hands:[29]

> He hit me, cut me, pulled my arms behind my back, and kicked me. I was pregnant with our oldest daughter, even then he hit me and cut me until the last minute when the ambulance came to fetch me. If I so much as looked at someone [a man], he became jealous.

History had repeated itself. Rózsi's younger daughter, Ilona, fled from her husband, who was settled in a large provincial city with his parents, because of his jealous rages and his repeated violence towards her. While Ilona had returned to live with her mother, her husband and his family had insisted that the couple's two-year-old boy remain with them. They refused to allow the boy to see her mother. Ilona was already pregnant with their second child, whom she would raise on her own with the support of Rózsi. However, Ilona became increasingly depressed as a result of losing all contact with her elder son. Already slim, Ilona began to lose an alarming amount of weight following the birth of her second child, which she attributed to her despair over her separation from her older boy.

Ilona's male relatives could be strangely insensitive to the psychological distress that she was experiencing. I visited Rózsi and Ilona some months after the latter had left her husband. At the time, Ilona was pregnant with her second child. A male cousin happened to be with the women when I called, a handsome, broad-shouldered young man of about 30. He was clearly a great favourite of Rózsi. When I remarked that it must be awful for Ilona to be separated from her child, the cousin replied breezily, '[i]t's OK, she'll soon have another'.

The theme of sexual jealousy amongst Romani men, an irrational and obsessive fear that a wife is scheming to betray her husband, is a recurrent one. A young research assistant whom I employed for some months in Budapest, who came from a provincial Beás Gypsy family, told me that her father had beaten her mother almost every day of their married life, using his fists and his boots. Once, when her mother was heavily pregnant, he had stabbed her in the stomach with a kitchen knife. The cause of her father's sudden rages was a groundless fear that his wife was consorting with other men.

In Chapter 6, I described the descent into homelessness, acute poverty and alcoholism of a middle-aged Romani couple, Eszti and Lajós, in the Romanian city of Cluj. On one occasion, when the couple were irritable and distressed because they were being evicted from a shed in which they'd found temporary refuge, I noticed that Eszti had a black eye. Her explanation, that she'd fallen over inside the shed because it was dark, was not entirely convincing. A young Romani social worker, who kept in contact with the couple for a while, thought that there was a pattern of domestic violence, although he suspected that sometimes Eszti was the perpetrator rather than the victim.

Ágnes Diósi is a respected and widely published sociologist in Hungary who has written extensively on the Roma. Her books include *Eye to Eye with Hungarian Gypsies*, a text that is intended primarily for trainee teachers and social workers in Hungary who need some background knowledge about the country's large Romani population.[30] In an article published some years ago in the *Hungarian Quarterly*, Diósi writes about a Vlach Romani girl from a village who went on to become a successful journalist in Budapest. The article describes the abusive relationship that she had with a Gadjo boy when she was 19. At the time, the girl had moved away from her village home and was working as an untrained kindergarten teacher in a provincial town:[31]

> it was...a relationship full of conflicts. He enjoyed the subordinate position Romany women had with their men, while I had feminist traits and revolted against it. We lived together for two years. It wasn't good. He took on the ways of Roma men. He had a friend who humiliated his girlfriend in company by stubbing his cigarette on her body. He too tried to humiliate me in front of others. There was a moment when I felt I would either go crazy or quit.

In some Romani communities, there have been reports of men abducting young women whom they wish to marry. Such cases should be carefully distinguished from elopements where the woman's consent has been freely given and where the stratagem is employed by the young couple in order to circumvent an arranged marriage.[32] The Protestant pastor of a village not far from the town of Târgu-Mureş in Romania told me that, amongst lower-class Gábor Gypsies in the area, the practice of abducting young girls was 'quite common'.[33] When I pressed her on this, asking how many instances of abduction she actually knew of, the pastor replied that two girls from her village had been taken in this fashion, one of whom was snatched from the yard of her own house. The more recent of the two abductions, involving a 15-year-old Gábor girl, had occurred five years ago. Although the young woman was eventually released by her captor and allowed to return to her family, her marriage prospects had been seriously compromised as she was now considered to be 'damaged goods'. According to the pastor, many young Gábor girls were afraid to leave their homes after dark, even to attend confirmation classes.

Isabel Fonseca reports that the rate of female abductions has risen sharply amongst the Roma of Bulgaria: '[m]ore and more young men were resorting to the simple method of kidnapping; with or without the complicity of the girl, this constituted betrothal'.[34] Whatever the true rate of abduction of Romani girls, in either Romania or Bulgaria,[35] such measures constitute gross acts of coercion and intimidation, with far-reaching consequences for the young women. As indicated by Fonseca, abduction generally leads inexorably to marriage. Even if a girl can avoid marrying her abductor, her reputation will have been tarnished.

Much of the anthropological literature on Romani women focuses on ancient Romani beliefs concerning 'pollution' or 'shame'. Romani women, particularly of childbearing age, are said to be a potential source of pollution (as are Gadje). According to these accounts, elaborate though variable codes govern relations between the sexes, the washing of clothes and other domestic chores.[36] Infraction of these rules may imperil the purity or, at the very least, social standing, of a Romani household or individual. Traditionally, those deemed 'impure' could be subject to the ultimate sanction of social exclusion.

So far, I have avoided any discussion of these beliefs in this analysis of the current condition of Romani women. For one thing, as indicated in Chapter 2, I simply couldn't find much evidence of the continued recognition of these rules amongst most of the Romani communities and families that I came to know. Time after time, I was presented with behaviour that seemed to flatly contradict the pollution practices I'd read about.[37] Of course, this does not mean that such practices never existed, or that they're not observed elsewhere, amongst other Romani communities. However, it does suggest that ideas about pollution or shame have ceased to be of universal importance amongst the Roma, that they may be slowly disappearing, or at least changing, under the relentless pressure of social adaptation and exposure to new ways of behaviour through the TV, through interaction with Gadje or with other, less observant Roma.[38]

In some Romani communities that do place an emphasis on the observation of various distinct cultural practices, some of these norms are of surprisingly modern origin. For example, Péter Szuhay has described recent changes in the funeral rites observed by Vlach Roma in a number of Hungarian villages. These changes have apparently resulted, at least in part, from the fact that videos of elaborate Vlach funerals began to circulate privately amongst the Vlach Roma of the region. Men who had not attended the funerals depicted in the videos, and who lived in other villages or towns, began to emulate what they had seen on their TV screens.[39] The video recorder, it seems, has become a potent agent of cultural change.

However, there has been another reason for my reluctance to dwell on traditional Romani beliefs concerning pollution or shame in this discussion of Romani women. Such talk can have the effect of exoticising the Roma, of portraying them as a quaint, colourful people with their roots in Asia, obstinately clinging to a host of bizarre yet intriguing customs. The reality is that the bulk of the Roma were born and have lived their whole lives in European states that, since 1990 at least, proclaim their commitment to human rights.[40] Consequently, while making due allowance for notions of cultural pluralism, the treatment of Romani women must ultimately be judged in terms of the political philosophies and constitutional norms of the societies in which they live and of which they're citizens, as well as in accordance with the principles laid down in the numerous human rights treaties that these states are bound by. Institutionalised violence against Romani women, the denial of opportunities to pursue education and careers, or even to participate fully in fundamental decisions affecting themselves and their families should not be seen as the legitimate expression of cultural diversity but as the denial of basic freedoms that most of us take for granted.[41] At the very least, it should be openly recognised that there is a tension between the way in which many women are treated and perceived, especially in traditional Romani communities, and the broadly egalitarian, individualistic values espoused by the societies in which these Romani communities are located. This is a tension that urgently needs to be acknowledged and addressed.[42]

The clearest evidence I found of the survival of notions of 'purity' and 'shame', connected to women, was amongst the Gábor Roma of Transylvanian Romania. The Gábor Roma are intensely proud of their distinctive culture and traditions that have served to distance them from both other Romani groups and from Gadje, as well as assuring many of them an enviable standard of living.[43] In the spaceous, marble-tiled home of a successful Gábor trader, in a village some distance from the Romanian town of Târgu-Mureş, I was given the following explanation by two Gábor men, with children of their own, of why Gábor girls are only permitted to attend school for a few years:[44]

> *Gábor man 1*: Now a girl isn't allowed to attend school past the age of twelve, or even ten.
>
> *Gábor man 2*: Until the age of ten. They should go [to school] until the age of ten. Two or three classes [i.e. years] for girls.
>
> *Me*: After that girls aren't allowed to attend school?
>
> *Gábor man 1*: This is what's laid down in Gypsy tradition, because according to Gypsy tradition girls are married at the age of 13 or 14.
>
> *Gábor man 2*: And it's forbidden [for unmarried girls] to go about on the streets, so that no-one can say of them that they did something; because then comes the shame, not just on her but on her whole family.
>
> *Gábor man 1*: On her parents.
>
> *Gábor man 2*: Yes, on her parents. And so to keep her pure and to avoid any shame happening, the parents help to pick out the couple [i.e. select a husband for their daughter].

It's clear from this exchange that, amongst the traditionally-minded Gábor Roma of north-west Romania, the survival of long-standing notions of 'shame' and of 'purity' serves to reinforce and justify the continuing subordination of women, placing severe and wide-ranging limits on the freedoms that they are permitted to enjoy. Although many Gábor women, particularly prosperous ones, exhibit an evident pride and self-confidence (like Gábor men), their lack of autonomy sits uneasily with the individualistic norms of contemporary society. The not infrequent confinement of adolescent Gábor girls to their homes, to avoid any imputation of scandalous conduct (or, in some cases, from fear of abduction), is scarcely compatible with modern ideas of liberty and personal choice.

THE LIMITS OF HUMAN RIGHTS

The revolution in human rights that accompanied the ousting of Communist regimes, in Central and Eastern Europe, has already been discussed. As noted in Chapter 6, the post-Communist states have enshrined fundamental human rights norms, chiefly civil and political rights, in new or revised constitutions. At the same time, the states in question have become parties to a broad range of human rights instruments including the European Convention on Human Rights and Fundamental Freedoms. The recognition of minority rights, analysed in Chapter 5, has also been a feature of the post-Communist transitions. In theory, at least, the Roma, along with their fellow citizens, have been invested with an unprecedented range of rights and freedoms.

In practice, as suggested in chapters 5 and 6, poverty, mass unemployment and social marginalisation have partially disenfranchised the Roma, rendering many of their newly-recognised rights nugatory. Rights of freedom of expression or of political participation have little meaning to people living on the edge of subsistence in stinking settlements, or squatting in crumbling tenement buildings without electricity. As a growing feminist literature makes clear, at least by implication, Romani women are in a still more precarious position than their menfolk. Many of the most common threats to their liberty and physicial integrity aren't even recognised by the law (whether national or international) as breaches of their human rights. In part, this is because human rights instruments generally associate threats to life, liberty or physical security with the actions of *public*, that is, state, authorities.[45] For women, who are frequently subject to physical assault (or restrictions on their liberty) by partners, fathers or other members of their own families, such catalogues of rights are of very little help. Referring to the right to life contained in the International Covenant on Civil and Political Rights and in various regional treaties, including the European Convention, Charlesworth and Chinkin note that:[46]

> The right is primarily concerned with the arbitrary deprivation of life through public action. Protection from arbitrary deprivation of life or liberty through public actions, important as it is, does not, however, address...the special ways in which women need legal protection to be able to enjoy their right to life...The significant documented violence against women around the world remains unaddressed by the international legal notion of the right to life because that legal system is focused on 'public' actions by the state.

The authors offer a similar critique of the proscription of torture under international law which, in construing 'torture' as having a necessary public element, excludes domestic violence from the scope of the prohibition.[47] The leading multilateral treaty concerned with the rights of women, the UN Convention on the Elimination of all Forms of Discrimination against Women, is rightly criticised for, 'its relatively weak language, the reservations states parties have made to its terms and...the limited monitoring methods provided for in the Convention itself'.[48]

The subordination of women in traditional Romani culture and the resilience of sexist ideas even amongst educated young Romani women today – as well as the apparent pervasiveness of domestic violence and of restrictions on the freedom or opportunities available to Romani women within their families and communities – confirm the need for the recognition and effective protection of the fundamental rights of Romani women at the levels of both national and international law. Yet, as noted in Chapter 6, human rights have come under increasing attack from scholars sceptical of the ability of the concept (and its application through law) to help in satisfying basic human needs and aspirations. To me at least, the notion that 'rights' are somehow unhelpful or even unnecessary, or that there may be some other and better means of assuring the legitimate and neglected interests of Romani women, is unconvincing. Such critiques, while robustly deconstructing rights, rarely set out a plausible alternative vision of ethics or of the scope and meaning of individual freedom. While exposing various weaknesses in the legal recognition and enforcement of rights, such critiques fail to indicate what other legal or political mechanisms are likely to be more effective in identifying and protecting vulnerable sections of society. Both as conceptual tools and as practical devices rights remain indispensable for disadvantaged groups such as Romani women.

Improvements in criminal codes and criminal justice systems – sensitising them to the actual experience of Romani women and making the systems more accessible – are also needed. Criminal law systems in Central and Eastern Europe, as elsewhere, proscribe assaults on women, abduction and various other interferences with their liberty. However, a range of social and other factors frequently inhibit Romani women (or their families) from having recourse to the law. Traditionally, the Roma have been wary of state agencies, including police and criminal justice systems. Police and criminal justice systems in the post-Communist states are broadly assumed to be unsympathetic to the Roma, mirroring the anti-Roma prejudice found in the societies at large.[49] Additionally, having recourse to the law is likely to draw further and unwelcome attention to the problems experienced by a Romani family (such as the abduction of a daughter) thereby aggravating the sense of shame experienced by the family, as well as generating criticism from other

Roma for involving 'external' agencies, such as the police, in the 'internal' affairs of the Roma. Encouraging greater use of criminal justice systems by the Roma, particularly by Romani women – and assuring sympathetic or at least fair-minded treatment by police, courts and medical personnel – is clearly necessary.

However, such prescriptions with regard to criminal justice systems do not negate the importance of human rights. In modern, secular societies it is human rights ideology that underpins the recognition of the entitlement of women, including Romani women, to freedom from assault, torture or deprivation of liberty. It was human rights ideology that led to the formal recognition of the Roma – along with other marginalised groups – as fully 'human'. Those are scarcely negligible gains. In addition, there is increasing evidence that human rights law and human rights ideology are beginning to make a contribution to improving the general status and treatment of the Roma in Central and Eastern Europe. As discussed in various parts of this book, particularly in chapters 1, 5, 6 and 8, pressure from a range of international organisations, from bodies overseeing human rights treaties and from NGOs has compelled the post-Communist states to revise their legal codes and institutions and to institute sizeable (though as yet inadequate) programmes aimed at tackling some of the root causes of Romani poverty and underdevelopment. To date, however, the gains have been overshadowed by the massive losses attendant upon the withdrawal of guaranteed employment and of a range of welfare benefits available to the Roma under Communism.

Nevertheless from the perspective of Romani women, the potential benefits of an increased focus on human rights, even civil and political rights, are clear. As indicated above, a significant proportion of Romani women, particularly those living in more traditional communities, have limited choice over how they live their lives. Many Romani women, it seems, are subject to the threat of physical assault from their partners. However, in order to extend the protection of human rights norms to Romani women, the ambit of such rights must be widened to cover actions that take place in the *private sphere* – notably within the family and the community – where much of the actual abuse of women (including Romani women) takes place.[50]

8
The Lambada

THE INCIDENT AT THE LAMBADA

Armed with *nunchuks*, Chinese martial arts weapons, the three youths burst into the village bar at around half past ten at night. 'The walls were covered with blood', says Olga, the bar's proprietor. 'They attacked everyone including me and my son. Seven of us were taken to hospital.'

Olga shows me her arm, although it's several months since the assault and most of the bruises have faded. 'They smashed everything! Bottles, chairs, even the ashtrays!'

Árpád, one of Olga's sons, was helping out in the bar on the night of the attack. During the incident he was struck on the forehead with a *nunchuk*. 'For a long time afterwards he was dizzy whenever he tried to stand up', says his mother. 'He had to spend two weeks in bed.'

The bar, known as the Lambada, is a one-room extension of Olga's home in the village of Tismana. Located in gently undulating countryside north of the city of Cluj-Napoca, in the Transylvanian region of Romania, the area was once famous. The aristocratic and wealthy Bánffy family maintained a splendid and enormous country house not far away. In the nineteenth century the building was known as the Versailles of Transylvania. But the Bánffys, ethnic Hungarians, are long gone and their mansion lies in ruins.

Olga's home is situated at an intersection in the village close to the Gypsy quarter, a few dozen ramshackle houses clustered around an unpaved track. Gypsies, or Roma, provided Olga with most of her customers. But the bar has been shut for some time now. Olga can't afford to reopen the Lambada even though it was her only source of income after her late husband fell ill. A skilled shoemaker, his hand-crafted leather boots were highly prized by the local villagers. 'People paid for the boots with money, if they had it, or in kind', says Jancsi, one of Olga's cousins.

For some time now, Olga has been caught in a vicious 'Catch 22': she can't reopen the bar until she's bought new stock and replaced the broken furniture. But, without the money that was generated by the business, she hasn't enough funds for either. Olga has no savings to

8   Romani men standing outside their village home

fall back on and the bar and its contents weren't insured. On top of that, the local police chief has informed her that she didn't have all the right paperwork and that she'll have to apply for a licence if she wants to reopen the bar. So the Lambada remains shut and Olga is growing desperate. 'Can you help me find a job in England?' she asks. 'I could work in a restaurant, look after an old person, anything.' Olga is 56 years old and has never travelled beyond the borders of her native Romania. She doesn't speak a word of English or of any other language that would be of use to her in the West. But she realises that, while the bar is closed, she can't support herself in the village.

Olga knows her assailants; she recites their names to me without hesitation. The three young men who attacked her and her customers are brothers; they live nearby with their widowed father. Olga points their house out to me while we stand in her front yard, close to the padlocked bar.

'They used to come to my place from time to time but I had to tell them to stay away', she says, referring to the brothers. 'They'd grab peoples' drinks from under their noses and snatch cigarettes from their mouths.' Olga says that she put up with their rowdy behaviour until one time she caught them pawing a terrified young woman. 'I seized a piece of firewood [from the hearth] and chased them out!' Olga recalls, with satisfaction. Sturdily built and above average height, Olga is an imposing woman. Some weeks later the brothers returned, armed with *nunchuks*, attacking everyone in the bar and smashing the furniture.

CRIMINAL JUSTICE IN A TRANSYLVANIAN VILLAGE: OLGA'S STORY

Olga doesn't have a telephone but she sent word to the village police station as soon as she could after the assault. A young policeman came out the same night and took several photographs of the blood-spattered bar. 'You could see he was frightened', Olga says. 'He was afraid of what the brothers might do to him. They have a bad reputation.'

Despite Olga's testimony and those of several customers who had been injured in the drunken attack, the three brothers weren't arrested. They remained free to go about their business, as before. Olga says that the photographs that the young policeman had taken, which formed an important part of the evidence against the youths, disappeared from the police station.

'The police chief we had in the village back then was a crook', says Olga. 'He accepted gifts and favours from the brothers and their father.' Not badly off, by the modest standards of the village, the assailants' family own a tract of forest land, although none of the brothers has a steady job. According to people in the village, the former police chief received a wagon-load of firewood not long after the incident at Olga's bar. The same people report seeing the brothers doing odd jobs for him on his plot of land.

Olga was determined to press charges. She also wanted compensation for the injuries that she and Árpád had suffered in the attack, as well as for the extensive damage to her bar. But over a year went by before the authorities completed their leisurely investigation of the incident. Only then were the papers finally sent to the local court, in the town of Gherla, so that proceedings could begin. Under Romanian law, a victim seeking civil damages arising from a criminal act is normally unable to proceed until those responsible have been indicted for the crime.[1] Once a trial has started, civil and criminal arguments are heard in the same court. So, while the police spun out their investigation, Olga was left broke and without any means of earning money to support herself.

In this unequal struggle with her assailants and the former police chief, Olga wasn't only handicapped by her poverty and her ignorance of legal process. The brothers who attacked her and her customers are ethnic Romanians while Olga and most of the people who drank at her bar are Gypsies. If the brothers picked on Olga and her customers at will, helping themselves to drinks and cigarettes and harassing women, their choice of victims wasn't random. Gypsies are despised, the lowest stratum of Romanian society.[2] Fuelled by alcohol and an inchoate sense of their own precarious status, as peasants in an impoverished village, the brothers selected their targets from a people even lower down Romania's pecking order.

Olga and her son didn't have enough money to hire a lawyer to represent them at the hearings before the court. In any event, many Romanian lawyers are reluctant to take on Romani clients.[3] Olga and Árpád could have applied for a court-appointed lawyer to handle their case free of charge. However, this is not an automatic entitlement. Only some lawyers are prepared to undertake such work and authorisation to use the services of a court-appointed lawyer must be granted in each case by the Dean of the Bar Association.[4] So Olga and Árpád represented themselves.

After several hearings before the court in Gherla, the parties asked for the proceedings to be suspended so that they could seek an amicable settlement of their dispute, as allowed under Romanian law. In due course, Olga and her son returned to the court and declared that they had been able to agree on the terms of a settlement with the defendants. They requested that the civil and criminal suits be discontinued.[5] For reasons that are not immediately apparent, the judge agreed to terminate the case without endorsing the terms of the private settlement. Normally, such settlements are approved in written form by the judge, giving them the same status as a court order.[6]

Olga says that the assailants and their father had agreed to pay 8 million Romanian Lei, a little over $250 at the then rate of exchange. However, Olga says that she has only received 3 million Lei from the defendants and that they have refused to pay her anything more. She says that, when she approached them in the village and asked for the rest of the money, the brothers threatened to beat her and her family. Without the 5 million Lei that Olga says are owed to her, she hasn't enough funds to reopen the bar or to start another business.

A young Romanian lawyer, whom I asked to look into Olga's case, went to the courthouse in Gherla and read the relevant files. Afterwards, he wrote to me indignantly:[7]

The Romani family did not hire a lawyer, but this did not interfere with the development of the suit…In fact, the lack of a lawyer cannot be taken into consideration when analysing this case, given the way in which this legal case ended: *the petitioners (namely the Romani family) dropped the legal action and gave up their requests,* as they declared in front of the Court out of their own will and without any constraint that *they amicably settled the matter with the aggressors* and *did not wish to continue the penal suit initiated by them*...Consequently, there is only one reasonable conclusion that can be drawn from the...file, namely that *THE HUMAN RIGHTS WERE ENTIRELY OBSERVED* in this case and any other pretence is unreasonable and founded on total lack of information.

The lawyer's anger, though perhaps excessive, was understandable. Romanians believe that their country's reputation abroad has suffered as a result of regular reports in the media that Romania's substantial Gypsy minority are routinely denied basic rights. From a rather legalistic perspective (even for a lawyer), Olga had nothing to complain of. She had opted, for whatever reason, not to apply for the services of a court-appointed attorney. And, without any coercion on the part of police, prosecutors or court officials, she had exercised her *right* to ask for the civil and criminal suits to be dropped. While the defendants may have reneged on the terms of their private settlement, that was no concern of the authorities. After all, Olga is an adult and must accept responsibility for her decisions. Though, in retrospect, Olga's judgement may have been flawed, she had freely decided that the settlement was satisfactory and that the defendants could be trusted to honour it.

Of course, the young lawyer's rather idealised view of human behaviour fails to take account of the social context. This is not a 'level playing field' in which everyone can be expected to understand the consequences of their actions, particularly where these involve abstruse issues of law. When she petitioned the court, asking for the trial to be discontinued, Olga didn't have a lawyer to advise her. Whether the judge even informed her of the consequences of dropping the case remains unclear.[8] Perhaps Olga didn't understand that it would be impossible for her to go back to the court later on and ask for the case to be reopened, or for the terms of the private settlement to be enforced. Or maybe she had persuaded herself that the defendants and their father would pay her the sum of money that they had promised. Olga was guilty of naïvety in assuming that the family could be relied upon. She was foolish not to have applied for the services of a court-appointed lawyer. Perhaps she imagined that, if she weren't paying the lawyer herself, he would lack the motivation to represent her properly. Olga is an unsophisticated woman who has lived all her life in a village. Although she can read and write to a reasonable standard, she has scant knowledge of legal process.

István Haller is a human rights specialist working for Liga Pro Europa, a highly respected NGO in the city of Târgu-Mureş in Romania. He grimaced when I told him about Olga's predicament. 'A simple village woman wouldn't have understood the profound significance of discontinuing a case. Now she can't do anything.'

THE ESCALATION OF VIOLENCE AGAINST THE ROMA
SINCE THE COLLAPSE OF COMMUNISM

No journalist from Bucharest or Cluj bothered to make the journey to Olga's village to interview the victims for one of the newspapers or the radio; the incident went unreported in the media.[9] The assault on Olga and her customers is an unremarkable story in present-day Romania. It's just one more example of an upsurge of violence against Gypsies that has been noted in many parts of Central and Eastern Europe since the overthrow of Communism. A detailed report, issued in 2000 by the OSCE's High Commissioner on National Minorities, confirms this trend:[10]

Widespread civilian violence against Roma has been documented in recent years. Although the largest number of skinhead attacks against Roma have been recorded in the Czech Republic, Bulgaria and the Slovak Republic, instances of such violence have also been registered in Albania, Austria, Bosnia, Croatia, Hungary, Poland, Romania, Russia, Ukraine and Yugoslavia.

Several examples of assaults on Roma are cited in the High Commissioner's report. Amongst these is the fatal attack on a 33-year-old Bulgarian Romani woman, Nadezda Dimitrova:[11]

On 15 June 1999, a 33-year-old Romani woman, Nadezda Dimitrova, was beaten to death by a group of teenaged boys in Sofia, Bulgaria. The suspects reportedly came across a group of younger children provoking the victim, and joined in attacking her. Three of the suspects hit and kicked her in the head repeatedly until she died.

The spate of vicious attacks on Roma in much of Central and Eastern Europe has not abated as yet. Human Rights Watch, a US-based NGO, reports several incidents of anti-Roma violence in Slovakia in its 2002 World Report. Noting 'a continuing pattern of police failure to prevent racist violence against Slovak Roma', the Report states:[12]

In a week of incidents, racist gang members beat and harassed Roma in the town of Holic, culminating in an August 13 assault on Milan Daniel that left him needing brain surgery. Roma residents asserted that the police had failed to protect them despite repeated complaints. On August 20, police finally charged two youths with the attack on Daniel. On August 30, Peter Bandur was sentenced to seven years' imprisonment for his part in the beating to death of a Roma woman, Anastazia Balasova, a year earlier...While Bandur was convicted of the more serious crime of racially motivated assault, his two accomplices received three and five years respectively for simple assault (without racist intent).

The 2002 World Report, issued by Human Rights Watch, is also damning about anti-Roma violence in the Czech Republic noting that, '[r]acist attacks on Roma continued, but police and prosecutors frequently failed to adequately investigate and prosecute Roma complaints'. The Report contains several examples of assaults on the Roma that have met with a limited or inappropriate response by the authorities:[13]

The July stabbing to death of a thirty-year-old Romani man, Ota Absolon, by a skinhead – racist gang-member – in Svitany, eastern Bohemia, renewed public attention to the failure of state and local authorities to protect minorities victimized by racially motivated violence and abuse. In the Absolon case, the accused was a repeat offender, having received a suspended sentence in 1997 for seriously injuring a Romani man by stabbing him in the stomach. In another incident, forty-five skinheads reportedly attacked a group of twenty Romani men with baseball bats in the town of Novy Bor on April 24, leaving eight Roma injured. According to local Romani representatives, approximately ten Roma and ten skinheads were charged in connection with the incident. The arrested Roma men claimed that they were being punished unjustly for acting out of self-defense. They also criticized the police for failing to pursue Polish and German skinheads who participated in the attack.

While the Communists held power in Central and Eastern Europe, for almost half a century following the end of World War II, violence was the prerogative of the state. Like much of the economy it was taken into state hands or 'nationalised'. The police and the security apparatus resorted to occasional brutality and, chiefly in the early years, to terror, internment in labour camps and even to executions and torture in order to stifle opposition to fundamentally alien and unpopular regimes.[14] But if the Communist states could be ruthless, particularly in their handling of political dissent, many were comparatively humane, if paternalistic, in their treatment of the Roma.[15] And Communist regimes demanded discipline and orderly conduct from the general public. The harassment or intimidation of ethnic minorities by their fellow citizens was, with rare exceptions, not tolerated. During the Communist era, Olga and the other Roma in her village had jobs or, in some cases, worked as self-employed artisans. They went about their lives free from fear of assault or humiliation at the hands of drunken thugs. Though conditions were far from perfect for the village's Roma they were probably as satisfactory as they have ever been, before or since. 'Life was good under Ceauşescu', is a phrase that I have heard over and over again from poor, working-class Gypsies in Romania.[*]

The common, overly simplistic perception of the Communist epoch – as a time of arbitrary and persistent abuse of fundamental rights – stands in need of partial correction. The Communist authorities *were* brutal in imposing the new Soviet-inspired order in Central and Eastern Europe. But it was a brutality that was focused rather than indiscriminate, and it recognised certain limits. Paradoxically, certain ethnic groups who were subject to escalating levels of persecution during the inter-war period and the war years, mainly by Fascist and extreme-right regimes committed to spurious notions of racial 'purity', were granted a degree of protection by the incoming Communists. This applied, above all, to Gypsies and Jews.[16] Although officially sanctioned anti-Semitism, of varying levels of severity, re-emerged in parts of Central and Eastern Europe during the Communist era,[17] many Jews in the CEE states retained a degree of gratitude, even affection, for the Communist regimes. As an elderly Jewish survivor of the Holocaust once remarked to me in Budapest, after the Communists had been swept from power in democratic elections held in the spring of 1990, '[a]t least they [the Communists] kept the people in check'. In her mind, the Communists represented discipline and some kind of order, a physical as well as an ideological barrier that held back the 'mob'. Her feelings were understandable in the light of her family history. As a young woman, in the winter of 1944, she had seen the body of her father shortly after he had been murdered by rampaging Hungarian Arrow Cross thugs.

---

[*] Of course, in the West, Ceauşescu, the long-serving and increasingly egomaniacal Communist ruler of Romania, was identified with bizarre dictatorial excesses and with the ruthless oppression and exploitation of his people.

As noted above, an upsurge of violence against Gypsies has been reported in almost every country in the region since the end of Communist rule. In Hădăreni, a village in Mureş County just a couple of hours by road from Olga's home, a 'pogrom' was instigated against the local Roma.[18] In September 1993, after a fight between a Gypsy and a Romanian in which the Romanian was killed, an angry mob of peasants drove all the Roma, including women and children, out of the village. Fourteen Romani-owned houses were burnt to the ground and a further five were demolished. Three Roma, including the man who had killed the Romanian, were lynched. Throughout these bloody events the local police apparently did nothing to pacify or restrain the peasants. According to eyewitnesses, one of the policemen on the scene even incited the violence, shouting 'let's go after the Gypsies!' As the peasants began to torch Romani-owned houses the police allegedly collaborated, warning the mob if a particular house belonged to an ethnic Romanian or Hungarian.

For almost four years, no-one was even indicted for the murderous assault on Hădăreni's Roma, although several villagers were eventually convicted of offences including aggravated murder.[19] In June 2000, in a startling display of clemency, Romania's President granted pardons to two of the villagers convicted of aggravated murder, setting them free.

Some of the victims and their families brought applications under the European Convention on Human Rights and Fundamental Freedoms. They alleged, *inter alia*, that Romania was in breach of Article 2 of the European Convention on Human Rights (the right to life) as a result of the authorities' failure to conduct an effective investigation leading to the identification and punishment of the policemen and others responsible for the deaths of three Romani men in the village.[20] The applicants argued, in addition, that they had been reduced to living in inhuman conditions, contrary to Article 3 of the Convention, as a result of the destruction of their homes during the pogrom. At the time of writing, the complaints have been declared partly inadmissible, by a Chamber of the European Court of Human Rights, on the grounds that the events in question occurred before the European Convention had entered into force for Romania.[21]

In neighbouring Hungary, an anti-Gypsy 'pogrom' took place in the village of Kétegyháza, close to the Romanian border, about a year before the violence in Hădăreni. It started with an incident over some melons in which a burly Gypsy, Péter Csurár, is said to have assaulted two Hungarians.[22] According to the newspapers, the Csurár family were notorious for their rowdy and sometimes violent conduct. Several articles suggested that they had been forced to move to Kétegyháza some years before, after being driven out of another village as a result of their persistently anti-social behaviour.

Whatever the truth about the incident involving Péter Csurár, the following night 15 or more peasants, riding in the back of a truck, went looking for him and for his elder brother, Gábor. Finding Gábor Csurár at home, in Kétegyháza's Roma quarter, they beat him severely about the head and body and rammed his house with their truck. Tiles were ripped from the roof rendering the property uninhabitable. Before leaving, the peasants also smashed a bicycle that was lying in the yard and Gábor Csurár's Russian-made car. On the following night, two Romani-owned properties in Kétegyháza, including Péter Csurár's house, were set on fire. The police descended *en masse*, arresting six of the suspected peasant vigilantes who were placed in custody.

The arrests prompted Kétegyháza's angry smallholders to convene a series of all-night meetings in the village's culture house, each of which was attended by several hundred people. The smallholders demanded the immediate release, on bail, of all the peasants who had been arrested, the opening of a police station in Kétegyháza and the prompt departure from the village of the Csurár brothers.

Many of the Roma, fearing for their lives, took to sleeping in the fields in case their houses were fire-bombed in the night. Some even started a petition amongst their fellow Roma, calling for the release of the peasant vigilantes from jail. Lajós Faragó, a successful horse-coper and the unofficial spokesman of the village's Romani community, gave an undertaking that the Roma would not seek revenge for the torching of the two properties. In interviews with journalists from Budapest, some Roma complained of a climate of racial hatred. They said that all the Roma were being treated as if they had behaved like the Csurár brothers. In reality, they were reported as saying, Roma and peasants alike had been victims of the Csurárs' reign of terror in the village.

Peace was finally restored with the release from custody of the peasants and with the 'voluntary' exile of the hated Csurár brothers from Kétegyháza. But the underlying resentment, fear and mutual suspicion between Gypsies and peasants in the village remained. As a front-page article in *Népszabadság*, Hungary's most widely read newspaper, stated: '[a]lthough the crisis appears to be over, everyone in Kétegyháza, peasants and Gypsies alike, is afraid'.[23]

Like Roma elsewhere in Central and Eastern Europe, Hungary's Roma complain of racist assaults, of exclusion from bars and cafés, of routine harassment by the police and of a climate of intolerance towards Gypsies. These views are underscored by Human Rights Watch. In its World Report, issued in 2002, the NGO concluded that, '[d]iscrimination against Roma remained pervasive' in Hungary. The report roundly condemned the Hungarian authorities for their failure to tackle the predicament of the country's Romani minority:[24]

> The situation for many Hungarian Roma remained precarious. With average life expectancy ten years shorter than the rest of the population and an unemployment rate ten times higher than the national average, Roma faced discrimination in employment, housing, education, and the criminal justice system, as well as physical attacks. The French government's decision in March to grant asylum to fifteen Hungarian Roma underscored the gravity of their difficulties.

In an application to the European Court of Human Rights, in Strasbourg, 25 Gypsies from the Hungarian village of Zámoly alleged that the authorities had failed to protect them from racist attacks, that their houses had been unlawfully demolished and that some of their children had been placed in classes for the educationally subnormal simply on the grounds of their ethnic origins. The petition was dismissed as inadmissible by a committee of three judges, in June 2001, solely on the grounds of non-exhaustion of domestic remedies. In other words, the applicants had failed to pursue all available legal remedies in Hungary before turning to Strasbourg.[25] The exhaustion of domestic remedies is a basic requirement of International Law and of human rights treaties such as the European Convention.[26] As noted above, a significant number of Hungarian Gypsies have been granted political asylum in France, to the dismay of the government in Budapest. In granting asylum, the French authorities had to be satisfied that the Roma in question had a 'well-founded fear of being persecuted for reasons of race, religion, nationality, membership of a political group or political opinion'.[27]

Set against this background, the assault on Olga and her customers can be seen as part of a wave of anti-Roma incidents in Central and Eastern Europe, since 1990. This phenomenon reflects increased levels of animosity towards (and scapegoating of) Gypsies throughout the region. However, as described in the following section of this chapter, the police chief in Olga's village tried to suggest that the incident at the Lambada had not been racially motivated.

AN INTERVIEW WITH THE LOCAL CHIEF OF POLICE

After I had heard Olga's account of the attack on the Lambada, I tried to make an appointment to see the new chief of police in the village. At this stage, Olga had not yet reached a private settlement with her assailants and was anxious for court proceedings to begin. I wanted to check Olga's story and to get the policeman's version of events. Tismana's former chief of police, the target of Olga's wrath, had been transferred to another village some months after the incident at the Lambada.

Alina, my Romanian research assistant, spoke several times on the phone with Ms Todea, the newly appointed press officer at the regional police headquarters in Cluj-Napoca. At first, Ms Todea was helpful and friendly. Gradually, though, as Alina persisted in seeking authorisation to interview the new police chief in Tismana, Ms Todea became increasingly irritable. Any hopes of preserving cordial relations were dashed when I asked Alina to enquire whether Romania had passed a law prohibiting incitement to racial hatred. Alina told me that, after she had put my question to Ms Todea, the latter replied rather icily: '[t]here is no need for such a law in Romania as everyone lives in harmony. There is no discrimination against the Roma and minority rights are guaranteed by the Romanian Constitution.' But, all the same, the police authorities in Cluj-Napoca finally relented and granted our request to speak to the new police chief in Olga's village.

Tismana's police station lies on the main road running through the straggling village. A young policeman, dressed in a coarse and over-large uniform, was standing guard on the front steps as Alina and I arrived. The police chief, burly and around 40 years of age, was waiting for us inside. Smiling and clearly anxious to make a good impression, he led us into his sparsely furnished office at the back. There were no computers or other trappings of modern technology anywhere in sight. Apart from a battered table, some shelving, chairs, a couple of law books and an old typewriter, the room was bare.

Before Alina or I had had a chance to say anything the police chief told us that he'd only been posted to Tismana a few months previously. So he hadn't been in the village when the incident at Olga's bar had taken place.

To put him at his ease I didn't ask about the fight at the Lambada straight away. Instead, I enquired about any changes that he may have noticed in the pattern of crime in Romania's villages since the end of Communist rule, some ten years before. The police chief told me that, in recent years, there had been a 40–50 per cent increase in levels of criminal activity in the surrounding villages. Mostly, the crimes involved thefts of animals or of agricultural produce. 'Some steal to eat, others steal to sell', he said, taking care to emphasise that the thieves comprised ethnic Romanians as well as Gypsies.

During the previous decades the bulk of the Roma in the area had worked for agricultural co-operatives. As indicated in Chapter 1 such co-operatives had been established throughout Romania, as elsewhere in Central and Eastern Europe, by post-War Communist administrations using land and livestock 'voluntarily' contributed by the peasants.[28] When the co-operatives were either dissolved or drastically scaled down, as a result of legislation permitting the restitution of land to the peasants, the Roma were left without land of their own on which to farm, or regular jobs. As in Hungary, the bulk of the Roma were excluded from the process of land reprivatisation in the 1990s because they had not owned any land prior to the formation of co-operatives under Communism. The policy of 'turning back the clock' with respect to the ownership of land, often trumpeted as an act of historic justice and of moral regeneration by populist, right-of-centre politicians in the region, conspicuously failed to produce fairness for marginalised and chronically underprivileged groups such as the Roma. In effect, restitution policies partially restored the iniquitous conditions that had existed in rural areas before the heavy-handed but undeniably egalitarian policies initiated by the Communists. As Ivan Berend has persuasively argued:[29]

> In social homogenization a great role was played by postwar land reforms and the collectivization of agriculture. The countryside of the region was strictly hierarchical before World War II... Collectivization, in spite of its tragic social, economic, and personal consequences, resulted in a homogeneous rural society. Former landless and well-to-do peasants became equal members of collective farms, receiving their 'working units' and having the same size of private plots.

The village police chief assured me that Roma who wanted to work could always get jobs as day labourers on privately owned farms.[30] 'Most of the Roma in Tismana work', he said. Tismana's Romani community, comprising around 1,200 persons, was pretty well integrated. 'They use the same shops and bars as the Romanians, although some fancy places may not admit them.' The police chief seemed neither surprised nor concerned that some establishments, the so-called 'fancy places', chose to keep the Roma off-limits.

After half an hour or so, I steered the conversation towards the incident at the Lambada that had occurred some seven months previously. 'The fight at the bar was a big scandal in the village', the police chief said, assuring me that the case would go to trial within 30 days. In fact, as things turned out, hearings at the court in Gherla would not start for several months.

The police chief told me that the three Romanian youths responsible for starting the fight at the Lambada had been charged with destruction of property and with assault. He reckoned that, in accordance with the Romanian Criminal Code, the defendants could expect a term of imprisonment or at least a substantial fine. He was confident that the court would also award Olga compensation. The authorities, I was told, had already estimated the total value of the property that had been destroyed in the incident at 3 million Romanian Lei. That is a much smaller sum than the 8 million Lei that Olga said she had been promised under the terms of the private settlement she'd reached with the defendants. But Olga had sought compensation for the injuries that she and Árpád had sustained in the fight, as well as for the destruction of property. The offer made to her by the defendants no doubt included an additional element as well. After all, if Olga could not be persuaded to reach a private settlement with her assailants, the defendants could face a term of imprisonment in one of Romania's poorly funded and chronically overcrowded jails.

'The three youths weren't known criminals', the police chief said, rejecting one of Olga's contentions. 'They got drunk, that's all, and they caused some trouble.' He was keen to point out that, in the ensuing fight, people on both sides had been injured. 'No-one was kept in hospital for more than ten days', he added, implying that the injuries had not been particularly serious. As for the Lambada, the police chief said that Olga had never sought the various licences that were needed to run such an establishment. The semi-legal bar may have been tolerated in the past but he was resolved to enforce the letter of the law from now on. The Lambada had to remain closed until Olga had secured all the necessary paperwork. In view of Olga's almost total lack of funds, that was likely to take a very long time.

In Olga's eyes, the assault on her bar was racially motivated, a premeditated attack by three brothers who had plagued her mostly Romani customers for some time. According to the police chief it was a regrettable incident triggered by alcohol, with no particular racial overtones. The victims could just as easily have been Romanians.

In refusing to characterise the attack on the Lambada as racist, Tismana's police chief is in good (or at least plentiful) company. There has been a tendency in much of Central and Eastern Europe for courts and criminal justice systems to hesitate – sometimes to the point of absurdity – in ascribing racist motives to attacks on Gypsies. In its 1999 World Report, Human Rights Watch refers to an attack by a group of up to 30 skinheads on two Romani families in a village in the Czech Republic. Although the gang 'fired guns and threw bricks and stones into the houses', causing one Romani man to be hospitalised, the police 'refused to recognize any racial motivation behind the attack'.[31] In its 2000 World Report, Human Rights Watch notes that, following an assault on a Romani man by a skinhead in Car, in Slovakia, the local police 'described the incident as one of "youthful imprudence" and ruled out a racial motive'.[32] In the same World Report, HRW also refers to a fatal attack on a middle-aged Romani woman in Slovakia:

> On August 20, three men shouting racial epithets beat Anastazia Balazova, a fifty-year-old Roma woman, and two of her daughters. She died from her injuries two days later. Deputy Prime Minister Csaky called the crime 'deplorable', but the chief investigator said that police had no evidence that the crime was racially motivated.

During the transition from Communist rule the countries of Central and Eastern Europe have gone to considerable lengths to revise and strengthen their domestic laws and institutions so as to improve the protection of human and minority rights, including the rights of the Romani people.[33] In part, this stems from a genuine commitment to reform and to bridging the 'gap' with Western Europe in political and legal (as well as in economic and material) terms. In part, though, recent efforts by the CEE states to provide more comprehensive legal protection to vulnerable minorities, particularly the Roma, have been founded on calculations of political or economic self-interest. In some instances, they have been a response to pressures deriving from membership of international organisations, such as the United Nations and the OSCE, or to obligations assumed under human rights treaties.[34]

In 1993, at the European Council meeting in Copenhagen, member states resolved that the admission of new states (including former Communist states) to the European Union depended on their compliance with various economic and political conditions, the so-

called 'Copenhagen Criteria'. Each candidate country must satisfy
the EU that it has fulfilled various targets. These include 'stability of
institutions guaranteeing democracy, the rule of law, human rights and
respect for and protection of minorities'.[35]

Since 1998 the European Commission has monitored the progress
made by each candidate country in complying with the admission
criteria. As recently as 2000, the Commission emphasised that Romani
minorities in the Czech Republic, Hungary, Poland, Romania and
Slovakia, 'suffer from discrimination and social hardship' and drew
attention to the urgent need to improve the situation of the Roma in
these countries.[36] The Commission's reports for 2002, while emphasising considerable progress, note certain deficiencies. These include
gaps in the anti-discrimination legislation in several candidate states.[37]
At the same time, the Commission praises some of the programmes
adopted by candidate countries to alleviate the chronic problems of
the Roma. For example, the Commission's 2002 report on Romania
applauds the adoption of a 'National Strategy for Improving the Conditions of the Roma'.[38]

Genuine reforms aimed at alleviating the deep-seated problems of the
Romani minorities in the CEE states are to be applauded. By contrast,
'paper reforms' will lead to 'paper results'. It is by no means clear
that the Commission has evaluated the Roma programmes adopted by
some of the CEE states with sufficient thoroughness. While Romania's
'National Strategy for Improving the Conditions of the Roma' is to be
welcomed, in principle, some tough questions need to be asked. In the
first place, what resources have been made available by the government
to give effect to these wide-ranging and expensive reforms? On what
basis have experts been hired to fill the new posts created by the
National Strategy? Do these experts have the appropriate qualifications
and work experience needed to discharge their responsibilities? And
how has the Romanian bureaucracy responded, at the national and
local levels, to the National Strategy? Unless the Romanian authorities
(both regional and national) are committed to the ideals of the National
Strategy there is little prospect that it will yield significant results.
Much the same questions can be posed with regard to the package of
affirmative measures introduced by the Czech Republic for its Romani
minority in January 2002.[39] The institutional commitment to such
large-scale initiatives has been patchy, at best, in a number of the CEE
states and the selection of personnel to implement the reforms has not
always been based on objective criteria.

As suggested above, recent efforts by the states of Central and Eastern Europe to 'clean up their act' – with respect to the treatment of their Romani citizens – also result from pressures exerted by international organisations of which they are already members. Such organisations include the United Nations, the Council of Europe, the Organisation for Security and Cooperation in Europe, and the International Bank for Reconstruction and Development.[40] Various UN bodies, including the Sub-Commission on Human Rights, have drawn attention to the difficulties experienced by the Roma in the transition from Communism.[41] For its part the Council of Europe, which maintains an assortment of programmes aimed at improving the situation of the Roma, has established a Specialist Group on Roma/Gypsies and a Coordinator Concerning Roma/Gypsy Activities.[42] In a series of resolutions, the Council of Europe's Parliamentary Assembly has drawn attention to the continuing deficiencies in the status and treatment of the continent's Romani minority. In Recommendation 1557 on 'The Legal Situation of Roma in Europe', which was adopted on 25 April 2002, the Assembly emphasised that:[43]

> Today Roma are still subjected to discrimination, marginalisation and segregation. Discrimination is widespread in every field of public and personal life, including access to public places, education, employment, health services and housing, as well as crossing borders and access to asylum procedures. Marginalisation and the economic and social segregation of Roma are turning into ethnic discrimination, which usually affects the weakest social groups.

Within the Organisation for Security and Cooperation in Europe both the OSCE High Commissioner on National Minorities and the Office for Democratic Institutions and Human Rights (ODIHR) have addressed the acute problems experienced by Roma in the CEE states.[44] In addition, the ODIHR Contact Point for Roma and Sinti Issues, established after the 1994 OSCE summit in Budapest, has a broad mandate to: 'develop, maintain and facilitate contacts on Roma and Sinti issues between participating States, international organizations and institutions, and NGOs, as well as between OSCE institutions and other international organizations and institutions'.[45]

Obligations assumed under multilateral human rights treaties have also played a part in inducing the CEE states to improve their domestic policies concerning their Romani minorities. As noted in Chapter 1, such treaties include the International Covenant on Civil and Political

Rights and the International Covenant on Economic, Social and Cultural Rights.[46] They include, in addition, the International Convention for the Elimination of all Forms of Racial Discrimination. In August 2000, the Committee established under the Convention adopted General Recommendation XXVII on 'Discrimination against Roma'.[47] Although not confined to the treatment of Roma in the CEE states, the instrument applies with particular force to the predicament of the sizeable Romani minorities in the region. As emphasised throughout this book, Gypsies have experienced severe and wide-ranging problems in the transition from Communism, many of which are associated with forms of discrimination.

Reference should also be made to the UN Convention against Torture and other Cruel, Inhuman or Degrading Treatment or Punishment.[48] In a recent decision the Committee Against Torture, established under the Convention, ruled that the failure of the police in the Federal Republic of Yugoslavia to prevent the destruction of a Romani settlement by elements of the local population amounted to a breach of Article 16(1) of the Convention:[49]

> the burning and destruction of houses constitute, in the circumstances, acts of cruel, inhuman or degrading treatment or punishment. The nature of these acts is further aggravated by the fact that some of the complainants were still hidden in the settlement when the houses were burnt and destroyed, the particular vulnerability of the alleged victims and the fact that the acts were committed with a significant level of racial motivation. Moreover, the Committee considers that the complainants have sufficiently demonstrated that the police (public officials), although they had been informed of the immediate risk that the complainants were facing and had been present at the scene of the events, did not take any appropriate steps in order to protect the complainants, thus implying 'acquiescence'.

Throughout the incident, in which an enraged mob of several hundred people destroyed a Romani settlement, a contingent of police stood idly by. Most of the settlement's residents had already fled, fearing for their lives. The 'pogrom' occurred after the alleged rape of a non-Romani minor by two Romani youths.

Unsurprisingly, the Committee established to monitor compliance with the Convention on the Rights of the Child has repeatedly criticised the predicament of Romani children in the CEE states.[50] For example, in January 2003, in its concluding observations on the second periodic report submitted by Romania, the Committee made certain concrete recommendations while emphasising its concern at: 'the negative attitudes and prejudices among the general public, in the political discourse, media representations, incidents of police brutality, and discriminatory behaviours on the part of some teachers and doctors'.[51]

Several judgments of the European Court of Human Rights are concerned with the treatment of the Roma in Central and Eastern Europe. At the time of writing, these judgments deal with the often brutal treatment meted out to Romani suspects and detainees by the police.[52] A number of other cases, brought under the European Convention on Human Rights and Fundamental Freedoms, involve the hasty and indiscriminate expulsion from Western Europe of Roma originating in the CEE states.[53] As yet, wider issues, such as the failure of the authorities in the CEE states to assure the protection of their Romani minorities from racially motivated assaults, have not resulted in an authoritative ruling by the Court.[54]

However, several important cases are currently before the European Court of Human Rights. One of these, discussed in Chapter 1, concerns the institutionalised discrimination that has been practised, allegedly, within the Czech educational system. The Romani applicants claim that children of Romani descent are far more likely to be sent to schools for the educationally sub-normal than their Czech peers, with disastrous consequences for their employment prospects and future lives.

The Framework Convention for the Protection of National Minorities, negotiated under the auspices of the Council of Europe, entered into force in 1998.[55] In recognising the specific rights, interests and concerns of persons belonging to national minorities the instrument complements and reinforces the European Convention on Human Rights and Fundamental Freedoms. The Advisory Committee established under the Framework Convention has regularly reviewed and commented on the situation of the Roma in the CEE states. Composed of independent experts the Advisory Committee, whose function is to assist the Council of Europe's Committee of Ministers, issues opinions on the reports submitted periodically by contracting states (Art. 26). In its Opinion on the Czech Republic, adopted on 6 April 2001, the Advisory Committee noted with 'deep concern' that:[56]

> many Roma in the Czech Republic face considerable socio-economic difficulties in comparison to both the majority and other minorities, in particular in the fields of education, employment and housing... Attitudes of intolerance and hostility towards national minorities,

especially Roma, are still widespread...the media continue to project negative stereotypes of certain national minorities, especially the Roma.

The Advisory Committee has also commented unfavourably on the treatment of Roma in other post-Communist states, including Hungary, Slovakia and Romania.[57] Though the opinions of the Advisory Committee are not binding they have considerable moral and political weight. They are generally endorsed by the Committee of Ministers, which has overall responsibility for evaluating the adequacy of the measures taken by contracting states.[58]

POSTSCRIPT

As yet, Romania's much-trumpeted 'National Strategy for Improving the Conditions of the Roma', introduced in 2002, has failed to improve Olga's circumstances, although it has resulted in several score jobs for special advisors on Romani affairs. The last time I saw Olga she was pulling a cart laden with apples along one of the rutted lanes in her village. Smiling, she led me back to her house. Looking around for something to give me, because of my efforts to help her in her claim against the brothers who had wrecked her business, Olga gave me a fading, black and white photograph of her father, Árpád. It shows a vigorous, handsome man, about 40 years of age, playing a violin at a village wedding in the mid 1960s. Árpád had been a respected violinist who had led his own band of Romani musicians from the village of Tismana. The band was much in demand at weddings, baptisms and at other family occasions; they were hired by Romanians and Gypsies alike.[59] Now, as a result of the poverty and falling living standards of the local smallholders, as well as changes in musical tastes, there are no longer any Gypsy bands in Tismana. Olga stays because she has nowhere else to go.

9

The Roma Café

THE ROMA CAFÉ

It was the Hungarian Romani activist, community leader and former parliamentary deputy, Aladár Horváth, who suggested that I visit the Roma Café. I had been talking to him in his cramped, paper-strewn office at the Romani Civil Rights Foundation, in Budapest. A meeting was to be held that evening, at the Café, to consider the Hungarian media and its handling of Romani affairs. The immediate catalyst for the discussion had been the sudden and unexplained replacement, by one of the country's main television channels, of a leading Romani intellectual, Ágnes Daróczi, who had fronted the only weekly television programme dealing exclusively with Romani issues.

I spent a long time looking for the Roma Café. Aladár Horváth had told me that it was in Almássy Square, in Budapest's Seventh District. Although I scrutinised every shop, bar and apartment building lining the perimeter of the square, I could find no trace of the Café. There weren't even any placards advertising the discussion I had come for. Eventually, long after the meeting was scheduled to start, I located the Roma Café; it had been convened in a room of a municipal building situated at one corner of the square. I had misunderstood Aladár Horváth; the Roma Café isn't a place but an idea. It's an occasional gathering of Romani politicians, activists, writers, intellectuals and artists, supplemented by a handful of sympathetic Hungarians, many of them journalists or university teachers, who are committed to improving the conditions of the country's Gypsies. The Roma Café is convened from time to time whenever there is an issue in the Romani community that needs airing. It's not the sort of café where you can buy a drink. Not for the first time I had been too literal minded.

In many ways, the notion of a 'Roma Café' is an apt metaphor for the Roma of Central and Eastern Europe. In contrast to the crude, two-dimensional stereotypes about Gypsies, that abound in the region, the image of a café is peculiarly empathetic. It conjures up scenes of warmth, of an eclectic mix of people and personalities, of lively conversation and of good music. As a metaphor, the notion of a 'Roma Café' is also corrective, reinvesting the Roma with the human attributes that have been relentlessly stripped away from them in Gadje representations of

9   A Gábor family in front of their house in north western Romania

Gypsies.[*] My initial misunderstanding of the nature of the Roma Café
neatly mirrors the failure of much of non-Romani society to understand
or to engage with the Roma, their culture(s), or the problems that they're
facing. Even in an age ostensibly committed to multiculturalism, there
is very little knowledge or even interest amongst non-Gypsies about
Romani traditions or values.

That evening, I spent several hours at the Roma Café listening to
an impassioned debate about the possible reasons for the removal of
Ágnes Daróczi from her post, as well as the airing of wider discontents.
With the Roma so often a minority in Central and Eastern Europe, the
normal demographic realities had been reversed; for the space of an
evening, at least, it was the Roma who constituted a majority. When I
left, a little before eleven, the heated discussion was still proceeding.

TACKLING THE PROBLEMS OF THE ROMA
OF CENTRAL AND EASTERN EUROPE

The mounting problems experienced by the mass of the Roma of
Central and Eastern Europe, since the collapse of Communism, are also

---

[*] A middle-aged vet in a Transylvanian village recounted the following local saying to me,
with a chuckle, when I told him that I was writing a book about the Roma: '[e]veryone
was made with some end in view. With Gypsies, it was the end of the village.'

matters of urgent concern for the wider societies in which the Roma live. Mass unemployment, long-term dependency on over-stretched welfare systems, a deepening sense of social alienation are not simply 'costs' borne by the Roma themselves. The prosperity, social cohesion and future dynamism of several post-Communist states with substantial Romani minorities depend, to a significant degree, on the ability of these countries to tackle the social and economic difficulties besetting their Romani communities. There is growing awareness of this elementary fact amongst both policy makers and academic researchers. For example, a recent study commissioned by the World Bank notes:[1]

> National governments have a large stake in the welfare of Roma, for human rights and social justice concerns, but also for reasons of growth and competitiveness. In countries where Roma constitute a large and growing share of the working-age population, increasing marginalization of Roma in poverty and long-term unemployment threatens economic stability and social cohesion.

Human Rights Strategies and the Roma of Central and Eastern Europe

As noted in Chapter 1, discussions of the problems experienced by the Roma in Central and Eastern Europe almost invariably invoke the language of human rights. Human rights have become the ultimate (sometimes the exclusive) standard by which a state's treatment of its citizens is judged – particularly by lawyers, journalists, political activists and by an increasing number of NGOs. The most prominent and certainly best-funded of the NGOs exclusively concerned with the promotion of Romani interests is the European Roma Rights Center (ERRC). The incorporation of the term 'rights' in the ERRC's name – and in that of other leading Romani NGOs such as the Budapest-based Romani Civil Rights' Foundation – suggests a particular way of under-standing (and of combating) the problems of the region's Roma.[2] In other words, the predicament of the Roma is presented (and perceived) primarily in terms of the denial of basic rights, including freedom from physical assaults by the police, and the need for non-discriminatory treatment by employers and in the provision of public services.

Similarly, human rights NGOs that are not concerned exclusively or even primarily with Romani affairs, such as Amnesty International or Human Rights Watch, inevitably characterise many of the problems experienced by the Roma as violations of specific rights enshrined in the Universal Declaration of Human Rights and in other texts. Bodies that are mandated to oversee or to enforce human rights instruments, including the International Covenant on Civil and Political Rights and the European Convention on Human Rights and Fundamental Freedoms, are limited by jurisdiction (and predisposed by culture) to evaluate the practice of state agencies in terms of the breach of specific rights included in the relevant treaties. Accordingly, 'in seeking legitimacy for their struggle Roma politicians have no choice but to lock onto the same concepts of human rights and anti-racism that operate in international organizations and relations between existing states'.[3]

The experience of the Roma during the post-Communist transition, in Central and Eastern Europe, bears witness to the widespread denial of human rights.[4] The recognition and enforcement of basic rights including the right to life, to freedom from inhuman or degrading treatment, to non-discrimination on grounds of race or ethnicity in the provision of public services and in employment matters, constitute necessary goals of any civilised society and vital steps in assuring improved conditions for the Roma. As indicated in various chapters of this book, there is compelling evidence of systematic discrimination against the Roma, across much of Central and Eastern Europe, in access to health care, education and housing, while criminal justice systems routinely treat the Roma in a less favourable manner than their non-Romani peers.[5] Similarly, Romani job applicants and Roma seeking promotion at work, are often subject to discriminatory practices. For this reason, I am not persuaded by one author who draws a distinction between human rights and 'the real needs' of Romani communities.[6] Recognition and enforcement of a range of basic rights must form an integral part of any concerted programme directed at overcoming the social and economic problems experienced by the region's Roma in the transition from Communism.

However, it remains true that observance of the basic rights of the Roma will not, of itself, resolve many of the underlying problems that the minority is currently facing. In fact, the general focus on rights may have partially obscured other modes of analysis and understanding. To put it another way, the chronic difficulties experienced by the bulk of the Roma in Central and Eastern Europe – including poverty, undereducation, mass unemployment and social marginalisation – are not simply a function of the denial of rights.

To take one example, the massive scale of Romani unemployment in the region since 1990, often as high as 70 per cent of Romani men of working age, is not only a result of discriminatory treatment by employers in the CEE states.[7] Although anti-Roma discrimination remains pervasive and virulent,[8] the appalling and socially divisive levels of Romani unemployment also reflects comparatively low levels of educational attainment and of marketable skills amongst the Roma as compared with their non-Romani peers.[9] While discriminatory or at least insensitive and culturally uninformed treatment of Romani pupils by teachers and by educational authorities goes some way towards explaining this phenomenon,[10] there are also important cultural factors at work that should not be overlooked.

Attitudes towards formal, school-based education amongst poorer as well as more traditional sections of the Romani community are sometimes negative or at least sceptical.[11] Historically, the Roma have tended to construe 'education' as the inter-generational transmission within families of skills or practices with which to earn a living, whether through collecting scrap metal, horse trading or other forms of commerce, mending pots, making stills or wooden spoons.[12] As this catalogue of occupations also shows, the Roma – except for those elements who have integrated to some degree – generally prioritise forms of economic activity that allow them to be self-employed, thus enabling them to retain a degree of independence and autonomy.

During the socialist era, as discussed in chapters 4 and 6, the Roma came under considerable if, in some states, fitful pressure to integrate economically within the societies of Central and Eastern Europe, often as unskilled or semi-skilled workers in the construction industry, in the agricultural cooperatives, or in the heavy industries that were rapidly established across the region. However, in increasingly technology-driven societies, many traditional Romani ways of earning a living have become obsolete, or the demand for them has largely disappeared.[13] At the same time, the need for unskilled or semi-skilled labourers, whether in industry or in agriculture, has sharply declined. Consequently, attitudes towards formal education amongst some poorer as well as more traditional Romani communities will have to change if future generations of Roma are to have a realistic chance of finding comparatively secure and well-paid jobs, or of taking advantage of new opportunities for self-employment. This will entail a difficult process of cultural adaptation on the part of sections of the Roma of Central and Eastern Europe. Targeted and generously funded schemes of social assistance are also necessary. Many Romani families make the point that they do not send their children to school because they fear that the kids will be ridiculed because the parents cannot afford to clothe them properly, or to provide them with exercise books, pens, pencils, or money for lunch.

The Principal Problems Facing the Roma and some Tentative Solutions

One of the clearest, most elegant expositions of the principal problems facing the Roma – and of some of the means needed to tackle them – has been set out in the form of a diagram by Géza Ötvös, the Romani director of the Romanian NGO Wassdas. Unlike the leaders of some high-profile Romani NGOs, who have been castigated for their alleged ignorance of, and indifference to, the perspectives of 'ordinary' Roma,[14] Géza Ötvös does not lead a sopisticated, urban lifestyle remote from the people whose interests he represents. He lives in the Transylvanian village in which he spent much of his childhood, amongst a mixed population of Roma, ethnic Hungarians and ethnic Romanians. His catalogue of the problems confronting the mass of the Roma and of the means needed to address them is pragmatic, lacking any hint of the 'naive ideological agendas' identified by one critic of NGO involvement in Romani affairs.[15]

Géza Ötvös' refusal to ascribe the problems of the Roma solely to racism or to a lack of political commitment on the part of the region's governments is refreshing – although these factors should not be discounted. At the same time, his carefully thought out approach to overcoming the difficulties experienced by the Roma, in the transition from Communism, illustrates the need for a broadly-based strategy involving legislation, generous and well-targeted schemes of social assistance, as well as innovative approaches in teaching. Each of the eight issues identified by Géza Ötvös' diagram has some bearing on all the others. Efforts to tackle one problem in isolation, or to pursue a single strategy (for example based on the recognition and enforcement of basic rights), are unlikely to succeed. The same point is made in the World Bank report cited above: 'a comprehensive policy approach is required to address multiple and interrelated causes of Roma poverty simultaneously'.[16]

Romani culture and the Roma contribution to the arts

As indicated in Chapter 2, the Roma are, in broad terms, a people without much sense of their own history, often living in societies where the public at large (including most professional historians) are ignorant of and indifferent to their past. The reasons for this situation are examined in Chapter 2. However, the consequences are far-

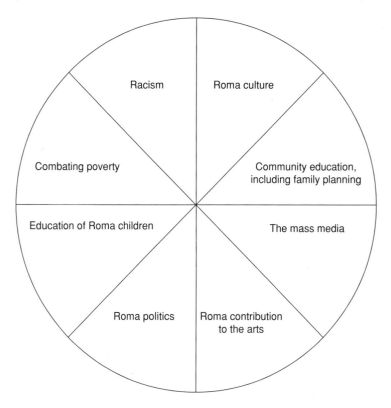

Géza Ötvös' diagram depicting the principal problems of Romania's Roma

reaching. The fact that the bulk of the Roma in the CEE states have little or no knowledge of their history and, frequently, a fading sense of their traditions and customs has impacted negatively on their sense of self-worth, compounding the effects of the social and economic marginalisation that they have been subject to in much of Central and Eastern Europe.

Education about Romani culture and history is as necessary for Gadje as for the Roma. It may help to stimulate greater respect for the Roma as well as shame at how they have been treated by the supposedly 'civilised' European states.[17] As described in Chapter 2, the Roma were held as slaves in much of present-day Romania, often in appalling and inhuman conditions, until as late as the middle of the nineteenth century. As emphasised in Chapter 3, the genocide and widespread persecution of the Roma during World War II were largely ignored by both statesmen and historians until comparatively recently. During the Communist era, there was an ideologically-fuelled reluctance in the CEE states to acknowledge that the Nazis and their allies had targeted specific ethnic or religious groups, that is to say, Gypsies and Jews.

Although Géza Ötvös' diagram treats the Romani contribution to the arts separately from Romani culture and history, there are several reasons for linking the two. For the Roma, the creative arts, above all music, represent ways of preserving (or of re-creating) vital aspects of their traditional culture(s). In addition, the arts, whether music, painting, dance or literature, offer means of self-expression and of communicating with the outside, Gadjo world. For a minority, the arts also represent a way of earning a living. Fostering and publicising the rich and diverse Romani contribution to the arts have become matters of some importance. In addition to benefiting the Roma directly, an enhanced awareness of Romani artistic achievements could highlight the massively talented nature of this community, something that is frequently overlooked in popular images of the Roma in Central and Eastern Europe.

Community education

Working with the Roma of Pata Rât Géza Ötvös became keenly aware that some of the problems experienced by significant numbers of Roma, particularly those living in such settlements, can only be alleviated through a process of social education, often in combination with the allocation of adequate resources by central or local government (or resulting from improved opportunities for the Roma to find regular employment). These are, admittedly, complex and sensitive issues. For the inhabitants of settlements such as Pata Rât, lack of money for toiletries and other items, as well as grossly unsatisfactory living conditions, make it difficult to maintain reasonable standards of health and of hygiene. Until Médecins sans Frontières paid for the installation of water pipes, for example, the Roma of Pata Rât lacked access to uncontaminated water.

For some, poorly educated sections of the Romani community, instruction about basic medical matters, nutrition, family planning and related subjects remains necessary, both in terms of the health and quality of life of the Roma themselves as well as their prospects of social and economic adjustment. The need for community education for elements of the Romani community – a point that is emphasised by social workers throughout the region – should not be dismissed out of some misguided notion of political correctness.

The mass media

Representations of the Roma in the mass media are of obvious and critical importance in shaping public attitudes towards Gypsies. As noted in Chapter 1, since the collapse of Communist rule the media across much of the region has repeatedly drawn attention to the ethnicity of Romani defendants charged with various offences, thereby confirming widely held assumptions about the 'innate' criminality of the Roma.[18] An article published in 2002 in a serious Romanian broadsheet was cited in Chapter 5 as an illustration of the way in which the region's media not infrequently portrays the Roma. There is a clear and compelling need for restraint amongst the region's media if public perceptions of the Roma are to be slowly tranformed. Articles suggesting that the Roma share certain collective and ineradicable traits are not only nonsensical but dangerous.

Romani politics

In multi-party democracies with sizeable Romani minorities, such as Romania, Slovakia, Bulgaria, the Czech Republic, Hungary and Macedonia, the Roma have the potential to exert considerable political pressure on governments. Put simply, the Roma have a lot of votes, although in practice many do not bother to register. Apathy or ignorance about political affairs, a feeling that politicians of the left and of the right are united in their lack of genuine concern for the Roma, as well as an understandable preoccupation with more immediate concerns, have tended to translate into comparatively limited Romani participation in the political process.[19]

A related problem has been the absence of a unified sense of Romani ethnicity or nationhood. This has hampered Romani politicians and activists seeking to influence government policy in the CEE states. As explained in Chapter 1, the Roma comprise a *multiplicity* of minorities with little sense, as yet, of a common cultural or ethnic identity.[20] Unsurprisingly, it has proved extremely difficult for Romani politicians and activists to establish a common platform within particular states, uniting the members of the various Romani subgroups as well as semi-integrated Roma with a diminished sense of Romani identity.

The education of Romani children

A growing body of literature has been devoted to the subject of the education of Romani children. One of the most original and inspirational books on the subject contains several essays about the children and elementary school in Csenyéte, a tiny Hungarian village.[21] In

1996, of Csenyéte's 328 inhabitants, 91.5 per cent were Gypsies, reflecting the gradual concentration (that is, 'ghettoisation') of the Roma in poorer agricultural regions and in impoverished inner suburbs of towns and cities in the CEE states.

The importance of improving the educational levels of Romani children, which lag behind those of their non-Romani peers, has been stressed at various points in this book. This is, perhaps, the key to transforming the socio-economic position of the Roma in Central and Eastern Europe. At present, the proportion of Romani pupils attending or completing secondary education, or going on to either university or to various specialist colleges, is tiny. According to research conducted in Hungary, in the mid 1990s, only 2 per cent of Roma aged 25–29 had completed secondary school.[22] Levels of educational attainment amongst Roma elsewhere in Central and Eastern Europe are broadly comparable. According to a Romanian study, carried out in 1998, 18.3 per cent of Romani children aged 7–16 had not even attended elementary school.[23] In the mid 1990s, 2.5 per cent of Czech Roma and 2.8 per cent of Slovak Roma attended (but did not necessarily complete) secondary school.[24] As little as 0.2 per cent of Hungarian Roma, 0.7 per cent of Romanian Roma and 0.9 per cent of Bulgarian Roma went on to tertiary education.[25]

This massive educational underperformance must be addressed as a matter of urgency. However, a significant improvement in the educational standards of all sections of the Roma is only likely to be achieved through the intensive education (or re-education) of teachers and educational authorities throughout Central and Eastern Europe, a process that has already begun to some extent. Too often, teachers have had low expectations of their Romani pupils, or have failed to understand the cultural context that may shape their behaviour in class.[26] Of course, the influence of Romani parents from poorer or more traditional communities has not always been helpful. For example, until Wassdas intervened, offering a variety of incentives and material support, many parents at the Pata Rât settlement had chosen to keep their school-age children at home, or working alongside the adults at the adjacent rubbish dump. These children were growing up without even basic literacy and numeracy skills, scarcely a preparation for a secure or fulfilling future. Notwithstanding traditional Romani expectations concerning the productive role of children, the latter should not be treated as an economic resource by their families. In this respect, it is helpful to view children as possessing rights – both in relation to schools and education systems, and vis-à-vis their parents. However, in practical terms, as some experts have noted, it may be easier to secure parental support for education through a system of incentives rather than sanctions.

Combating poverty

Combating Roma poverty is, without doubt, the greatest challenge facing the Roma and the societies in which they live. As noted above, a recent World Bank report confirmed that the scale of Roma poverty threatens the economic performance and social cohesion of several states in Central and Eastern Europe. The same report rightly emphasises that:[27]

> Roma poverty has multiple and interrelated causes. These tend to reinforce one another in a vicious cycle of poverty and exclusion, and require a multifaceted approach. Roma often have poor access to labor markets because of low education levels, geographic isolation and discrimination...Roma often face discrimination at school and feel that schools ignore Roma language and culture. In addition, Roma sometimes lack sufficient food or clothing to support school attendance. Thus, attitudes, experiences, and social conditions conspire to reduce Roma education levels and labor market performance. Because of their interconnected roots, one cannot adequately address Roma poverty by focusing on a single aspect. Rather, a comprehensive approach is needed.

Turning the clock back, that is returning to the material certainties of the socialist era, is not an option. The right to work cannot be assured in societies that have transformed themselves into market economies; states in Central and Eastern Europe can no longer dictate how many jobs there are. In any event, as emphasised by Michael Stewart, many of the jobs created for the Roma under state socialism were artificial, they 'disappeared as soon as consumers had any choice over what they purchased'.[28]

At the same time, levels of social provision, whether for the unemployed, for the chronically sick, for the elderly, or for large families, are necessarily limited by each country's economic performance, as well as by competing priorities for state funding. Should long-term unemployment benefits take precedence over increased funding for education, even though the latter option may mean that the next generation of Romani children enjoy significantly enhanced employment prospects? These are difficult choices, even for well-intentioned governments that are committed to improving the conditions of the Roma.

The scope of the social and economic rights that the states of Central and Eastern Europe can deliver is constrained by the fact that they have become market economies, as well as by the inevitable swings of economic performance. However, basic entitlements to health care, to reasonable housing and to other forms of social provision could be made available as of right in most countries in the region. This would benefit overwhelmingly impoverished groups such as the Roma, many of whom exist at or outside the margins of society. It is worth noting that the post-apartheid South African Constitution, of 1996, guarantees a range of social and economic rights. These include the right to housing, enshrined in Article 26:[29]

(1) Everyone has the right to have access to adequate housing.
(2) The state must take reasonable legislative and other measures, within its available resources, to achieve the progressive realisation of this right.

In addition, Article 27 of South Africa's Constitution contains rights to health care, food, water and social security:

(1) Everyone has the right to have access to health care services, including reproductive health care; sufficient food and water; and social security, including, if they are unable to support themselves and their dependants, appropriate social assistance.
(2) The state must take reasonable legislative and other measures, within its available resources, to achieve the progressive realisation of each of these rights.
(3) No one may be refused emergency medical treatment.

Crucially, these rights are not simply rhetorical affirmations of political or moral intent but fully justiciable undertakings, that is, the courts in South Africa both construe and enforce the social and economic rights contained in the Constitution.[30]

Unsurprisingly, the approach adopted in the above-mentioned World Bank report is markedly different. Rather than calling for a reversion to social and economic rights, even on a much more modest scale than under state socialism, it advocates well-targeted schemes of social assistance and 'creating a better environment for job creation'.[31] In addition, the report calls for fiscal policies that do not 'discourage employers from hiring unskilled laborers'. However, such initiatives would not be incompatible with the recognition of a limited range of social and economic rights, similar to those found in the South African Constitution.

Though wary of social and economic rights, the World Bank report acknowledges that a number of civil and political rights are needed in the struggle to overcome the causes of Roma poverty.[32] These include the right to non-discrimination, on grounds of race or ethnicity, in the provision of public services and in employment matters. Arguably, programmes of affirmative action and schemes of targeted assistance are also required for a minority, such as the Roma, that has been subject to long-term social, economic and political marginalisation.

However, enacting and enforcing rights is not enough. Tackling the 'multiple and interrelated causes' of Roma poverty ultimately entails a transformation of the educational levels and skills of the mass of 'ordinary' Roma. Achieving this will require enormous and concerted effort on the part of governments, education authorities, teachers, social workers, Romani NGOs and a variety of other bodies – as well as by the Roma themselves.[33] The societies of Central and Eastern Europe, including employers, churches and other institutions, must be willing and enthusiastic partners in this process of social transformation. Competent, educated, enthusiastic Romani job applicants won't succeed unless employers in the region are willing (or can be induced) to discard ingrained prejudices. This is unlikely to prove a simple task.

At the same time, the goal of economic integration, or inclusion,[34] must not be permitted to prejudice Romani cultural autonomy or self-determination, a process that has accelerated since 1990. As emphasised in Chapter 4, the Communist project was initially directed at the economic, cultural and social integration or, more properly, *assimilation* of the Roma. In the former Czechoslovakia and in Bulgaria these objectives were never abandoned by the Communist regimes. Such unashamedly assimilationist policies mirrored the efforts of Habsburg rulers, in the mid eighteenth century, to eliminate the Roma as a distinct cultural group. The challenge for post-Communist societies in the region is to reverse the relentless deterioration in the living standards of the mass of the Roma, while supporting their right to cultural self-expression and self-awareness. At the same time, the fostering of Romani group identities must not be at the expense of individual autonomy. Human rights include the right *not* to be treated as a member of a particular national or ethnic group.

Racism

As noted in Chapter 8, racially-motivated assaults have been an ugly and recurrent feature of the transition process in many post-Communist states. More fundamentally, popular stereotypes about the Roma in much of Central and Eastern Europe have contributed to the process of Romani marginalisation. As discussed in Chapter 5, successful, educated Roma, including distinguished classical musicians, sometimes prefer to draw a veil over their ethnicity out of fear for their social standing and careers.

Combating racism requires a complex, multifaceted strategy. As suggested above, the media bear a heavy responsibility in this regard. Their portrayal of the Roma inevitably colours and reinforces popular perceptions. Educational systems can also play an important part, as already suggested, contributing to an enhanced awareness of the enormous contribution that the Roma have made, particularly in music, the arts, handcrafts and commerce. Institutions of civil society in Central and Eastern Europe, including the churches, could be much more active in combating 'anti-Gypsyism'. The established churches in the region, many of which are enormously influential, have often (though not invariably) chosen to ignore the Gypsies, in part because of the perception that they lack genuine religious devotion. As a teacher at the elementary school in the Hungarian village of Csenyéte remarked: '[f]or a number of reasons, the churches haven't concerned themselves with the village's Gypsies so far'.[35]

As suggested in Chapter 8, police and criminal justice systems, in much of Central and Eastern Europe, could help to combat racism by treating assaults on Romani victims as both serious breaches of the criminal law and, where the facts warrant it, as racially motivated acts. Rehousing the Roma who have drifted to settlements, small ghettoes of deprivation and marginality, also represents a priority. As a recent study on Romani deprivation concluded, 'geographic and social exclusion are important correlates of poverty'.[36]

Combating anti-Roma racism, which involves challenging and overturning entrenched prejudices, is a long-term project. In particular, the societies of Central and Eastern Europe must learn (or re-learn) greater tolerance of cultural, religious and ethnic difference.[37] The price of securing freedom from material insecurity and deprivation, racist assaults and the general opprobrium of society should not have to be the surrender (or continued denial) of Romani identity. Roma should not have to turn themselves into Gadje in order to be treated with respect.

Notes

INTRODUCTION

1. The figure of 6 million Roma living in Central and Eastern Europe, cited in some European Union texts, is an estimate. See *EU Support for Roma Communities in Central and Eastern Europe* (May 2002), p. 4, available at <http://europa.eu.int/comm/enlargement/docs/pdf/brochure_roma_may2002.pdf > (accessed 3 September 2003). For a discussion of Roma numbers in the CEE states see D. Ringold, M. Orenstein, E. Wilkens, *Roma in an Expanding Europe: Breaking the Poverty Cycle* (Washington, D.C.: International Bank for Reconstruction and Development, 2003), p. 12. For a variety of reasons, including the reluctance of many Roma to acknowledge their ethnicity in societies where anti-Romani prejudice remains rampant, it is impossible to ascertain the size of Romani populations in the various CEE states with complete accuracy.

2. For details of the pattern of violence against Roma in the CEE states see, for example, the Country Reports Series issued by the Budapest-based European Roma Rights Center. See, also, the World Reports published annually by Human Rights Watch. These are available at <http://www.hrw.org/reports/world/reports/> (accessed 28 March 2003). See, in addition, infra, Chapter 8.

3. For an excellent and detailed discussion of the living conditions of the Romani people in the Czech Republic, Slovakia, Romania, Bulgaria and Macedonia see I. Zoon, *On the Margins: Roma and Public Services in Romania, Bulgaria and Macedonia* (New York: Open Society Institute, 2001), pp. 115–89; I. Zoon, *On the Margins: Roma and Public Services in Slovakia* (New York: Open Society Institute, 2001), pp. 77–101. See, also, infra, Chapter 6.

4. The numbers of Roma living in settlements in Slovakia increased during the 1990s, reaching over 124,000 persons by 1998. See Zoon, *On the Margins: Slovakia*, pp. 79–80.

5. My translation. An extract from Forgács' poem is available, in Hungarian, at <http://www.romapage.hu/kultura/index.php?kozep=irodn019.htm> (accessed on 7 November 2002). In Romani the term 'Gadjo' (plural 'Gadje'), which is somewhat disparaging, is used to denote someone who is not a Gypsy.

6. Interview recorded in April 1999 (on file with the author).

7. *A Magyarországban 1893 január 31-en végrehajtott Cigányösszeirás Eredményei* (Budapest: Athenaeum R. Társulat Könyvnyomdája, 1895), p. 69.

8. For a more detailed analysis of Communist policies towards the region's Roma see Z. Barany, *The East European Gypsies* (Cambridge: Cambridge University Press, 2002), Chapter 4. See also infra, Chapter 4.

9. A study conducted in 1971, in Hungary, found that 73–74 per cent of young Roma were almost entirely illiterate. Levels of illiteracy amongst older Roma were, of course, significantly higher. See I. Kemény, 'Tennivalók a cigányok/romák ügyében' in F. Glatz (ed.), *A cigányok Magyarországon* (Budapest: Magyar Tudományos Akadémia, 1999), p. 229.

10. On attitudes towards literacy amongst British Gypsies, which are not dissimilar to those of traditionally-minded Gypsies elsewhere, see J. Okely, *The Traveller-Gypsies* (Cambridge: Cambridge University Press, 1983), pp. 160–2.

11. On the worsening poverty experienced by the bulk of the Roma since the end of Communism see, for instance, Barany, *East European Gypsies*, pp. 157–83. See, also, Ringold, Orenstein, Wilkens, *Roma in an Expanding Europe*, Chapter 2. On the economic gains experienced by many Roma during the socialist era see Barany, *East European Gypsies*, pp. 125–43. See, also, infra, Chapter 4.

12. European Union's 2002 Regular Report on Hungary, p. 31. This is available at <http://europa.eu.int/comm/enlargement/report2002/ > (accessed 28 March 2003).

13. As noted above, the size of Romani minorities in the CEE states cannot be given with any degree of precision. However, according to figures cited by the European Commission, there are up to 800,000 Roma in Bulgaria, 300,000 in the Czech Republic, 600,000 in Hungary, 2.5 million in Romania, and 520,000 in Slovakia. In Poland, where the bulk of the Roma were killed during World War II, it is estimated that there are up to 60,000 Gypsies. See *EU Support for Roma Communities in Central and Eastern Europe*, p. 4.

14. See, generally, Ringold, Orenstein, Wilkens, *Roma in an Expanding Europe*, Chapter 2. On the dismantling of social and economic rights in the CEE states see infra, Chapter 6.

15. Ina Zoon provides many examples of this phenomenon. See, for example, Zoon, *On the Margins*, pp. 184–5, 188.

16. Information supplied by the Roma rights NGO Wassdas on 2 and 26 April 2002 (on file with the author).

17. On post-Communist land reforms in Romania see A. Cartwright, *The Return of the Peasant* (Aldershot: Dartmouth, 2001), Chapter 7.

18. Until 1989, there had only been five dwellings at Pata Rât.

19. See, generally, Barany, *East European Gypsies*, Chapter 4.

20. Interview recorded on 24 and 25 September 2002 (on file with the author). However, there were exceptions to this relentless process of social and economic integration. Members of the Gábor Romani community, concentrated in parts of Transylvanian Romania, mostly preferred to retain their economic independence and to earn a living, as before, through their skills as traders, metal workers and tinsmiths. To a considerable extent, Romania's Communist authorities accommodated the Gábor Roma, allowing them to practise their traditional occupations provided that they obtained the necessary licences.

21. See, in particular, Zoon, *On the Margins*; Zoon, *On the Margins: Slovakia*.

22. See, for example, European Roma Rights Center, *A Special Remedy: Roma and Schools for the Mentally Handicapped in the Czech Republic* (Budapest: ERRC, Country Report Series No. 8, June 1999).

23. Ibid., p. 11.

24. G. Havas, 'A cigány tanulók elkülönitése az általános iskolában' in T. Reisz and M. Andor (eds), *A Cigányság Társadalomismerete* (Pécs: Iskolakultúra, 2002), p. 152, at pp. 166–72.

25. Ibid., p. 170.

26. Ibid., p. 158.

27. For the past two years an idealistic general practitioner in a nearby suburb of Cluj has been treating Romani residents of Pata Rât. Previously, no doctor would agree

to receive Gypsies from the settlement. Information supplied by Géza Ötvös, Director of the NGO Wassdas, 14 April 2003.

28. See, generally, on the problems faced by Romania's Gypsies in obtaining medical care, Zoon, *On the Margins*, pp. 79–101. On the difficulties experienced by Gypsies in registering with family doctors see ibid., pp. 82–4.

29. See, for instance, Barany, *East European Gypsies*, p. 311. In Hungary, however, it is unconstitutional to collect (let alone disseminate) information about the ethnicity of suspects, defendants or those convicted of crimes.

30. See, generally, H. Moutouh, *Les Tsiganes* (Paris: Flammarion, 2000), pp. 34–46. See, also, Barany, *East European Gypsies*, pp. 241–9.

31. On the Oláh, or Vlach, Roma of Hungary and their propensity for trade and commerce as means of earning a living, in preference to wage labour, see M. Stewart, *The Time of the Gypsies* (Boulder: Westview Press, 1997), especially chapters 9 and 10. For a vivid description of a prominent and wealthy Kalderash family in Romania see I. Fonseca, *Bury me Standing* (Vintage: London, 1996), pp. 283–8.

32. For example, there are a number of huge and extraordinarily ornate mansions in and around the town of Turda in Transylvanian Romania, that have been built for Romani families.

33. For a discussion of the implications for the Roma of the new rights-based political cultures established in the post-Communist states and the enhanced concern for minority rights see infra, Chapter 5.

34. See, for example, Barany, *East European Gypsies*, pp. 143–51.

35. Ringold, Orenstein, Wilkens, *Roma in an Expanding Europe*, pp. 1–2.

36. See, generally, Barany, *East European Gypsies*, pp. 325–39. For an evaluation of how successful these programmes have been in practice see, for example, the European Union's 2002 regular reports on the applicant countries. These are available at <http://europa.eu.int/comm/enlargement/report2002/> (accessed 28 March 2003).

37. On the role of NGOs concerned with promoting Roma interests see, for example, N. Trehan, 'In the name of the Roma? The role of private foundations and NGOs' in W. Guy (ed.), *Between Past and Future: The Roma of Central and Eastern Europe* (Hertfordshire: University of Hertfordshire Press, 2001), p. 134.

38. For a detailed discussion of these international factors see infra, Chapter 8.

39. For the text of General Recommendation XXVII of the Committee on the Elimination of Racial Discrimination see, for example, <http://www.unhchr.ch/tbs/doc.nsf/(symbol)/CERD+General+recom.+27.En?Opendocument> (accessed 8 September 2003).

40. Although not expressly confined to the treatment of Roma in the CEE states, the General Recommendation applies with particular force to the predicament of the sizeable Romani minorities in the region. As emphasised throughout this book, Gypsies have experienced severe and wide-ranging problems in the transition from Communism, many of which are associated with forms of discrimination.

41. These cases are discussed infra, Chapter 8. However, the Court will not link the abuse of a Romani victim's basic rights to his/her ethnicity where compelling evidence of racial motivation is lacking. See, for instance, *Anguelova* v. *Bulgaria* (Application no. 38361/97), especially at paras. 166–8.

42. For example, in *The East European Gypsies*, an otherwise a highly informative book about the Roma of Central and Eastern Europe, there is little evidence that Barany, a political scientist, actually spoke to any Roma other than leading political

activists who were far removed, both by education and lifestyle, from the mass of ordinary Roma in the countries concerned.

43. On Romani and its various dialects see, for example, A. Fraser, *The Gypsies* (Oxford: Blackwell, 2nd ed., 1995), pp. 10–22.

44. See, for example, I. Kemény, (ed.), *A Magyarországi Romák* (Budapest: Press Publica kiadó, 2000), p. 28.

45. On the Roma and the extent to which they currently recognise a sense of national identity see, for example, I. Pogany, 'Accommodating an emergent national identity: The Roma of Central and Eastern Europe' in S. Tierney (ed.), *Accommodating National Identity* (The Hague: Kluwer Law International, 2000), pp. 175–88.

46. Fraser, *The Gypsies*, p. 8.

47. Linguistic competence always imposes limits on what any individual can read. For the most part, I relied on materials published in English, French, Hungarian and, latterly, Romanian.

48. See, generally, on the significance of the personal characteristics of researchers engaging in participant observation, M. Hammersley and P. Atkinson, *Ethnography* (London: Routledge, 2nd ed., 1995), pp. 92–9.

49. As Hammersely and Atkinson rightly observe, in some circumstances, 'the dividing line between participant observation and interviewing is hard to discern' ibid., p. 139. On interviews as participant observation see ibid., pp. 139–51.

50. On the importance of triangulation, that is the use of multiple sources of evidence, see, for example, R. Yin, *Case Study Research* (London: Sage Publications, 2nd ed., 1994), pp. 90–4.

51. Ringold, Orenstein, Wilkens, *Roma in an Expanding Europe*, p. 4.

52. See, generally, the country reports and other publications of the Budapest-based European Roma Rights Center.

53. The contrast between the situation of the Roma during the Communist era and their predicament now is discussed in various chapters of this book. See, in particular, Chapter 2, Chapter 4 and Chapter 6.

54. For an excellent ethnographic account of the subsistence strategies pursued by various Vlach Romani families in a Hungarian village, following the disappearance of Communist-era jobs, see P. Szuhay, 'Foglalkozási és megélhetési stratégiák a magyarországi cigányok körében' in F. Glatz (ed.), *A cigányok Magyarországon* (Budapest: Magyar Tudományos Akadémia, 1999), p. 139. See, generally, on ethnography Hammersley and Atkinson, *Ethnography*. On oral history see, for instance, R. Perks and A. Thomson (eds), *The Oral History Reader* (London: Routledge, 1998).

55. R. Perks and A. Thomson, 'Introduction' in Perks and Thomson, *Oral History Reader*, p. ix.

56. On *szociográfia*, or 'sociography', see, for example, L. Kelecsényi, *Atlasz: Magyar Irodalom* (Budapest: Athenaeum, 2nd ed., 2002), pp. 217, 219.

57. L. Bárdos, I. Szabó, G. Vasy (eds), *Irodalmi Fogalmak Kisszótára* (Budapest: Korona Kiadó, 1996), pp. 226–7.

58. L. Nagy, *Kiskunhalom* (Budapest: Osiris Kiadó, 1999).

59. G. Illyés, *Puszták népe* (Budapest: Osiris Kiadó, 1999). The book is also available in English. See G. Illyés, *People of the Puszta* (Budapest: Corvina, 2nd rev. ed., 1979).

60. Z. Csalog, *Kilenc cigány* (Budapest: Komosz Könyvek, 1976).

61. U. Baxi, *The Future of Human Rights* (New Delhi: Oxford University Press, 2002), pp. 2–3.

62. The adoption of new constitutions emphasising civil and political rights and the impact of a range of human rights treaties and of various 'soft-law' commitments on the ex-Communist states are discussed in Chapter 6.

63. In Romani, the term 'porajmos' literally means 'devouring'.

64. The same technique is used in several other chapters, including Chapter 2 and Chapter 4.

65. See Ringold, Orenstein, Wilkens, *Roma in an Expanding Europe.*

66. See I. Hancock, *We are the Romani people* (Hertfordshire: University of Hertfordshire Press, 2002), pp. xviii–xxii.

67. See Ringold, Orenstein, Wilkens, *Roma in an Expanding Europe.*

2   THE HAIRY THING THAT BITES, OR WHY GYPSIES SHUN GADJE

1. On Romani and its affinities with various Indic languages see, for example, A. Fraser, *The Gypsies* (Oxford: Blackwell, 2nd ed., 1995), pp. 10–22.

2. See, for instance, M. Stewart, *The Time of the Gypsies* (Boulder, Colorado: Westview Press, 1997), especially Chapter 12; J. Okely, *The Traveller-Gypsies* (Cambridge: Cambridge University Press, 1983), pp. 80–94, 206–12; I. Fonseca, *Bury me Standing* (Vintage: London, 1996), pp. 42–4, 49–50, 106–7. Dr Péter Szuhay, a curator at the Museum of Ethnography in Budapest, has written extensively on the Roma of Central and Eastern Europe. He argues that many of the practices which western anthropologists have interpreted as evidence of distinctive Romani beliefs regarding purity or shame are actually peasant customs that have been adopted by Romani communities who settled in the area. See, generally, on the value systems of the various Romani groups found in Hungary, P. Szuhay, *A magyarországi cigányság kultúrája: etnikus kultúra vagy a szegénység kultúrája* (Panórama: Budapest, 1999), pp. 76–117.

3. Some of these aspects of Gábor culture are discussed in Chapter 7.

4. Z. Barany, *The East European Gypsies* (Cambridge: Cambridge University Press, 2002), p. 13.

5. *Sitiprinc*, a film directed by Edit Kőszegi, was released in Budapest in 1998. With the exception of the leading roles many of the parts are played by Roma from Hungary and Transylvanian Romania, none of whom had any previous experience of acting or film-making. Rózsi had a small part in the film which recounts the remarkable life of Rudolf Horváth, an ethnic Hungarian who spent several years living with nomadic Gypsies at the end of the nineteenth century and who eventually joined the Hussars. Like the Gadjo youth in Rózsi's story, Rudolf Horváth 'betrayed' the Gypsies who had accepted him into their midst.

6. On the clash of cultures and outlook dividing peasants and their Vlach Romani neighbours, as revealed in the village of Patakrét in Hungary, see, for example, P. Szuhay, 'Arson on Gypsy row' in *The Hungarian Quarterly*, Winter 1995, p. 81.

7. See, generally, Stewart, *Time of the Gypsies*, Chapter 2.

8. Szuhay, 'Arson on Gypsy row', p. 90.

9. Interview recorded in April 1999 (on file with the author).

10. On Vlach Romani attitudes towards theft see Szuhay, 'Arson on Gypsy row', p. 90.

11. On traditional Vlach Roma attitudes towards theft from Gadje see Stewart, *Time of the Gypsies*, pp. 17–19.
12. For a fuller discussion of Gypsies and criminality, particularly in Hungary, see S. Póczik, 'Roma bűnelkövetők a sztatisztikák tükrében. A romákkal kapcsolatos kriminológiai kutatás mai állása' in F. Irk (ed.), *Kriminológiai Tanulmáyok XXXVIII* (Budapest: Országos Kriminológiai Intézet, 2001), p. 266.
13. Okely, *The Traveller-Gypsies*, p. 30.
14. See, for example, D. Crowe, *A History of the Gypsies of Eastern Europe and Russia* (New York: St. Martin's Griffin, 1996), pp. 74–5. See, generally, P. Nagy, *A magyarországi cigányok története a rendi társadalom korában* (Kaposvár: Csokonai Vitéz Mihály Tanítóképző Főiskola Kiadója, 1998), pp. 247–56.
15. Nagy, *magyarországi cigányok története*, p. 252.
16. Crowe, *History of the Gypsies*, p. 84.
17. *A Magyarországban 1893 január 31-en végrehajtott Czigányösszeirás Eredményei* (Budapest: Athenaeum R. Társulat Könyvnyomdája, 1895), p. 30.
18. Ibid., pp. 1, 29.
19. Ibid., p. 30.
20. See Chapter 5.
21. Stewart, *Time of the Gypsies*, pp. 27–8; Fonseca, *Bury me Standing*, p. 243.
22. See, generally, Fraser, *The Gypsies*, Chapter 1; Crowe, *History of the Gypsies*, p. xi.
23. Fraser, *The Gypsies*, Chapters 2–3.
24. Crowe, *History of the Gypsies*, pp. 69–70, 107.
25. Fraser, *The Gypsies*, Chapter 6.
26. In *A History of the Jews* (London: Phoenix, 1995) Paul Johnson recounts that in 1817, in Ferrara:

> the little daughter of Angelo Ancona was forcibly taken away from her parents by armed men employed by the archbishop's tribunal, on the grounds that five years before, aged two months, she had been privately baptized by her nurse, later dismissed for dishonesty. The case led to a reign of terror in the Ferrara ghetto. (p. 304)

27. See, generally, Crowe, *History of the Gypsies*, pp. 107–20. See, also, V. Achim, *Tiganii în istoria Romănei* (Bucharest: Editura Enciclopedica, 1998), Chapters 2, 3.
28. Quoted Crowe, *History of the Gypsies*, pp. 114–15.
29. Ibid., pp. 121–2.
30. Okely, *The Traveller-Gypsies*, pp. 167–8, 207–9; Stewart, *Time of the Gypsies*, pp. 207–11; Fraser, *The Gypsies*, p. 245.
31. Stewart, *Time of the Gypsies*, p. 224.
32. Rózsi's recollections of the War and of the occupation of her village by Soviet troops are discussed in Chapter 3.
33. For further consideration of the importance of notions of 'pollution' or 'shame' in Romani culture(s), see Chapter 7.

3 THE DEVOURING

1. Florin's knowledge of what happened at Birkenau is accurate enough. Birkenau, a German corruption of the Polish 'Brzezinka', was the site of the second and larger

Auschwitz camp constructed by the Nazis in World War II. Auschwitz-Birkenau was equipped with four gas chambers and crematoria. Tens of thousands of Roma perished at Auschwitz and at other camps. See, generally, on Auschwitz, O. Friedrich, *The Kingdom of Auschwitz* (London: Penguin Books, 1996).

2. In *The Time of the Gypsies* (Boulder, Colorado: Westview Press, 1997) Michael Stewart records that:

> At almost any time of night or day, unless one saw a towel hung over the door as a sign that someone was washing, one might enter a house without any preparatory greeting or warning. Rarely did I see a Gypsy make another feel that an unexpected visit fell at an inconvenient time. (p. 67)

3. See, generally, on the wartime ghetto in Cluj, R. Braham, *The Politcs of Genocide* (New York: Columbia University Press, 1981), Vol. I, pp. 571–73.

4. The Hungarian Second Army evacuated Cluj and the surrounding area in the second week of October 1944, as Soviet forces approached. Cluj was thus spared the vicious street fighting which later enveloped Budapest. See, for example, P. Gosztonyi, *A Magyar Honvédség a Második Világháborúban* (Budapest: Európa Könyvkiadó, 1995), pp. 174, 208.

5. Of the available literature on the Roma Holocaust see, in particular, G. Lewy, *The Nazi Persecution of the Gypsies* (Oxford: Oxford University Press, 2000). See, also, D. Kenrick, and G. Puxon, *Gypsies under the Swastika* (Hertfordshire: University of Hertfordshire Press, 2nd ed., 1995). The first edition of Kenrick and Puxon's book, under the title *The Destiny of Europe's Gypsies*, was published in 1972. See, also, K. Fings, H. Heuss and F. Sparing (eds), *From 'Race Science' to the Camps* (Hertfordshire: University of Hertfordshire Press, 1997); D. Kenrick (ed.), *In the Shadow of the Swastika* (Hertfordshire: University of Hertfordshire Press, 1999); L. Karsai, *A cigánykérdés Magyarországon 1919–1945* (Budapest: Cserépfalvi Kiadás, 1992).

6. Stewart, *Time of the Gypsies*, p. 165.

7. G. Havas, *Gazdálkodó Cigányok* (Budapest: Autonómia Alapítvány, 2001), p. 16.

8. The American historian Lucy Dawidowicz famously invoked the concept of the Nazis' *war* against the Jews. See L. Dawidowicz, *The War against the Jews 1933–45* (London: Penguin Books, 10th Anniversary ed., 1990). As Michael Marrus has pointed out, the term 'war', although evocative, is only partially accurate. The Jews, who lacked armaments and had no military organisations of their own, never had the means to prosecute a war against the Nazis or the Germans. M. Marrus, *The Holocaust in History* (Toronto: Key Porter Books, 2nd ed., 2000), p. 6.

9. For the testimonies of Roma who endured severe persecution in various parts of Hungary during the War because of their ethnicity, particularly after October 1944 when the Nazi-style Hungarian Arrow Cross party seized power, see G. Bernáth, *Porrajmos* (Budapest: Roma Sajtó Központ, 2000).

10. Lewy, *Nazi Persecution of the Gypsies*, p. 38.

11. Ibid., p. 43.

12. Professor Lewy places considerable emphasis on the fact that 'pure' Jews were considered by the Nazis to represent much more of a threat to Germans than persons with mixed Jewish and Gentile ancestry, whereas 'pure' Gypsies were viewed more favourably than *Zigeunermischlinge*, that is Gypsies of mixed ancestry. See Lewy, *Nazi Persecution of the Gypsies*, p. 55. While true, it is doubtful whether this quirk of Nazi ideology is of particular importance. Even 'pure' Gypsies were seen as

sufficiently corrupting to require sexual segregation from Germans, while at least 90 per cent of all Gypsies in Germany were thought to be *Mischlinge* and thus deemed particularly dangerous. Ibid., p. 49.

13. I. Kershaw, *Hitler, 1889–1936* (London: Penguin Books, 1999), p. 541.

14. See, generally, D. Crowe, *A History of the Gypsies of Eastern Europe and Russia* (New York: St. Martin's Griffin, 1996), pp. 88–91. See, also, Karsai, *A cigánykérdés Magyarországon*, especially Chapters 3, 5, 6, 7.

15. See, variously, Karsai, *A cigánykérdés Magyarországon*, p. 144; Crowe, *History of the Gypsies*, p. 91.

16. See, for example, D. Cesarani, 'Introduction' in D. Cesarani (ed.), *Genocide and Rescue* (Oxford: Berg, 1997), p. 1 at p. 5.

17. Lewy, *Nazi Persecution of the Gypsies*, pp. 150–1. For a somewhat understated account, by a Czech historian, see C. Necas, 'Bohemia and Moravia – two internment camps for the Gypsies in the Czech lands' in Kenrick (ed.), *In the Shadow of the Swastika*, p. 149, at pp. 149–70. See, also, C. Necas, *The Holocaust of Czech Roma* (Prague: Prostor, 1999, S. Pellar trs.), especially at pp. 49–151.

18. See, for example, Crowe, *History of the Gypsies*, pp. 49–50. See, also, Kenrick and Puxon, *Gypsies under the Swastika*, pp. 55–9; A. Fraser, *The Gypsies* (Oxford: Blackwell, 2nd ed., 1995), p. 266.

19. Fraser, *The Gypsies*, p. 267. See, generally, on the Jasenovac camp, M. Glenny, *The Balkans 1804–1999* (London: Granta Books, 2000), p. 501; Kenrick and Puxon, *Gypsies under the Swastika*, at pp. 115–94.

20. Crowe, *History of the Gypsies*, pp. 219–20. See, generally, on the treatment of Gypsies in wartime Croatia, which included much of present-day Bosnia, Kenrick and Puxon, *Gypsies under the Swastika*, at pp. 112–20.

21. See, generally, on the deportation of Romanian Gypsies to Transnistria during World War II, M. Kelso, 'Gypsy deportations from Romania to Transnistria 1942–44' in Kenrick (ed.), *In the Shadow of the Swastika*, p. 95, at pp. 95–130. See, also, R. Ioanid, *The Holocaust in Romania* (Chicago: Ivan R Dee, 2000), Chapter 7; Crowe, *History of the Gypsies*, pp. 133–5; C. Iancu, *La Shoah en Roumanie* (Montpellier: Université Paul-Valéry, 1998), pp. 25–7. The number of Gypsy deportees is taken from Ioanid, at p. 235. The other sources tend to give slightly higher figures.

22. Quoted in Kelso, 'Gypsy deportations from Romania', p. 114.

23. Ibid., p. 130. For a significantly higher estimate of Romani fatalities in Transnistria during World War II see I. Fonseca, *Bury me Standing* (Vintage: London, 1996), p. 243.

24. On the conflation of Jews and Communists in Nazi thinking see, for example, Dawidowicz, *The War against the Jews*, pp. 163–5.

25. R. Overy, *Russia's War* (London: Penguin Books, 1999), p. 140. See, also, Lewy, *Nazi Persecution of the Gypsies*, pp. 117–22; Kenrick and Puxon, *Gypsies under the Swastika*, pp. 90–8.

26. Lewy, *Nazi Persecution of the Gypsies*, p. 122.

27. Fraser, *The Gypsies*, p. 266. See, also, Kenrick and Puxon, *Gypsies under the Swastika*, at pp. 61–2, who give slightly different figures.

28. M. Gilbert, *The Holocaust* (London: Fontana Paperbacks, 1987), p. 239.

29. Lewy, *Nazi Persecution of the Gypsies*, at p. 221.

30. See, generally, ibid., pp. 113–15.

31. Ibid., pp. 140–9.

32. Ibid., p. 148.

33. Ibid., pp. 158–62. See, also, K. Fings, 'Romanies and Sinti in the concentration camps' in Fings, Heuss and Sparing (eds), *From 'Race Science' to the Camps*, p. 71, at pp. 104–6.

34. Gilbert, *Holocaust*, p. 807. See, also, M. Gilbert (ed.), *The Dent Atlas of the Holocaust* (London: J M Dent, 2nd ed., 1993), p. 232, Map 301.

35. Reliable statistics of Romani fatalities during the War are not available. However, it has been estimated that the number of Roma who perished in the Nazi death camps, or who were murdered elsewhere during World War II, may have been of the order of 200,000 to 500,000. See, for example, M. Brearley, *The Roma/Gypsies of Europe: A Persecuted People* (London: Institute for Jewish Policy Research, 1996), p. 9. Donald Kenrick and Grattan Puxon, authors of one of the best-known texts on the Roma Holocaust, conclude that around 200,000 Gypsies were deliberately killed by the Nazis and their allies. Kenrick and Puxon, *Gypsies under the Swastika*, p. 150.

36. See, in particular, Lewy, *Nazi Persecution of the Gypsies*, pp. 221–4. For similar, though somewhat more muted, views see, for example, Marrus, *Holocaust in History*, p. 24. Unlike Lewy, Marrus does not focus on the term 'genocide' but rather identifies an important distinction between the parallel persecution of Jews and Gypsies in the fact that the Nazis intended to kill *all* Jews without exception, whereas policies regarding the Roma were less draconian. Relying on the same distinction, a leading Holocaust scholar, Yehuda Bauer, suggests in a recent book that the treatment of the Roma during the War, though satisfying the legal test of 'genocide', should be distinguished from the concept of a 'Holocaust' as the Nazis had no demonstrable intention of killing every single Gypsy, in contrast to their exterminationist policies towards the Jews. See Y. Bauer, *Rethinking the Holocaust* (New Haven: Yale University Press, 2001), p. 66.

37. Professor Lewy argues persuasively that Gypsies, who were widely perceived in German society as work-shy and as inclined to criminality, were initially characterised by the Nazis as a social problem. Gradually, however, the Nazis began to formulate racial theories about the Gypsies, classifying them as alien and inferior. See Lewy, *Nazi Persecution of the Gypsies*, pp.15–16.

38. The quotation, which is from the Preamble of the 1935 Law, is reproduced in S. Friedländer, *Nazi Germany and the Jews*, Vol. 1 (London: Phoenix, 1998), p. 142.

39. The additional restrictions on sexual relations were effected by means of a decree of 14 November 1935, which extended the scope of the 1935 Law, and a subsequent circular from the German Ministry of the Interior which explicitly refers to Gypsies. See Friedländer, *Nazi Germany and the Jews*, p. 153.

40. Quoted in Lewy, *Nazi Persecution of the Gypsies*, p. 97.

41. Ibid., pp. 154–8.

42. Ibid., at pp. 187–93.

43. Ibid., p. 190.

44. The legal construction of 'genocide' and of 'complicity in genocide' is far from straightforward. Following the establishment of the International Criminal Tribunals for the former Yugoslavia and Rwanda, both of which have considered allegations of genocide and of complicity in genocide, there is now an expanding jurisprudence on these concepts. See, generally, S. Ratner and J. Abrams *Accountability for Human Rights Atrocities in International Law* (Oxford: Oxford University Press, 2nd ed., 2001), Chapter 2.

45. My emphasis. For the text of the Genocide Convention see, for instance, <http://www.1.wmn.edu/hamanrts/instree/x1cppcg.htm> (accessed 18 November 2003).

46. For an analysis of the Nuremberg Tribunal's consideration of the persecution of the Roma see M. Rooker, *The International Supervision of Protection of Romany People in Europe* (Nijmegen: Nijmegen University Press, 2002), pp. 38–46. Dr Rooker concludes that, although the 'Romany people were not explicitly named in the judgment', the Nuremberg Tribunal implicitly recognised that the treatment of the Roma amounted to 'Crimes against Humanity' and 'War Crimes'. Ibid., pp. 45–6. For a general analysis of the concepts of Crimes Against Humanity and War Crimes see, for instance, Ratner and Abrams, *Accountability for Human Rights Atrocities in International Law*, chapters 3, 4.

47. The term 'forgotten Holocaust' was first used in a French text. See C. Bernadac, *L'Holocauste oublié* (Paris: Éditions France Empire, 1979).

48. Fonseca, *Bury me Standing*, p. 243.

49. See Chapter 1, note 9.

50. See, generally, on the significance of diasporas in the modern world, R. Cohen, *Global Diasporas* (London: UCL Press, 1997).

51. For example, and without wishing to pander to anti-Semitic stereotypes, there are a number of Jewish organisations, both national and international, which aim to promote Jewish interests of various kinds. The World Jewish Congress is, perhaps, the best known international organisation while, in Britain, the Board of Deputies of British Jews and the Institute for Jewish Policy Research are examples of national organisations.

52. The omnipresent issue of Roma poverty is considered in various chapters of this book, including Chapter 1, Chapter 4 and Chapter 6.

53. Several examples could be given of Israeli aid to beleaguered Jewish communities around the world. In comparatively recent times the rescue of the Falashas, the Jews of Ethiopia, several thousand of whom were spirited to Israel in 1984 after years of hardship and persecution, deserves particular mention. See, for example, H. Sachar, *A History of Israel*, Vol. 2 (Oxford: Oxford University Press, 1987), pp. 108–9; M. Gilbert, *Israel a History* (London: Doubleday, 1998), pp. 497–8.

54. India helped to finance the First World Romany Congress, convened in London in 1971. Subsequently, Indian governments have offered limited diplomatic and material support to the Roma. See, for example, I. Hancock, 'The struggle for the control of identity', originally published in *Transitions*, Vol. 4, No. 4 (September 1997), now available at <http://www.geocities.com/paris/5121/identity.htm> (accessed 29 July 2003).

55. On Gypsies' general lack of interest in their history see, for instance, M. Stewart, *The Time of the Gypsies*, p. 28. See, also, Fonseca, *Bury Me Standing*, p. 243.

56. The relative lack of concern with the War years shown by the elderly Roma I interviewed may also have been due to the fact that my field work was carried out in parts of Romania and Hungary where the Gypsies had been saved from the worst forms of persecution by the timely arrival of Soviet troops. However, the Soviet troops often behaved with conspicuous brutality themselves, raping thousands of women in the occupied states, including Gypsies. Yet even memories of this terrifying episode were suppressed until I began to question my elderly Romani interviewees.

4 MAYBE TOMORROW THERE WON'T EVEN BE BREAD

1. The information about András Balogh Balázs in this chapter, as well as the statements attributed to him, are drawn from two lengthy interviews. The first of these was carried out by Péter Szuhay, at András' home in the town of Salgótarján. The interview was filmed, with a view to the preparation of a documentary about András' life. I am grateful to Péter Szuhay and to Edit Kőszegi for giving me the opportunity to see the rushes in their entirety several times, thus enabling me to compile detailed notes. In December 2001, I visited András and his wife, Jolán Oláh, at their apartment in Salgótarján. Over the course of several hours, I recorded a lengthy interview with them about their lives.

2. See, generally, on the Austro-Hungarian monarchy during the latter part of the nineteenth century and on the growing discontent of the national minorities, including the Slovaks, M. Molnár, *A Concise History of Hungary* (Cambridge: Cambridge University Press, 2001), pp. 208–40. See, also, R. Okey, *The Habsburg Monarchy c. 1765–1918* (Basingstoke: Macmillan, 2001), especially at pp. 325–30.

3. See, for example, J. Rothschild, *East Central Europe between the Two World Wars* (Seattle: University of Washington Press, rev. ed. 1977), p. 179.

4. On the Roma Holocaust, or Porajmos, see Chapter 3.

5. Rózsi, in talking about her family's experiences during the War, describes this type of bread as 'cigány bokoli'. See Chapter 3. The bread is flat and round, resembling the nan bread popular in northern India, or the unleavened breads that are consumed in much of the Near and Middle East. Rózsi still bakes *bokoli* on special occasions and I have tasted it for myself.

6. On contrasting Roma and Gadje attitudes to cleanliness and hygiene, particularly as observed amongst English Gypsies, see, for example, J. Okely, *The Traveller-Gypsies* (Cambridge: Cambridge University Press, 1983), pp. 78–87.

7. On the loss of employment opportunities for Eastern Europe's Roma in the transition from Communism see, for example, Z. Barany, *The East European Gypsies* (Cambridge: Cambridge University Press, 2002), pp. 172–6.

8. For an excellent overview of Communist policies towards the Roma in Central and Eastern Europe see Barany, *East European Gypsies*, Chapter 4. Barany's account places due emphasis on the increasingly significant differences that emerged within the region in terms of national policies towards the Roma. See, also, A. Fraser, *The Gypsies* (Oxford: Blackwell, 2nd ed., 1995), pp. 274–82; M. Stewart, *The Time of the Gypsies* (Boulder: Westview Press, 1997), Chapter 6.

9. For the text of the 1961 Party decision (in Hungarian) see, for example, B. Mezey (ed.), *A magyarországi cigánykérdés dokumentumokban 1422–1985* (Budapest: Kossuth Könyvkiadó, 1986), p. 240.

10. For an excellent analysis of the 1961 decision see Sághy, E. 'A magyarországi cigányság története a Holocausttól az 1961-es Párthatározatig – A Politika tükrében' (unpublished dissertation submitted in the Department of Modern Hungarian History, Eötvös Loránd University, Budapest, Hungary, 1996), especially at pp. 56–61.

11. Ibid., p. 58.

12. Quoted in B. Mezey, (ed.), *A magyarországi cigánykérdés dokumentumokban*, p. 241. My translation.

13. Barany, *East European Gypsies*, pp. 117–19.

14. Ibid., p. 117.

15. Ibid., pp. 116, 121–2.

16. Ibid., pp. 119–20.

17. For example, Michael Stewart has denounced 'the creation of phantasmagorical "socialist" jobs for the Gypsies which disappeared as soon as consumers had any choice over what they purchased'. See M. Stewart, 'Communist Roma policy 1945–89 as seen through the Hungarian case' in W. Guy (ed.), *Between Past and Future: The Roma of Central and Eastern Europe* (Hertfordshire: University of Hertfordshire Press, 2001), p. 71, at p. 87.

18. See, generally, Stewart, *The Time of the Gypsies*, Chapter 2.

19. Ibid., Chapter 6.

20. See D. Crowe, *A History of the Gypsies of Eastern Europe and Russia* (New York: St. Martin's Griffin, 1996), p. 84.

21. See, for example, P. Szuhay, *A magyarországi cigányság kultúrája: etnikus kultúra vagy a szegénység kultúrája* (Panórama: Budapest, 1999), pp. 18–19.

22. Stewart, *The Time of the Gypsies*, pp. 107–8.

23. Molnár, *Concise History of Hungary*, p. 332.

24. I. Berend, *Central and Eastern Europe 1944–1993* (Cambridge: Cambridge University Press, 1996), p. 208.

25. See, generally, Barany, *East European Gypsies*, Chapter 4.

26. See, generally, Stewart, 'Communist Roma policy 1945–89 as seen through the Hungarian case', at pp. 71–92.

27. See, generally, J. Kurczewski, *The Resurrection of Rights in Poland* (Oxford: Oxford University Press, 1993).

28. For a more detailed examination of the Roma and their contribution to music, particularly in Central and Eastern Europe, see Chapter 5.

29. See, for example, the series of Country Reports issued by the Budapest-based European Roma Rights Center. See, in particular, Reports nos. 2, 3, 8, 10 on Romania, Slovakia, The Czech Republic and Romania, respectively. In the face of overwhelming evidence, some politicians and scholars continue to resist the view that anti-Roma sentiment has increased in the transition from Communism.

5   THE CZARDAS

1. István Kemény is a little older than Miklós Rácz. He returned to live in Hungary in 1990, after a long exile in Paris. His book in which Miklós Rácz is listed (under a different name), was published in Hungarian: I. Kemény, (ed.), *A Magyarországi Romák* (Budapest: Press Publica Kiadó, 2000). As indicated above, 'Miklós Rácz' is not the real name of the classical musician whom I interviewed in Cluj. To protect his anonymity, I have changed both his name and his instrument. Although the news will surely displease him, I later discovered that another book about the Roma, which had been published in Budapest in 1994, gives details of Professor Rácz and even includes a photograph of him.

2. On the emergence of a Romani written literature in Hungary see, for example, Kemény (ed.), *A Magyarországi Romák*, pp. 37–41.

3. See, for example, S. Broughton, M. Ellingham and R. Trillo (eds), *World Music*, Vol. 1 (London: The Rough Guides, 1999), p. 152. See, also, Kemény (ed.), *A Magyarországi Romák*, p. 41.

4. Broughton, Ellingham and Trillo (eds), *World Music*, pp. 160–1.

5. R. Dullea, 'The role of Romani music in Hungarian nationalism' in *Central European Review*, Vol. 3, No. 13 (2 April 2001), at <http://www.ce-review.org/archiveindex.html> (accessed 7 April 2001).

6. G. Csemer, *Habiszti* (Budapest: privately published by the author, 1994), p. 304.

7. See, generally, T. Gallagher, *Romania after Ceauşescu* (Edinburgh: Edinburgh University Press, 1995), pp. 62–5. See, also, A. Süle, 'Románia Politikatörténete 1944–1990', in G. Hunya et al. (eds), *Románia 1944–1990* (Budapest: Atlantisz, 1990), p. 199, at pp. 251–8.

8. Broughton, Ellingham and Trillo (eds), *World Music*, pp. 161–5.

9. Ibid., pp. 239–41.

10. Interview recorded on 10 April 2003 (on file with the author).

11. See, for example, D. Goldstein, 'Re-imagining the Jew in Hungary: The reconstruction of ethnicity through political affiliation', in H.-R. Wicker (ed.), *Rethinking Nationalism and Ethnicity* (Oxford: Berg, 1997), p. 193, at p. 206.

12. On nationalism in the post-Communist states of Central and Eastern Europe see, for example, C. Giordano, 'Affiliation, exclusion and the national state: "ethnic discourses" and minorities in East Central Europe' in Wicker (ed.), *Rethinking Nationalism and Ethnicity*, pp. 175–92; R. Wistrich, 'Nationalism reborn', in Michael Hughey (ed.), *New Tribalisms* (Basingstoke, Hampshire: Macmillan Press Ltd., 1998), pp. 356–62; E. Hobsbawm, *Nations and Nationalism since 1780* (Cambridge: Cambridge University Press, 2nd ed. 1992), Chapter 6; E. Harris, *Nationalism and Democratisation* (Aldershot: Ashgate, 2002). The passage of Hungary's Status Law, in June 2001, provides a further example of the region's frequently nationalistic mindset. The Law extends preferential treatment in matters of work, education and health care to ethnic Hungarians in the post-Communist states bordering Hungary. See, for example, 'Hungary's "Status Law" irks neighbours', BBC News, 19 June 2001, available at <http://news.bbc.co.uk/1/hi/world/monitoring/media_reports/1397385.stm> (accessed 5 August 2003).

13. The Budapest-based viola player Marta Konrád expressed the view to me that 'music is very democratic'. Interview recorded on 17 September 2002 (on file with the author).

14. A. Diósi, *Szemtől szemben a magyarországi cigánysággal* (Budapest: Pont Kiadó, 2002), p. 125.

15. The CD was released in 2002 by Fréa Records in the Netherlands (MWCD 4039). For further details see <www.musicwords.nl>.

16. See, generally, A. Cartwright, *The Return of the Peasant* (Aldershot: Dartmouth, 2001).

17. For a CD offering an excellent introduction to the astonishing variety of Romani musicians and music available in Central and Eastern Europe, Turkey and elsewhere see *From an Early Age: The Incredible Music of the Gypsies*, (Manteca World Music, 2000, MANTCD009).

18. The band has recorded numerous CDs. These include *L'Orient est Rouge* (Cramworld, 1997, LC8689).

19. Romani unemployment, following the end of Communist rule, is discussed in various chapters of this book including Chapter 1, Chapter 4 and Chapter 6. See, also, Z. Barany, *The East European Gypsies* (Cambridge: Cambridge University Press, 2002), pp. 172–6.

20. See, for example, I. Pogány, 'Accommodating an emergent national identity: The Roma of Central and Eastern Europe', in S. Tierney (ed.), *Accommodating National Identity* (The Hague: Kluwer Law International, 2000), pp. 177–82.

21. A. Fraser, *The Gypsies* (Oxford: Blackwell, 2nd ed., 1995), pp. 8–9.

22. See, generally, M. Beissinger, 'Occupation and ethnicity: Constructing identity among professional Romani (Gypsy) musicians in Romania' in *Slavic Review*, Vol. 60, Issue 1, Spring 2001, p. 24, at p. 25.

23. For a brief discussion of the Pata Rât settlement in Cluj, Romania see Chapter 1, above.

24. See, generally, Barany, *East European Gypsies*, Chapter 5. See, also, above, Chapter 1.

25. Barany, *East European Gypsies*, p. 119.

26. English-language translations of the constitutions of the post-Communist states are available at <http://www.findlaw.com/12international/countries/> (accessed 5 August 2003).

27. For the text of the 1991 Romanian Constitution see <http://wiretap.area.com/ftp.items/Gov/World/romania.con> (accessed 5 August 2003).

28. For the text of the revised Hungarian Constitution see <http://wiretap.area.com/ftp.items/Gov/World/hungary.con> (accessed 5 August 2003).

29. For the texts of the European Convention on Human Rights and Fundamental Freedoms see <http://conventions.coe.int/treaty/en/Treaties/Word/005.doc> (accessed 5 August 2003). For the text of the Framework Convention see <http://conventions.coe.int/treaty/en/Treaties/Word/157.doc> (accessed 5 August 2003).

30. The texts of these and other human rights treaties are available from the University of Minnesota Human Rights Library at <http://www1.umn.edu/humanrts/instree/ainstls1.htm> (accessed 6 August 2003).

31. OSCE texts, including the Charter of Paris, are available at <http://www.osce.org/docs/> (accessed 6 August 2003).

32. In 1990, when the Charter of Paris was adopted, the OSCE was known as the CSCE, that is the Conference on Security and Cooperation in Europe. For the text of the Charter of Paris for a New Europe see <http://www.osce.org/docs/english/1990-1999/summits/paris90e.htm> (accessed 6 August 2003).

33. See, also, Recommendation 1203 of the Parliamentary Assembly of the Council of Europe, adopted in February 1993. Paragraph 3 of the Recommendation states that: 'As a non-territorial minority Gypsies greatly contribute to the cultural diversity of Europe. In different parts of Europe they contribute in different ways, be it by languages and music, or by their trades and crafts.' See <http://assembly.coe.int/Main.asp?link=http%3A%2F%2Fassembly.coe.int%2FDocuments%2FAdoptedText%2Fta93%2FEREC1203.htm> (accessed 6 August 2003).

34. On nationalism in Central and Eastern Europe see the sources cited supra, n. 12.

35. For the text of the Slovak Constitution see, for example, <http://www.slovakia.org/sk-constitution.htm> (accessed 18 November 2003).

36. On the need to avoid an overly simplistic view of the strength of ethnic nationalism and of chronic inter-ethnic tensions in the region see, for example, Harris, *Nationalism and Democratisation*, pp. 18–21.

37. Post-Communist states seeking admission to the Council of Europe were required to become parties to various human rights instruments including the European Convention on Human Rights and, after 1995, the Framework Convention for the Protection of National Minorities. These expectations were set out in various

'opinions' adopted by the Parliamentary Assembly of the Council of Europe. See, for example, Opinion No. 195 (1996) on Croatia's request for membership of the Council of Europe. See <http://assembly.coe.int/Main.asp?link=http%3A%2F%2 Fassembly.coe.int%2FDocuments%2FAdoptedText%2Fta96%2FEOPI195.htm> (accessed 6 August 2003). In 1993, the EU's Heads of State and Government drew up the 'Copenhagen criteria' which sets out a range of criteria which must be met by states seeking admission to the EU. The criteria include, 'stability of institutions guaranteeing democracy, the rule of law, human rights and respect for and protection of minorities'. See, generally, *EU Support for Roma Communities in Central and Eastern Europe* (May 2002), sec. 2.2, at <http://europa.eu.int/comm/enlargement/ docs/pdf/brochure_roma_may2002.pdf> (accessed 6 August 2003).

38.   *Szabadság*, 28 May 2002, p. 3 (my translation).

39.   See, for example, J. Waldron, 'Minority cultures and the cosmopolitan alternative' in *University of Michigan Journal of Law Reform*, Vol. 25, 1992, p.751.

40.   All of these rights may be found, for example, in the Council of Europe's Framework Convention for the Protection of National Minorities.

41.   In addition, Article 12(1) of the Framework Convention states: 'The Parties shall, where appropriate, take measures in the fields of education and research to foster knowledge of the culture, history, language and religion of their national minorities and of the majority.'

6   NOMADS

1.   On the process of industrialisation that was a feature common to all of all the Communist states of Central and Eastern Europe see, for example, I. Berend, *Central and Eastern Europe 1944–1993* (Cambridge: Cambridge University Press, 1996), at pp. 190–200.

2.   Ibid., p. 191.

3.   Ibid., p. 169.

4.   See, generally, G. Swain, and N. Swain, *Eastern Europe since 1945* (London: Macmillan, 1993), pp. 115–18.

5.   S.45(1), The Constitution of the Hungarian Peoples' Republic, 1949:XX tv.

6.   In principle, local authorities in Romania provide a small monthly sum to people who have no other means of support. However, local authorities often lack the financial resources to pay this money to all those who may be eligible. The level of social assistance is, in any event, extremely modest and is not enough to live on. Information supplied by a Legal Counsellor at the Department Fortelor de Munka, Cluj, Romania, April 2001.

7.   See, generally, Z. Barany, *The East European Gypsies* (Cambridge: Cambridge University Press, 2002), pp. 180–3, who comments that:

> The phenomenon of Romani crime ought to be viewed in its proper context. The majority of Gypsies have no regular source of earned income, and they are impoverished and ostracized by the majority population. Quite simply, many Roma have nothing to lose especially because incarceration in many cases signifies an improvement in their situation. Considering that their conditions include all the major socio-economic catalysts of criminal behavior in an acute form, one may wonder why Romani crime rates are not higher. (p. 183)

For studies of Romani criminality by a Hungarian criminologist see S. Póczik, *Cigányok és Idegenek* (Miskolc: Felsőmagyarország Kiadó, 1999), Part 2.

8. In *The Gypsies* (Oxford: Blackwell, 2nd ed., 1995) Sir Angus Fraser refers to Gypsies', 'underlying propensity for working on their own account, and a generalist repertoire which allows a degree of flexibility suited to their social structure and their desire for independence in organizing their lives' (pp. 305–6). However, it should be borne in mind that Lajós and Eszti (like increasing numbers of Roma in the region) no longer had any real 'social structure' to fall back on. They had limited contact with relatives and were largely reliant on themselves and on occasional assistance from state agencies and charities.

9. See, for instance, Péter Szuhay, 'Foglalkozási és megélhetési stratégiák a magyarországi cigányok körében' in F. Glatz (ed.), *A cigányok Magyarországon* (Budapest: Magyar Tudományos Akadémia, 1999), p. 139.

10. See Sections 45(1), 59, The Constitution of the Hungarian Peoples' Republic, 1949: XX tv.

11. Following an agreement with the West German government, concluded in 1978, Romania received 10,000 Deutschmarks for every ethnic German who left for Germany. See, generally, T. Gallagher, *Romania after Ceauşescu* (Edinburgh: Edinburgh University Press, 1995), p. 83.

12. The Communist constitutions guaranteed a range of social and economic rights to citizens. For example, Hungary's Constitution, as amended in 1972, guaranteed various rights including the 'right to the protection of health', and material support in the event of 'old age, illness and inability to work'. See Sections 57(1), 58(1), 1972:I tv.

13. For the text of the Charter of Paris for a New Europe, which was adopted under the auspices of the then Conference on Security and Co-operation in Europe (CSCE) see <http://www.osce.org/docs/english/1990-1999/summits/paris90e.htm> (accessed 11 August 2003).

14. My emphasis.

15. Apart from Hungary, which radically amended its Communist-era Constitution, every post-Communist state has adopted a new constitution.

16. For the text of the 1991 Romanian Constitution see <http://wiretap.area.com/ftp. items/Gov/World/romania.con> (accessed 5 August 2003).

17. My emphasis.

18. R. Weber, 'Constitutionalism as a vehicle for democratic consolidation in Romania' in J. Zielonka, (ed.), *Democratic Consolidation in Eastern Europe* (Oxford: Oxford University Press, 2001), Vol. 1, p. 212, at p. 239.

19. See, generally, P. Kopecký, 'The Czech Republic: From the burden of the old federal constitution to the constitutional horse trading among political parties' in Zielonka, *Democratic Consolidation in Eastern Europe*, Vol. 1, p. 319, at pp. 335, 342.

20. 43/1995. (VI. 30.) AB határozat, in *Az Alkotmánybíróság Határozatai* [1995], p. 188, at pp. 196–97.

21. Ibid., p. 198.

22. W. Sadurski, 'Conclusions: On the relevance of institutions and the centrality of constitutions in post-communist transitions' in Zielonka (ed.), *Democratic Consolidation in Eastern Europe*, Vol. 1, p. 455, at p. 466.

23. See U. Baxi. *The Future of Human Rights* (New Delhi: Oxford University Press, 2002), p. 132.

24. For an influential and widely cited critique of rights see C. Douzinas, *The End of Human Rights* (Oxford: Hart Publishing, 2000).

25. However, this should not blind us to the fact that, though challenging existing inequities, such human rights movements and ideologies were a product of their historical, economic and cultural context. Thus, they often failed to extend the scope of human rights to women, non-European peoples, and others. See, generally, Baxi, *The Future of Human Rights*, pp. 28–30.

26. These criticisms of rights have been set out in an elegant essay by Adam Tomkins. See A. Tomkins, 'Introduction: On being sceptical about human rights' in T. Campbell, K.D. Ewing and A. Tomkins (eds), *Sceptical Essays on Human Rights* (Oxford: Oxford University Press, 2001), p. 1.

27. Ibid., p. 9.

28. Ibid., p. 10.

29. Ibid., pp. 9–10.

30. B. De Sousa Santos, *Toward a New Legal Common Sense* (London: Butterworths, 2nd ed., 2002), pp. 280–3.

31. On the historical importance of factors including religion, ethnicity and class in Central and Eastern Europe see, generally, G. Schöpflin, *Politics in Eastern Europe 1945–1992* (Oxford: Blackwell, 1993). On the Nazi era, when ethnicity could be a matter of life or death in much of Europe, including Central and Eastern Europe, see above, Chapter 3.

7 ANIKÓ

1. On Hungarian Roma and illiteracy see, for example, chapters 2 and 4. On attitudes towards literacy amongst British Gypsies see J. Okely, *The Traveller-Gypsies* (Cambridge: Cambridge University Press, 1983), pp. 160–2.

2. At the time of writing, the documentary remains unfinished due to budgetary and other factors.

3. See, in particular, Chapter 4.

4. As noted in Chapter 1, in Hungary, for example, 73–74 per cent of Roma aged between twenty and twenty-nine were found to be almost totally illiterate in 1971. Chapter 1, Note 9.

5. Stalin had been responsible for millions of deaths amongst his fellow countrymen, whether through starvation, forced labour in the gulags, incompetent or callous military decisions during World War II, or almost random, terroristic executions. For a recent study of the Soviet Gulag system see A. Applebaum, *Gulag: A History of the Soviet Concentration Camps* (London: Allen Lane, 2003). On the deliberate starvation of millions of peasants under Stalin see R. Conquest, *The Harvest of Sorrow* (London: Pimlico, 2002). See, also, R. Conquest, *The Great Terror* (London: Pimlico, 1992).

6. P. Szuhay, *A magyarországi cigányság kultúrája: etnikus kultúra vagy a szegénység kultúrája* (Panórama: Budapest, 1999), p. 77. In large cities, where many Gypsies have settled, there is often greater freedom in the choice of marriage and life partners than in rural areas where the Roma have generally preserved a more traditional way of life. See M. Neményi, 'Biológia vagy kultúra? Termékenységgel kapcsolatos szerepviselkedések a roma nők körében' in Glatz (ed.), *A cigányok Magyarországon*, p. 103, at p. 117.

7. For a rather different experience of Vlach Romani attitudes towards Gadje who have adopted a Romani lifestyle, learnt the Romani language and integrated with a Romani community see M. Stewart, *The Time of the Gypsies* (Boulder: Westview Press, 1997), pp. 58–60. Stewart states that descent was not regarded as an essential component of Romani identity:

    > the Rom had no trouble admitting that it was possible to be born a *gažo* and become a Rom. Among the Rom of Harangos and nearby villages, there were several such people…I never heard it suggested that because of their non-Gypsy ancestry, these people were somehow less Rom than anyone else. Their children were also fully accepted as Gypsies…when I asked Gypsies how one might become a Rom, the answer, as often as not, was 'if you learn to speak Romany'. (p. 59)

    He concludes that, 'the Rom idea of reproduction was not so much rooted in an ideology of descent and inheritance of character as in an ideology of nurture and shared social activity'. (Ibid).

8. On Romani perceptions of the rampant, 'shameless' sexuality of Gadje women see, for example, Stewart, *Time of the Gypsies*, pp. 210–13.

9. Ibid., pp. 211–14. Michael Stewart suggests that even attending evening classes or driving lessons could pose a problem for teenage Vlach Romani girls, potentially threatening their marriage prospects. Consequently, the girls were accompanied on these trips by an older female relative (Ibid., p. 212). I have observed much the same phenomenon amongst young Catalan Romani women in Perpignan, France. Groups of teenage girls taking an evening stroll through the town are invariably accompanied by a soberly dressed Romani matron. However, it is difficult to generalise. As recounted in Chapter 2, I was told a singularly crude tale by an elderly Vlach Romani woman, whom I knew comparatively well, with her daughter in attendance. And it was the daughter, a young woman in her twenties, who laughingly asked me what the English word is for a woman's private parts. Whether such ribald banter is only acceptable with Gadje (as suggested by Stewart) or whether it indicates that old customs and norms are being gradually relaxed is not entirely clear.

10. P. Szuhay, 'Foglalkozási és megélhetési stratégiák a magyarországi cigányok körében' in Glatz (ed.), *A cigányok Magyarországon*, p. 139, at p. 152.

11. On the increase in anti-Roma sentiment in much of Central and Eastern Europe, following the removal of the Communist regimes, see Chapter 1.

12. See, generally, on these confiscatory laws I. Pogány, *Righting Wrongs in Eastern Europe* (Manchester: Manchester University Press, 1997), pp. 26–36. For an overview of the fate of Hungary's Jews in World War II see, for example, F. Fejtő, *Hongrois et Juifs* (Paris: Éditions Balland, 1997), pp. 265–337; R. Braham, 'The Holocaust in Hungary: A retrospective analysis' in D. Cesarani (ed.), *Genocide and Rescue: The Holocaust in Hungary 1944* (Oxford: Berg, 1997), p. 29, at pp. 29–46.

13. On the exclusion of Jews from white-collar employment see, for instance, Pogány, *Righting Wrongs in Eastern Europe*, pp. 82–9. On the Jewish labour battalions see ibid., pp. 89–93, and the sources cited at nn. 97–126.

14. On the nationalisation laws and related measures adopted by Hungary's post-War Communist administration see ibid., pp. 64–8.

15. See, for example, I. Fehérváry, *Börtönvilág Magyarországon 1945–1956* (Budapest: Magyar Politikai Foglyok Szövetsége, 1990), p. 148.

16. There is a certain ambivalence in the attitude of many Vlach Roma. While taking great pride in their cultural identity and feeling themselves superior to Gadje in many ways, there is nevertheless recognition of the fact that Gadje exercise ultimate power through the police and through other state agencies and that Gadje are, at best, condescending towards Gypsies. See, generally, Stewart, *Time of the Gypsies*, pp. 24–6, 40–3.

17. Of course, the fact that Anikó was being paid for her participation in the documentary, about the quest for her Gadje relatives, helped to make his wife's new-found interest in her Hungarian 'roots' more tolerable.

18. Stewart, *Time of the Gypsies*, p. 53.

19. Ibid., p. 38.

20. Ibid, p. 228.

21. Ibid., p. 54.

22. Many of the same domestic and other responsibilities – as well as expectations of sexual fidelity and of virginity until marriage – have been traditionally applied to Gypsy women in Britain. See Okely, *The Traveller-Gypsies*, pp. 203–5.

23. I. Fonseca, *Bury me Standing* (Vintage: London, 1996), p. 40.

24. Ibid., p. 47.

25. Interviews recorded with a Gábor family and with a local Protestant pastor in villages adjacent to the town of Târgu-Mureş in the Transylvanian region of Romania, September 2002 and April 2003 (on file with the author). For an overview of the Gábor Roma and their culture see, for example, Burcea, 'Gaborii – o naţie romă aparte' in Z. Varga (ed.), *Interetnica* (Cluj: Ethnocultural Diversity Resource Center, 2002), p. 75.

26. On the survival of notions of 'purity' and 'shame' amongst Gábor Roma, and on the impact of such notions on Gábor women, see below.

27. Gábor men are also denied any real right to determine the course of their own lives. A Gábor youth is expected to marry while still in his teens (his wife is selected by his parents), to have several children, to learn a trade or business from his father, and to establish his own home. The opportunity to continue his studies beyond elementary school does not exist in this rigid, conformist but, in both material and social terms, often highly successful community.

28. Interview recorded in Budapest in September 1998 (on file with the author). My translation.

29. Interview recorded in Patakrét in April 1999 (on file with the author). My translation.

30. A. Diósi, *Szemtől szemben a magyarországi cigánysággal* (Budapest: Pont Kiadó, 2002).

31. Á. Diósi, 'Brought up to be different' in the *Hungarian Quarterly*, Vol. 41, Winter 2000, p. 84, at p. 88.

32. Michael Stewart gives an example of a young Romani couple, much in love, who decided to elope to avoid an arranged marriage that was being planned for the young woman by her parents. Stewart, *Time of the Gypsies*, pp. 83–4. See, also, Fonseca, *Bury me Standing*, pp. 129–30.

33. Interview recorded in April 2003 (on file with the author).

34. Fonseca, *Bury me Standing*, p. 130.

35. When I recounted what I'd been told, about the abduction of Gábor girls, to Péter Szuhay, he thought it likely that the number of such incidents had been unconsciously inflated, resulting in an irrational degree of panic and alarm amongst the community at large.

36. See, for example, Okely, *The Traveller-Gypsies*, pp. 80–90, 206–12; Stewart, *Time of the Gypsies*, Chapter 12; A. Fraser, *The Gypsies* (Oxford: Blackwell, 2nd ed., 1995), pp. 244–6.

37. On one occasion, I happened to call on Rózsi, when she was busy doing the washing for the family with the assistance of two young nieces. Rózsi was energetically cramming clothes into an ancient top-loading washing machine. Seizing this unexpected opportunity to learn something about the pollution practices of the Roma, which I'd read about, I asked her how she went about doing the weekly wash. Looking at me as if I were crazy, she patiently explained that first she put white garments into the washing machine, later coloured items and finally anything that was dark. The principle governing this process was not some ancient custom about upper–lower body distinctions, or the need to wash female undergarments separately from male clothes, but the mechanical limitations of the washing machine that she was operating. The apparent impossibility of changing the water, once the machine was switched on, dictated the order in which the clothes had to be washed. Nor could I observe any cultural principle at work in the way that the clothes were hung up to dry by Rózsi's nieces.

38. Michael Stewart was told by the Vlach Roma in the community in which he did his fieldwork that they no longer adhere to many of the old customs regarding purity and pollution, which they referred to as superstitions. However, Stewart did find evidence of a continuing concern with 'shame' and with 'shameful acts'. Stewart, *Time of the Gypsies*, p. 210.

39. P. Szuhay, 'Örökös Lakás: a Kétegyházi Faragó Zsigmond Temetése a Magyarországi Oláh Cigány Temetések Rendszerében' (2001, unpublished manuscript, on file with the author).

40. On the incorporation of human rights norms in the legal systems of the post-Communist states of Central and Eastern Europe, and on the increasing impact of regional and global human rights treaties, see Chapter 6.

41. For an impassioned critique of cultural relativism as a justification for the denial of elementary rights see M. Ignatieff, 'Human rights as idolatry' in Amy Gutmann (ed.), *Human Rights as Politics and Idolatry* (Princeton: Princeton University Press, 2001), p. 53, at pp. 63–73.

42. There is a similar tension between the treatment of children in many impoverished or traditional Romani communities – where they are often expected to contribute to the family income from a comparatively early age – and the laws and moral assumptions of the broader society. On one occasion I happened to be in Cluj in late November. Almost everyone who ventured onto the freezing streets wore boots, a heavy overcoat, scarf and hat. Consequently, I was shocked to see two skimpily dressed Romani children, a boy and a girl aged about four and six, begging for money. Neither child wore a coat, jumper or shoes. Their feet were completely bare. Even allowing for the poverty of their families, it was hard to resist the conclusion that the children had been deliberately sent out with only minimal clothing in order to excite greater sympathy and larger hand-outs from bystanders.

43. See, generally, Burcea, 'Gaborii – o naţie romă aparte', pp. 75–8.

44. Interview recorded in September 2002 (on file with the author). My translation from the original Hungarian.

45. Of course, at the level of domestic law, criminal law systems proscribe assaults on women, abduction and various other interferences with their liberty. This is discussed below.

46. H. Charlesworth and C. Chinkin, *The Boundaries of International Law* (Manchester: Manchester University Press, 2000), pp. 233–4 (footnotes omitted).

47. Ibid., p. 234.

48. Ibid., p. 220.

49. Stewart, *Time of the Gypsies*, pp. 41–2.

50. Charlesworth and Chinkin, *The Boundaries of International Law*, pp. 56–9.

8   THE LAMBADA

1. In some circumstances, it may be possible to begin civil proceedings independently of a criminal prosecution. However, this would normally involve hiring a lawyer and incurring other expenses. Information supplied by Ms Ioana Banu, Staff Attorney, European Roma Rights Center, 7 April 2003. It is quite likely that Olga, who did not have a lawyer, would not have known of this option in any event.

2. On Romanian attitudes towards Gypsies see, for example, L. Boia, *Romania* (London: Reaktion Books, 2001), pp. 215–19.

3. Information supplied by Ms Ioana Banu, Staff Attorney, European Roma Rights Center, 7 April 2003.

4. Ibid.

5. Depending on the severity of the charges a criminal case may be discontinued at the request of a victim, in accordance with the Romanian Criminal Code.

6. Information supplied by Ms Ioana Banu, Staff Attorney, European Roma Rights Center, 7 April 2003.

7. Information supplied by an advocate in Cluj-Napoca, Romania, dated 3 October 2001 (on file with the author). The English translation was provided by Ms Mihaela Chiorean.

8. It would be customary for a judge to inform the victim in a case such as this of the consequences of asking for the proceedings to be discontinued.

9. There is, however, a reference to the incident in an ERRC text. See European Roma Rights Center, *State of Impunity: Human Rights Abuse of Roma in Romania* (Country Report Series, No. 10, September 2001), pp. 33–4.

10. See OSCE High Commissioner on National Minorities, Report on the Situation of Roma and Sinti in Europe (2000), at <http://www.osce.org/hcnm/documents/reports/>, p. 39 (footnotes omitted). Accessed 3 September 2003.

11. Ibid. (footnotes omitted).

12. See entry for 'Slovakia' in Human Rights Watch, World Report 2002, at <http://hrw.org/wr2k2/europe.html > (accessed 3 September 2003).

13. See entry for 'Czech Republic' in Human Rights Watch, World Report 2002, at ibid.

14. On the changing character of Communist regimes in Central and Eastern Europe and consequent fluctuations in patterns of state-orchestrated violence and brutality see, for example, J. Rothschild, *Return to Diversity* (Oxford: Oxford University Press, 2nd ed., 1993), chapters 3–7; G. Schöpflin, *Politics in Eastern Europe 1945–1992* (Oxford: Blackwell, 1993), chapters 4–9.

15. However, as noted in Chapter 4, Communist Romani policies in the former Czechoslovakia were oppressive. For example, the authorities encouraged the sterilisation of even young Romani women. On Communist policies concerning the Roma in Hungary see, for example, M. Stewart, *The Time of the Gypsies* (Boulder, Colorado: Westview Press, 1997) especially chapters 6–7. For a more general overview of Communist treatment of the Roma in Central and Eastern Europe see, for example, A. Fraser, *The Gypsies* (Oxford: Blackwell, 2nd ed., 1995), pp. 274–82 and Z. Barany, *The East European Gypsies* (Cambridge: Cambridge University Press, 2002), Chapter 4.

16. On the persecution of Roma and Jews during World War II see, generally, Chapter 3.

17. See, generally, P. Lendvai, *Anti-Semitism Without Jews* (London: Doubleday, 1971).

18. For details of the incident at Hădăreni and of other attacks against Roma in Romania see, for instance, European Roma Rights Center, *State of Impunity*, pp. 20–52; European Roma Rights Center, *Sudden Rage at Dawn: Violence Against Roma in Romania* (Country Report Series, No. 2, September 1996); I. Fonseca, *Bury me Standing* (Vintage: London, 1996), pp. 140–3. For details of attacks against Gypsies in the ex-Communist states more generally see, for example, the country reports in the annual World Report issued by Human Rights Watch. These can be found at: <http://hrw.org/> (accessed 3 September 2003).

19. European Roma Rights Center, *State of Impunity*, pp. 23–6.

20. For details of the complaints see *Moldovan and Others and Rostaş and Others* v. *Romania: Decision as to Admissibility* (Applications Nos. 41138/98 and 64320/01), at pp. 10–12.

21. Ibid., pp. 12–16.

22. Details of the following events are taken, in the main, from a series of articles published in national and regional newspapers in Hungary. See *Magyar Hírlap*, 10 September 1992, p. 15; ibid., 11 September 1992, p. 8; ibid., 15 September 1992, p. 4; *Népszabadság*, 14 September 1992, pp. 1, 7; *Békés Megyei Hírlap*, 10 September 1992, pp. 1, 4; *Magyar Narancs*, 17 September 1992, pp. 14–15.

23. *Népszabadság*, 14 September 1992, pp. 1, 7.

24. For Human Rights Watch's World Report 2002, see <http://hrw.org/wr2k2/europe. html > (accessed 3 September 2003).

25. *Krasznai and Others* v. *Hungary* at <www.echr.coe.int/Eng/Press/2001/June/Decis onKrasznai&Othersepress.ht> (accessed 24 July 2001).

26. Art. 35(1) of the European Convention on Human Rights provides: 'The Court may only deal with the matter after all domestic remedies have been exhausted, according to the generally recognized rules of international law.' For the text of the Convention see, for example, <http://www.echr.coe.int/Convention/webConvenENG.pdf.> (accessed 3 September 2003).

27. Art. 1(2), Convention Relating to the Status of Refugees (1951), as amended by Art. 1(2) of the 1967 Protocol relating to the Status of Refugees. For the text of these treaties see 189 U.N.T.S. 150 and 606 U.N.T.S. 267.

28. On the collectivisation of agriculture in Communist Romania see, for example, A. Cartwright, *The Return of the Peasant* (Aldershot: Dartmouth, 2001), chapters 5, 6.

29. I. Berend, *Central and Eastern Europe 1944–1993* (Cambridge: Cambridge University Press, 1996), pp. 213–14.

30. Some Romanians whom I consulted expressed doubts as to whether even work of this kind would be available for the local Roma.

31. Human Rights Watch, World Report 1999, at <http://www.hrw.org/wr2k/Eca-08.htm> (accessed 3 September 2003).

32. Human Rights Watch, World Report 2000, at < http://www.hrw.org/wr2k1/europe/slovakia.html> (accessed 3 September 2003).

33. See, generally, the essays in J. Zielonka, (ed.), *Democratic Consolidation in Eastern Europe* (Oxford: Oxford University Press, 2001), Vols 1–2.

34. See, generally, M. Rooker, *The International Supervision of Protection of Romany People in Europe* (Nijmegen: Nijmegen University Press, 2002).

35. See, generally, *EU Enlargement – A Historic Opportunity* at <http://europa.eu.int/comm/enlargement/intro/criteria.htm> (accessed 3 September 2003).

36. See *EU Support for Romani Communities in Central and Eastern Europe*, p. 5 at <http://europa.eu.int/comm/enlargement/docs/pdf/brochure_roma_may2002.pdf> (accessed 3 September 2003).

37. 2002 Regular Report on Hungary's Progress Towards Accession, p. 27, at <http://europa.eu.int/comm/enlargement/report2002/hu_en.pdf> (accessed 3 September 2003); 2002 Regular Report on Romania's Progress Towards Accession, p. 28, at <http://europa.eu.int/comm/enlargement/report2002/ro_en.pdf> (accessed 3 September 2003); 2002 Regular Report on Slovakia's Progress Towards Accession, p. 27, at <http://europa.eu.int/comm/enlargement/report2002/sk_en.pdf> (accessed 3 September 2003); 2002 Regular Report on the Czech Republic's Progress Towards Accession, p. 32, at <http://europa.eu.int/comm/enlargement/report2002/cz_en.pdf> (accessed 3 September 2003).

38. See 2002 Regular Report on Romania's Progress Towards Accession, p. 36.

39. 2002 Regular Report on the Czech Republic's Progress Towards Accession, p. 31.

40. For details of the recent World Bank-sponsored report on Romani poverty and on strategies for combating it see D. Ringold, M. Orenstein, E. Wilkens, *Roma in an Expanding Europe: Breaking the Poverty Cycle* (Washington, D.C.: International Bank for Reconstruction and Development, 2003). The report is discussed in detail in Chapter 9.

41. See, for example, Decision 2000/109, Sub-Commission on Human Rights, at <http://www.unhchr.ch/Huridocda/Huridoca.nsf/(Symbol)/E.CN.4.SUB.2.DEC.2 000.109.En?Opendocument> (accessed 3 September 2003). See, also, a working paper endorsed by the Sub-Commission: 'On the human rights problems and protections of the Roma' (E/CN.4/Sub.2/2000/28).

42. For details see, for example, <http://www.coe.int/T/E/social_cohesion/Roma_Gypsies/Contacts/> (accessed 3 September 2003).

43. Para. 3, Recommendation 1557 (25 April 2002), See, previously, Recommendation 1203 (2 February 1993). Recommendations and other texts adopted by the Parliamentary Assembly can be found at <http://assembly.coe.int/Main.asp?Link=/asp/doc/ATMenu(SQL).asp?Language=E> (accessed 3 September 2003).

44. See, generally, on the OSCE High Commissioner for National Minorities <http://www.osce.org/hcnm/> (accessed 3 September 2003). For the text of the High Commissioner's Report on the Situation of Roma and Sinti in the OSCE Area (April 2000), see <http://www.osce.org/hcnm/documents/reports/roma/report_roma_sinti_2000.pdf> (accessed 3 September 2003). On the activities of the Office for Democratic Institutions and Human Rights see <http://www.osce.org/odihr/> (accessed 3 September 2003).

45. On the functions of the ODIHR Contact Point for Roma and Sinti Issues see, for example, <http://www.osce.org/odihr/cprsi/index.php3?s=1a> (accessed 3 September 2003).

46. For the text of these treaties see, for example, <http://www.unhchr.ch/html/menu3/b/a_ccpr.htm> and <http://www.unhchr.ch/html/menu3/b/a_cescr.htm> (accessed 3 September 2003). In reviewing periodic reports submitted by contracting states, the committees established under these treaties have commented on the problems experienced by the Roma in Central and Eastern Europe.

47. For the text of General Recommendation XXVII of the Committee on the Elimination of Racial Discrimination see, for example, <http://www.unhchr.ch/tbs/doc.nsf/(Symbol)/CERD+General+recom.+27.En?Opendocument> (accessed 8 September 2003).

48. For the text of the Convention see, for instance, <http://193.194.138.190/html/menu3/b/h_cat39.htm> (accessed 8 September 2003).

49. See Para. 9(2), Communication No 161/2000: Yugoslavia. 02/12/2002 (CAT/C/29/D/161/2000). Article 16(1) of the Convention provides:

> Each State Party shall undertake to prevent in any territory under its jurisdiction other acts of cruel, inhuman or degrading treatment or punishment which do not amount to torture as defined in article I, when such acts are committed by or at the instigation of or with the consent or acquiescence of a public official or other person acting in an official capacity.

50. For the text of the Convention on the Rights of the Child see, for example, <http://www.unhchr.ch/html/menu2/6/crc/treaties/crc.htm> (accessed 3 September 2003).

51. See Concluding Observations of the Committee on the Rights of the Child: Romania, para. 64, UN Doc. CRC/C/15/Add. 199 (31 January 2003), at <http://www.unhchr.ch/html/menu2/6/crc/doc/co/co-romania-2.pdf> (accessed 3 September 2003). For the Committee's earlier criticism of the situation of Romani children in Poland see UN Doc. CRC/C/15/Add. 194 (30 October 2002), para. 52, at <http://www.unhchr.ch/tbs/doc.nsf/(Symbol)/CRC.C.15.Add.194.En?OpenDocument> (accessed 8 September 2003):

> The Committee is concerned that, despite pilot programmes aimed at improving the situation of the Roma in certain provinces, they still suffer from widespread discrimination which has in some instances impeded Romani children's right to education, health and social welfare.

52. See *Assenov and others* v. *Bulgaria* (Application no. 90/1997/874/1086); *Velikova* v. *Bulgaria* (Application no. 41488/98); *Anguelova* v. *Bulgaria* (Application no. 38361/97).

53. See *Čonka* v. *Belgium* (Application no. 51564/99); *Sulejmanovic and Sultanovic* v. *Italy: Decision as to Admissibility* (Application no. 57574/00). The latter case was settled by means of a friendly settlement after a Chamber of the Court ruled that it was partially admissible.

54. In *Osman* v. *UK* (87/1997/871/1083), which was not concerned with the problems of the Roma, the European Court of Human Rights went as far as to say that the right to life, in Article 2, 'may also imply in certain well-defined circumstances a positive obligation on the authorities to take preventive operational measures to protect an individual whose life is at risk from the criminal acts of another individual' (para. 115). However, the Court emphasised that (para. 116):

such an obligation must be interpreted in a way which does not impose an impossible or disproportionate burden on the authorities. Accordingly, not every claimed risk to life can entail for the authorities a Convention requirement to take operational measures to prevent that risk from materialising...In the opinion of the Court where there is an allegation that the authorities have violated their positive obligation to protect the right to life in the context of their above-mentioned duty to prevent and suppress offences against the person..., it must be established to its satisfaction that the authorities knew or ought to have known at the time of the existence of a real and immediate risk to the life of an identified individual or individuals from the criminal acts of a third party and that they failed to take measures within the scope of their powers which, judged reasonably, might have been expected to avoid that risk...For the Court, and having regard to the nature of the right protected by Article 2, a right fundamental in the scheme of the Convention, it is sufficient for an applicant to show that the authorities did not do all that could be reasonably expected of them to avoid a real and immediate risk to life of which they have or ought to have knowledge. This is a question which can only be answered in the light of all the circumstances of any particular case.

55. For the text of the Framework Convention for the Protection of National Minorities see, for example, <http://conventions.coe.int/Treaty/EN/CadreListeTraites.htm > (accessed 8 September 2003).

56. See Opinion on the Czech Republic, adopted on 6 April 2001 (ACFC/INF/ OP/I(2002)002), paras. 29, 38, available at <http://www.coe.int/T/e/human_ rights/Minorities/2._FRAMEWORK_CONVENTION_(MONITORING)/2._ Monitoring_mechanism/> (accessed 8 September 2003).

57. See the Opinion on Hungary, adopted on 22 September 2000 (ACFC/INF/OP/ I(2001)004); Opinion on Slovakia, adopted on 22 September 2000 (ACFC/INF/ OP/I(2001)001); Opinion on Romania, adopted on 6 April 2001 (ACFC/INF/OP/ I(2002)001). The opinions of the Advisory Committee are available at <http:// www.coe.int/T/e/human_rights/Minorities/2._FRAMEWORK_CONVENTION_ (MONITORING)/2._Monitoring_mechanism/> (accessed 8 September 2003).

58. However, the resolutions adopted by the Committee of Ministers are usually milder in tone and less detailed than the opinions of the Advisory Committee.

59. On the contribution of the Roma to music in Central and Eastern Europe see Chapter 5.

9   THE ROMA CAFÉ

1. See D. Ringold, M. Orenstein, E. Wilkens, *Roma in an Expanding Europe: Breaking the Poverty Cycle* (Washington, D.C.: International Bank for Reconstruction and Development, 2003), p. 1.

2. For a perceptive examination of the role of NGOs concerned with Romani affairs see N. Trehan, 'In the name of the Roma? The role of private foundations and NGOs' in W. Guy (ed.), *Between Past and Future: The Roma of Central and Eastern Europe* (Hertfordshire: University of Hertfordshire Press, 2001), p. 134.

3. N. Gheorghe and T. Acton, 'Citizens of the world and nowhere' in Guy (ed.), *Between Past and Future*, p. 54, at p. 57.

4. Violations of the rights of the Roma, particularly civil and political rights, are discussed in various chapters including Chapter 1 and Chapter 8.

5. On the less favourable treatment of Roma by criminal justice systems in Central and Eastern Europe see, for instance, Chapter 8.

6. Nidhi Trehan argues that some NGOs are preoccupied with 'popular concepts' such as human rights, 'without connecting them to the real needs of local [Roma] communities'. Trehan, 'In the name of the Roma?', p. 137.

7. Rates of Roma unemployment are discussed in Chapter 1.

8. A successful businesswoman in Hungary told me frankly that if a Gypsy and a non-Gypsy applied for a job, each of whom had comparable qualifications, she would unhesitatingly pick the non-Gypsy 'to avoid any hassle'. Following the collapse of Communism many employers in the region did not even bother to conceal their anti-Gypsy prejudices. 'We don't hire Italians', the father of a young Romani acquaintance of mine was told by the foreman, in the mid 1990s, when he went to enquire about a job as a garbage collector in a provincial Hungarian city. The reference to 'Italians' was the foreman's little joke, a way of showing he was aware that the job seeker was dark skinned and therefore a Gypsy. However, such brazenly discriminatory practices are finally being challenged as a result of the enactment of increasingly comprehensive anti-discrimination laws in the CEE states. See, for example, the European Commission's 'regular reports' on CEE states that examine, *inter alia*, developments in anti-discrimination legislation in the post-Communist states. These legal developments are discussed in Chapter 8.

9. Z. Barany, *The East European Gypsies* (Cambridge: Cambridge University Press, 2002), pp. 173–4. See, also, Ringold, Orenstein,Wilkens, *Roma in an Expanding Europe: Breaking the Poverty Cycle*, p. 2.

10. Some of the problems encountered by Roma pupils in Central and Eastern Europe, including allegations of institutionalised discrimination in the Czech educational system, are discussed in Chapter 1.

11. See, for example, J. Okely, *The Traveller-Gypsies* (Cambridge: Cambridge University Press, 1983), pp. 161–2. Amongst the Vlach Roma of Hungary, for example, entrepreneurial activity is seen as the optimum way to earn a living. There are very few instances of young people studying for specialist qualifications. As noted in Chapter 7, the Gábor Roma of north-western Romania have strong and generally negative views regarding formal education.

12. J. Okely, *The Traveller-Gypsies*, pp. 53–6

13. For example, as we saw in Chapter 5, musical tastes have changed in much of the region, leading to the loss of employment opportunities for traditional Romani musicians in Hungary and in Transylvanian Romania.

14. See, generally, Trehan, 'In the name of the Roma?' Whether these criticisms are entirely justified is open to debate.

15. Ibid., p. 137.

16. Ringold, Orenstein, Wilkens, *Roma in an Expanding Europe*, p. 6.

17. Much the same point is made in the recent World Bank report, cited above: '[m]ulticultural education and a curriculum which includes the history and culture of Roma and other minorities are critical vehicles for overcoming cultural barriers'. (Ringold, Orenstein,Wilkens, *Roma in an Expanding Europe*, p. 7)

18. See, for example, Barany, *East European Gypsies*, p. 311. However, in Hungary it is unconstitutional to collect (let alone disseminate) information about the ethnicity of suspects, defendants or those convicted of crimes.

19. See, for example, Barany, *East European Gypsies*, pp. 231–9.

20. On the Roma and the extent to which they currently recognise a sense of national identity see, for example, I. Pogány, 'Accommodating an emergent national identity: The Roma of Central and Eastern Europe' in Stephen Tierney (ed.), *Accommodating National Identity* (The Hague: Kluwer Law International, 2000), pp. 175–88.

21. Z. Kereszty and Z. Pólya (eds), *Csenyéte antológia* (Budapest: Bár Könyvek, 1998).

22. I. Kemény, 'Tennivalók a cigányok/romák ügyében' in F. Glatz (ed.), *A cigányok Magyarországon* (Budapest: Magyar Tudományos Akadémia, 1999), p. 229, at p. 230.

23. Barany, *East European Gypsies*, pp. 169–70. See, generally, ibid., pp. 164–72.

24. Ibid., p. 170.

25. Ibid., p. 171.

26. The educational 'ghettoisation' of Romani pupils in parts of Central and Eastern Europe and related problems are discussed in Chapter 1.

27. Ringold, Orenstein, Wilkens, *Roma in an Expanding Europe*, p. 4.

28. See M. Stewart, 'Communist Roma policy 1945–89 as seen through the Hungarian case' in Guy (ed.), *Between Past and Future*, p. 71, at p. 87.

29. For the text of the South African Constitution see, for example, <http://www.concourt.gov.za/constitution/const02.html#26> (accessed 1 September 2003).

30. A complaint that a right guaranteed by the Constitution has been infringed (or withheld) can be raised before the High Court in South Africa. In some circumstances, the matter may be referred to the Constitutional Court, either at the initiative of the High Court or on appeal. See, for example, *Information about the Constitutional Court* at <http://www.concourt.gov.za/about.html#cases> (accessed 1 September 2003).

31. Ringold, Orenstein, Wilkens, *Roma in an Expanding Europe*, p. 128.

32. Ibid., pp. 127–9.

33. For a thorough set of policy recommendations on addressing Roma poverty see ibid., pp. 133–9.

34. The recent World Bank report on Roma poverty uses terms such as 'inclusion' and 'participation' rather than 'integration' in calling for an end to Roma economic marginalisation, no doubt because 'integration' was sometimes a euphemism for 'assimilation' during the Communist era. See ibid, p. 6.

35. Kereszty and Pólya, *Csenyéte antológia*, p. 57.

36. Ringold, Orenstein, Wilkens, *Roma in an Expanding Europe*, p. 126.

37. On the rise of exclusivist and intolerant forms of nationalism in Central and Eastern Europe see, for example, I. Berend, *History Derailed* (Berkeley: University of California Press, 2003), pp. 114–19.

Bibliography

A Magyarországban 1893 január 31-en végrehajtott Czigányösszeirás Eredményei (1895) (Budapest: Athenaeum R. Társulat Könyvnyomdája).

Achim, V. (1998) *Tiganii în istoria Romănei* (Bucharest: Editura Enciclopedica).

Appelbaum, A. (2003) *Gulag: A History of the Soviet Concentration Camps* (London: Allen Lane).

Barany, Z. (2002) *The East European Gypsies* (Cambridge: Cambridge University Press).

Bárdos, L., Szabó, I. and Vasy, G. (eds) (1996) *Irodalmi fogalmak kisszótára* (Budapest: Korona Kiadó).

Bauer, Y. (2001) *Rethinking the Holocaust* (New Haven: Yale University Press).

Baxi, U. (2002) *The Future of Human Rights* (New Delhi: Oxford University Press).

Beissinger, M. (2001) 'Occupation and ethnicity: Constructing identity among professional Romani (Gypsy) musicians in Romania' in *Slavic Review*, Vol. 60, Issue 1, p. 24.

Berend, I. (1996) *Central and Eastern Europe 1944–1993* (Cambridge: Cambridge University Press).

—— (2003) *History Derailed* (Berkeley: University of California Press).

Bernadac, C. (1979) *L'Holocauste oublié* (Paris: Éditions France Empire).

Bernáth, G. (2000) *Porrajmos* (Budapest: Roma Sajtó Központ).

Boia, L. (2001) *Romania* (London: Reaktion Books).

Braham, R. (1981) *The Politics of Genocide*, Vols. 1–2 (New York: Columbia University Press).

—— (1997) 'The Holocaust in Hungary: A retrospective analysis' in D. Cesarani (ed.), *Genocide and Rescue: The Holocaust in Hungary 1944* (Oxford: Berg), p. 29.

Brearley, M. (1996) *The Roma/Gypsies of Europe: A Persecuted People* (London: Institute for Jewish Policy Research).

Broughton, S., Ellingham, M. and Trillo, R. (eds) (1999) *World Music*, Vol. 1 (London: The Rough Guides).

Burcea, A. (2002) 'Gaborii – o naţie romă aparte' in Z. Varga (ed.), *Interetnica* (Cluj: Ethnocultural Diversity Resource Center), p. 75.

Burleigh, N. (2001) *The Third Reich: A New History* (London: Pan Books).

Cartwright, A. (2001) *The Return of the Peasant* (Aldershot: Dartmouth).

Cesarani, D. (ed.) (1997) *Genocide and Rescue: The Holocaust in Hungary 1944* (Oxford: Berg).

Charlesworth, H. and Chinkin, C. (2000) *The Boundaries of International Law* (Manchester: Manchester University Press).

Cohen, R. (1997) *Global Diasporas* (London: UCL Press).

Commission of the European Communities (undated) *EU Enlargement – A Historic Opportunity* at <http://europa.eu.int/comm/enlargement/intro/criteria.htm> (accessed 3 September 2003).

—— (2002a) *EU Support for Roma Communities in Central and Eastern Europe* available at <http://europa.eu.int/comm/enlargement/docs/pdf/brochure_roma_may2002.pdf > (accessed 3 September 2003).

—— (2002b) EU Regular Reports on Bulgaria, the Czech Republic, Hungary, Romania and Slovakia, available at <http://europa.eu.int/comm/enlargement/report2002/> (accessed 9 September 2003).

Conquest, R. (1992) *The Great Terror* (London: Pimlico).

—— (2002) *The Harvest of Sorrow* (London: Pimlico).

Crowe, D. (1996) *A History of the Gypsies of Eastern Europe and Russia* (New York: St. Martin's Griffin).

Csalog, Z. (1976) *Kilenc cigány* (Budapest: Komosz könyvek).

Csemer, G. (1994) *Habiszti* (Budapest: privately published).

Davies, N. (1996) *Europe* (Oxford: Oxford University Press).

Dawidowicz, L. (1990) *The War against the Jews 1933–45* (London: Penguin Books, 10th Anniversary ed.).

De Sousa Santos, B. (2002) *Toward a New Legal Common Sense* (London: Butterworths, 2nd ed.).

Dempsey, J. (1986) 'Religion in the Soviet Union and Eastern Europe' in G. Schöpflin (ed.) *The Soviet Union and Eastern Europe* (London: Muller, Blond & White, rev. ed.), p. 565.

Diósi, A. (2000) 'Brought up to be different' in *Hungarian Quarterly*, Vol. 41, Winter, p. 84.

—— (2002) *Szemtől szemben a magyarországi cigánysággal* (Budapest: Pont Kiadó).

Don, Y. (1997) 'Economic implications of the anti-Jewish legislation in Hungary' in D. Cesarani (ed.), *Genocide and Rescue: The Holocaust in Hungary 1944* (Oxford: Berg), p. 47.

Douzinas, C. (2000) *The End of Human Rights* (Oxford: Hart Publishing).

Dullea, R. (2001) 'The role of Romani music in Hungarian nationalism' in *Central European Review*, Vol. 3, No. 13 at <http://www.ce-review.org/archiveindex.html> (accessed 7 April 2001).

European Roma Rights Center (1996a) *Sudden Rage at Dawn: Violence Against Roma in Romania* (Country Report Series, No. 2, September).

—— (1996b) *Time of the Skinheads: Denial and Exclusion of Roma in Slovakia* (Country Report Series, No. 3).

—— (1999) *A Special Remedy: Roma and Schools for the Mentally Handicapped in the Czech Republic* (Country Report Series, No. 8).

—— (2001) *State of Impunity: Human Rights Abuse of Roma in Romania* (Country Report Series, No. 10).

Fehérváry, I. (1990) *Börtönvilág Magyarországon 1945–1956* (Budapest: Magyar Politikai Foglyok Szövetsége).

Fejtő, F. (1997) *Hongrois et Juifs* (Paris, Éditions Balland).

Fings, K. (1997) 'Romanies and Sinti in the concentration camps' in K. Fings, H. Heuss and F. Sparing (eds), *From 'Race Science' to the Camps* (Hertfordshire: University of Hertfordshire Press), p. 71.

Fonseca, I. (1996) *Bury me Standing* (Vintage: London).

Fraser, A. (1995) *The Gypsies* (Oxford: Blackwell, 2nd ed.).

Friedländer, S. (1998) *Nazi Germany and the Jews*, Vol. 1 (London: Phoenix).

Friedrich, O. (1996) *The Kingdom of Auschwitz* (London: Penguin Books).

Gallagher, T. (1995) *Romania after Ceauşescu* (Edinburgh: Edinburgh University Press).

Gheorghe, N. and Acton, T. (2001) 'Citizens of the world and nowhere' in W. Guy (ed.), *Between Past and Future: The Roma of Central and Eastern Europe* (Hertfordshire: University of Hertfordshire Press), p. 54.

Gilbert, M. (1987) *The Holocaust* (London: Fontana Paperbacks).

—— (1993) *The Dent Atlas of the Holocaust* (London: J M Dent, 2nd ed.).

—— (1994) *First World War* (London: Weidenfeld and Nicolson).

—— (1998) *Israel a History* (London: Doubleday).

Giordano, C. (1997) 'Affiliation, exclusion and the national state: "Ethnic discourses" and minorities in East Central Europe' in H.-R. Wicker (ed.), *Rethinking Nationalism and Ethnicity* (Oxford: Berg), p. 175.

Glatz, F. (ed.) (1999) *A cigányok Magyarországon* (Budapest: Magyar Tudományos Akadémia).

Glenny, M. (2000) *The Balkans 1804–1999* (London: Granta Books).

Goldstein, D. (1997) 'Re-imagining the Jew in Hungary: the reconstruction of ethnicity through political affilliation' in H.-R. Wicker (ed.), *Rethinking Nationalism and Ethnicity* (Oxford: Berg), p. 193.

Gosztonyi, P. (1995) *A Magyar Honvédség a Második Világháborúban* (Budapest: Európa Könyvkiadó).

Hammersley, M. and Atkinson, P. (eds) (1995) *Ethnography* (London: Routledge, 2nd ed.).

Hancock, I. (1997) 'The struggle for the control of identity' in *Transitions*, Vol. 4, No. 4, September available at <http://www.geocities.com/paris/5121/identity.htm> (accessed 29 July 2003).

—— (2002) *We are the Romani people* (Hertfordshire: University of Hertfordshire Press).

Harris, E. (2002) *Nationalism and Democratisation* (Aldershot: Ashgate).

Havas, G.(2001) *Gazdálodó Cigányok* (Budapest: Autonómia Alapítvány).

—— (2002) 'A cigány tanulók elkülönitése az általános iskolában' in T. Reisz and M. Andor (eds), *A Cigánység Társadalomismerete* (Pécs: Iskolakultúra), p. 152.

Hilberg, R. (1985) *The Destruction of the European Jews*, Vols 1–3 (New York: Holmes & Meier, rev. ed.).

Hobsbawm, E. (1992) *Nations and Nationalism since 1780* (Cambridge: Cambridge University Press, 2nd ed.).

Human Rights Watch (1999–2003) World Report at <http://hrw.org/> (accessed 3 September 2003).

Iancu, C. (1998) *La Shoah en Roumanie* (Montpellier: Université Paul-Valéry).

Ignatieff, M. (1994) *Blood and Belonging* (London: Vintage).

—— (2001) 'Human rights as idolatry' in A. Gutmann (ed.), *Human Rights as Politics and Idolatry* (Princeton: Princeton University Press), p. 53.

Illyés, G. (1993) *Puszták népe* (Budapest: Századvég Kiadó).

Ioanid, R. (2000) *The Holocaust in Romania* (Chicago: Ivan R Dee).

Johnson, P. (1995) *A History of the Jews* (London: Phoenix).

Karsai, L. (1992) *A cigánykérdés Magyarországon 1919–1945* (Budapest: Cserépfalvi Kiadás).

Kedourie, E. (1993) *Nationalism* (Oxford: Blackwell, 4th rev. ed.).

Kelecsényi, L. (2002) *Atlasz: Magyar Irodalom* (Budapest: Athenaeum, 2nd ed.).

Kelso, M. (1999) 'Gypsy deportations from Romania to Transnistria 1942–44' in D. Kenrick (ed.), *In the Shadow of the Swastika* (Hertfordshire: University of Hertfordshire Press), p. 95.

Kemény, I. (1999) 'Tennivalók a cigányok/romák ügyében' in F. Glatz (ed.), *A cigányok Magyarországon* (Budapest: Magyar Tudományos Akadémia), p. 229.

—— (ed.) (2000) *A Magyarországi Romák* (Budapest: Press Publica Kiadó).

Kenrick, D. (1989) 'Letter to the editor' in *Holocaust and Genocide Studies*, Vol. 4, No. 2, p. 251.

—— (ed.) (1999) *In the Shadow of the Swastika* (Hertfordshire: University of Hertfordshire Press).

Kenrick, D. and Puxon, G. (1995) *Gypsies under the Swastika* (Hertfordshire: University of Hertfordshire Press, 2nd ed.).

Kershaw, I., (1999) *Hitler, 1889–1936* (London: Penguin Books).

Kereszty, Z. and Pólya, Z. (eds) (1998) *Csenyéte antológia* (Budapest: Bár Könyvek).

Kopecký, P. (2001) 'The Czech Republic: From the burden of the old federal constitution to the constitutional horse trading among political parties' in J. Zielonka (ed.), *Democratic Consolidation in Eastern Europe* (Oxford: Oxford University Press), Vol. 1, p. 319.

Kurczewski, J. (1993) *The Resurrection of Rights in Poland* (Oxford: Oxford University Press).

Lendvai, P. (1971) *Anti-Semitism Without Jews* (London: Doubleday).

Lewy, G. (2000) *The Nazi Persecution of the Gypsies* (Oxford: Oxford University Press).

Marrus, M. (2000) *The Holocaust in History* (Toronto: Key Porter Books, 2nd ed.).

Mérimée, P. (1996) *Carmen* (Paris: Le Livre de Poche).

Mezey, B. (ed.) (1986) *A magyarországi cigánykérdés dokumentumokban 1422–1985* (Budapest: Kossuth Könyvkiadó).

Molnár, M. (2001) *A Concise History of Hungary* (Cambridge: Cambridge University Press).

Moutouh, H. (2000) *Les Tsiganes* (Paris: Flammarion).

Nagy, L. (1999) *Kiskunhalom* (Budapest: Osiris Kiadó).

Nagy, P. (1998) *A magyarországi cigányok története a rendi társadalom korában* (Kaposvár: Csokonai Vitéz Mihály Tanítóképző Főiskola Kiadója).

Necas, C. (1999a) 'Bohemia and Moravia – two internment camps for the Gypsies in the Czech lands' in D. Kenrick (ed.), *In the Shadow of the Swastika* (Hertfordshire: University of Hertfordshire Press), p. 149.

—— (1999b) *The Holocaust of Czech Roma* (Prague: Prostor).

Neményi, M. (1999) 'Biológia vagy kultúra? Termékenységgel kapcsolatos szerepviselkedések a roma nők körében' in F. Glatz (ed.), *A cigányok Magyarországon* (Budapest: Magyar Tudományos Akadémia), p. 103.

Okely, J. (1983) *The Traveller-Gypsies* (Cambridge: Cambridge University Press).

Okey, R. (2001) *The Habsburg Monarchy c. 1765–1918* (Basingstoke: Macmillan).

OSCE High Commissioner on National Minorities (2000) Report on the Situation of Roma and Sinti in Europe (2000) at <http://www.osce.org/hcnm/documents/reports/> (accessed 3 September 2003).

Overy, R. (1999) *Russia's War* (London: Penguin Books).

Perks, R. and Thomson, A. (1998) 'Introduction' in R. Perks and A. Thomson (eds), *The Oral History Reader* (London: Routledge).

Pogány, I. (1997) *Righting Wrongs in Eastern Europe* (Manchester: Manchester University Press).

—— (2000) 'Accommodating an emergent national identity: The Roma of Central and Eastern Europe' in S. Tierney (ed.), *Accommodating National Identity* (The Hague: Kluwer Law International), pp. 175–88.

Póczik, S. (1999) *Cigányok és Idegenek* (Miskolc: Felsőmagyarország Kiadó).

—— (2001) 'Roma bűnelkövetők a sztatisztikák tükrében. A romákkal kapcsolatos kriminológiai kutatás mai állása', in F. Irk (ed.), *Kriminológiai Tanulmáyok XXXVIII* (Budapest: Országos Kriminológiai Intézet), p. 266.

Ratner, S. and Abrams, J. (2001) *Accountability for Human Rights Atrocities in International Law* (Oxford: Oxford University Press, 2nd ed.).

Ringold, D., Orenstein, M. and Wilkens, E. (2003) *Roma in an Expanding Europe: Breaking the Poverty Cycle* (Washington, D.C.: International Bank for Reconstruction and Development).

Rooker, M. (2002) *The International Supervision of Protection of Romany People in Europe* (Nijmegen: Nijmegen University Press).

Rosenbaum, R. (1998) *Explaining Hitler* (London: Macmillan).

Rothschild, J. (1977) *East Central Europe between the Two World Wars* (Seattle: University of Washington Press, rev. ed.).

—— (1993) *Return to Diversity* (Oxford: Oxford University Press, 2nd ed.).

Rupnik, J. (2002) 'The other Central Europe' in *East European Constitutional Review*, Vol. 11, Nos 1/2, p. 68.

Sachar, H. (1987) *A History of Israel*, Vol. 2 (Oxford: Oxford University Press).

Sadurski, W. (2001) 'Conclusions: On the relevance of institutions and the centrality of constitutions in post-communist transitions' in J. Zielonka (ed.), *Democratic Consolidation in Eastern Europe* (Oxford: Oxford University Press), Vol. 1, p. 455.

Sághy, E. (1996) 'A magyarországi cigányság története a Holocausttól az 1961-es Párthatározatig – A Politika tükrében' (unpublished dissertation submitted in the Department of Modern Hungarian History, Eötvös Loránd University, Budapest, Hungary).

Schöpflin, G. (ed.) (1986) *The Soviet Union and Eastern Europe* (London: Muller, Blond & White, rev. ed.).

—— (1993) *Politics in Eastern Europe 1945–1992* (Oxford: Blackwell).

Stewart, M. (1997) *The Time of the Gypsies* (Boulder, Colorado: Westview Press).

—— (2001) 'Communist Roma policy 1945–89 as seen through the Hungarian case' in W. Guy (ed.), *Between Past and Future: The Roma of Central and Eastern Europe* (Hertfordshire: University of Hertfordshire Press), p. 71.

Süle, A. (1990) 'Románia Politikatörténete 1944–1990' in G. Hunya et al. (eds), *Románia 1944–1990* (Budapest: Atlantisz), p. 199.

Swain, G. and Swain, N. (1993) *Eastern Europe since 1945* (London: Macmillan).

Szuhay, P. (1995) 'Arson on Gypsy row' in *Hungarian Quarterly*, Winter, p. 81.

—— (1997) 'Akiket cigányoknak neveznek – akik magukat romának, muzsikusnak vagy beásnak mondják' in *Magyar Tudomány*, No. 6, p. 656.

—— (1999a) *A magyarországi cigányság kultúrája: etnikus kultúra vagy a szegénység kultúrája* (Panóráma: Budapest).

—— (1999b) 'Foglalkozási és megélhetési stratégiák a magyarországi cigányok körében' in F. Glatz (ed.) *A cigányok Magyarországon* (Budapest: Magyar Tudományos Akadémia), p. 139.

—— (2001) 'Örökös Lakás: a Kétegyházi Faragó Zsigmond Temetése a Magyarországi Oláh Cigány Temetések Rendszerében' (unpublished manuscript).

Tomkins, A. (2001) 'Introduction: On being sceptical about human rights' in T. Campbell, K.D. Ewing and A. Tomkins (eds), *Sceptical Essays on Human Rights* (Oxford: Oxford University Press), p. 1.

Trehan, N. (2001) 'In the name of the Roma? The role of private foundations and NGOs' in W. Guy (ed.), *Between Past and Future: The Roma of Central and Eastern Europe* (Hertfordshire: University of Hertfordshire Press), p. 134.

Waldron, J. (1992) 'Minority cultures and the cosmopolitan alternative' in *University of Michigan Journal of Law Reform*, Vol. 25, p. 751.

Weber, R. (2001) 'Constitutionalism as a vehicle for democratic consolidation in Romania' in J. Zielonka (ed.), *Democratic Consolidation in Eastern Europe* (Oxford: Oxford University Press), Vol. 1, p. 212.

Wistrich, R. (1998) 'Nationalism Reborn' in M. Hughey (ed.), *New Tribalisms* (London: Macmillan), p. 356.

Yin, R. (1994) *Case Study Research* (London: Sage Publications, 2nd ed.).

Zielonka, J. (ed.) (2001) *Democratic Consolidation in Eastern Europe* (Oxford: Oxford University Press), Vols 1–2.

Zoon, I. (2001a) *On the Margins: Roma and Public Services in Romania, Bulgaria and Macedonia* (New York: Open Society Institute).

Zoon, I. (2001b) *On the Margins: Roma and Public Services in Slovakia* (New York: Open Society Institute).

Index